Revelations in Master Dominion

Actual Conversations with God

Part 1

Pastor Olabisi Kufeji

ISBN: 978-1-60383-004-1

Published by:
Holy Fire Publishing
Unit 116
1525-D Old Trolley Rd.
Summerville, SC 29485

www.ChristianPublish.com

Cover Design: Jay Cookingham

Printed in the United States of America and the United Kingdom

Table of Contents

INTRODUCTION

4. Vengeance is mine

5. Emotional pain is caused by deep spiritual innermost wound

6. Intercessory work affords graceful mercy to the sinner

7. Spiritual freedom is through perfect sacrificial atonement for the remissions of sins

8. The motional intelligence of the seventh sense

9. No man exist without me

CHAPTER 3 251

TO FORGIVE AND FORGET IS TO FULFILL DIVINE LAW

1. To forgive is to stop the offensive count

2. In my holy spirit comfort you are able to forgive and easily forget

3. Offensive baggage keeps a spirit in the condemnation of the past

4. All things work together for goodness sake of life

5. Forgive, forget and give thanks that you have done so

6. No man shall finish the race of time unless they abide by my royal law from beginning to the end

CHAPTER 4 291

TO HAVE THE DIVINE HEART OF LOVE IS TO BE A LIVING ADVOCATE IN LIFE

1. Only in divine heart of love will a man be able to choose good and resist evil
2. To preach the law in mind of hate is to be a hypocrite
3. To love is to have wisdom of life
4. To remain with the master is to face and win all challenges
5. The story of the wise son

CHAPTER 5

THE LIGHT IS SHINNING AND IT IS GAME OVER FOR THE HATEFUL BEAST

1. Victory for man is in only through the lamb
2. Death is the last enemy of man and to conquer death you must have courage of life
3. No man can be good on deeds except by my certifications
4. I am the way, the truth and the life and the father and the son is one
5. let the wise seek entrance to the kingdom by the straight line of covenant

Acknowledgements

I thank the Lord God Almighty the Father, the Son and the Holy Spirit who by his grace made me his vessel and enabled me to write this book for the proclamation of his goodness name.

I thank my immediate family starting from my father for all his word of encouragement throughout the years and my husband for all his support over the years. Most especially, I will like to thank my son also for his understanding and my eight-year-old daughter Precious for her entire patience and understanding with me during the course of my writing.

I thank all members of Freedom House International Ministries for believing in my God given mission and for all their support. In particular, I would like to say big thanks to all members of the women of virtue for all their support in my most difficult times.

Finally, I thank God for the life of the entire staff of Holy Fire publishers and for the life of you the reader of this book and for the life of my entire friends and supporters that had stood by me all this years. I pray that God goodness and mercies continue to rest and abide with you all forevermore. (Amen)

Introduction

Life they say is very complex and like most humans, I have had my share of complexities and difficulties in life.

As long as I could remember, I have always wanted answers to many questions. For example, where do we go when we die? Is there really life after death? Why do some in life seem to have it all and some merely get by. Why is there so much sorrow in the world? Is there really a God and if so where is he, who is he and who am I to him.

I was born into a Christian family but I am what you will call a mere churchgoer and I did not understand many things about my Christian beliefs particularly concerning Christ himself. Although I was unsure of the basis for my Christian beliefs, I believed there is a God as matter of logic even though I have no picture in mind who he is or what he stands for. I regarded this God as a super being with some kind of super power to provide for my needs and resolve my problems. It is mainly for this reason that I prayed to this God occasionally hoping he will answer my prayers.

I prayed usually when there is crisis in my life and as for crisis I have had my share of it. However, I always accredit my success in life to my hardworking efforts even when I have prayed to God to have the success. I never saw God in relationship context and my main reason for this is because I saw God as a hash judge especially towards those that are his chosen. I feared God would only be in mind to judge me if I were to be in any mind to know him beyond asking him to give me the things that I needed.

As for the bible, I was not into reading my bible and I had no idea how to find anything in the bible. The main use I had for my bible was putting it under my pillow especially after I have had a bad dream. I always believe that putting my bible under my pillow will give me some form of protection.

As a believed Christian, I consider going to church important to remain in God's favour. As such, over the years I changed from attending church once a year on New Year's Eve to regular Sunday attendance to satisfy my religious conscience.

Even though I started to attend church regularly, I was very sceptical about various aspects of the Christian idea concepts for instance the whole concept of speaking in tongues and the need to be born again. Besides, all I tend to hear from those that claim to be born again is death and judgement and as a result, I was even more hardened to the whole idea. I saw most people that claim to be born again as fanatics and as far as I was concerned all God expects from us is to be good.

Over the years of my believed Christianity, I had formulated my own beliefs and godly acceptable standards that suited me fine and this godly acceptable standard was very much concentrated on church attendance and nothing further. I have always believed there is a heaven however, from my own judgement standards; I could not see why I would not make heaven. According to my own standard of goodness, I believed I am a good person and as such, I could not see the need for me to be born again. I felt that by me not born again I could continue to follow my own judgement standards and that way the God of the born again people will not have any reason to judge me by the born again standards.

I never expected much from God given that I did not see him in any kind of relationship mind that is beyond attending church on Sundays. I did not see God as love or as a loving God. Love was something I looked for from my human counterparts and not once did it occur to me that the only one that can love me, as I desired to be loved is God.

My entire Christian beliefs and my life changed following an eventful encounter with God in the latter part of 2003. Leading up to this time starting from around late 2001 I started to feel as if my life was going nowhere and it was as if all doors were sealed and everything was at a stand still.
Naturally, I said my little prayers in manner of desperation hoping more than ever that he will answer my prayers in a convincing manner so that I give him the credit and not take the credit for success as I use to before.

However, instead of things getting better my prayer seem to be worsening my situation. As a result I concluded that if indeed there is a God he clearly hates me and he obviously has blocked his ears now completely to my prayers.

Leading up to my 2003 godly encounter, I became very depressed about everything. I hated everything about my life and I hated what to me I see as a world full of injustice, inequality and unfairness. I felt a kind of burden that I find hard to explain to anyone and the more I thought about my life the more frustrated I became. I felt as if I was trapped doing what I really do not enjoy doing and this made me to be even sadder because I could not see any way out. I have always enjoyed helping people and for some reason I felt that I am here on earth to offer people some genuine help and practical solutions and I was very frustrated by the fact that I felt I was not doing this as I am meant to.

Life in general as far as I was concerned has always appeared to me like a rat race that involves engaging in repeated daily routines.
Most of the time I felt completely alone and during this period I felt even more alone. The more I deliberated on my life the more hopeless I felt and the more this feeling of hopelessness increased the more depressed I got. The more depressed I got the more I kept thinking I was better off dead than to continue to live in what I consider a sorrowful world.

The strangest thing in all of this is that everyone around me often looks up to me and sees me as someone with high life potentials.

This made things even harder for me because I felt there is no one I could talk to that will understand what I was going through.

Things got from worse to worse for me emotionally and the worse things got the more I saw God as my enemy instead of my friend. Things got so bad to the point that I saw suicide more and more as my only option.

The turn around to my life came about in October 2003. I got so distressed and out of shear frustration, I sought God one night as I have never before. I asked too many questions such as why am I here on earth. What is my purpose and does he ever listen at all to me. I realised how hopeless and helpless I had become and wondered if God could see just how hopeless and helpless I was. I begged him to come to my rescue if he can hear me and said I was tired and in desperate need of his help. I also asked him to forgive me if at all I had offended him but at the same time I could not help but blame him for everything that had gone wrong in my life after all he has all the power. I was at a breaking point at this time and I was desperate for some form of breakthrough. Life had no meaning to me and I wanted to know the meaning of life.

I cried so much that night and when I woke up the following day, it was with a headache.

The following day was Sunday and at this point, I had stopped attending church on Sundays. Church was nice but I needed more than simply going to a church.

When I woke up I deliberated some more on the events of my life and after much deliberation and the usual daily routines I decided to watch the telly.

I switched my television on to the news channel and as usual, it was the same horror stories. The news was all about death, war and one disaster after the other.

I changed the channel after a few minutes of watching as it was making me to feel even more depressed and hopeless about my entire life. I choose one of the Christian Channels and found that a preacher that I had listened to a number of times was in the middle of a sermon.

I was about to change the channel again when I realised that the sermon was about life's purpose so I decided to listen.

The Preacher talked about our purpose in life and the main theme of his message was that God is a God of promises and if we look in the bible, we would find his promises to us.

 He stated that we should all be positive in our thinking and when we are down we should look through the bible for God's promises and when we read the bible we should form a habit of highlighting God's promises and knowing them by heart to encourage us.

The message cheered me up a bit and given the state of my mind, I could well do with some cheering up.

As I was listening to the message I wondered about the promises spoken about by the preacher and wondered also how it relates to me. After I finished listening, I decided to look through the bible for the promises the Preacher spoke about.

My only use for my bible as I said has always been for under my pillow and the only thing I am familiar with in the bible is Psalm 23. Therefore, when I picked up my bible on that day I had no clue where to begin.

It was like finding a needle out of a hay sack but I was desperate so I decided to read the bible like a novel.

I opened the first book Genesis and began to read from verse 1. By the time, I reached verse 3 something amazing happened to me that was beyond comprehension.

For some strange reason Genesis chapter 1 verse 1 to 3 meant so much to me and just from reading it, I felt like someone has lifted off a veil from my face. I heard a voice whispering some things to me and they were soothing to my ears.

At first I was not sure if it was my wishful thinking but even though I was not at this point sure what has happened I knew something has happened or better still about to happen.

After this experience, I suddenly became a lot more interested in praying not for the things that I had always wanted to have in the world but to know God and for God to draw me closer to him.

I also became interested in reading the bible but because I had no idea where to find anything I will simply just open it and read whatever page I have opened.

In February 2004, I had another experience that puts everything in higher perspective. I had continue everyday since my 2003 experience before going about my daily routine to read any bible page that open followed by a little prayer to God to draw me closer to him.

However, on this very day in 2004, something tells me to read Acts chapter 2 and after I had finished reading, I decided to say my little prayer as usual.

As I open my mouth to pray I could not say a word, instead, I busted into tears and I could not stop crying. I cried so much to the point of having a blocked nose and as I was crying I could not stop singing the song I love you Lord and Lord I give you my heart, I give you my soul. Then suddenly like a force of wind everywhere and beyond my imagination and human comprehension, I started to fall everywhere and each time I fell, I will get up only to fall down again.

After several fallings and as it became obvious that I could not stand without falling I choose to remain flat on the ground. I do not know how long I was flat on the ground for but when I rose up again, I open my mouth and I started to speak in tongues.

The amazing thing was that I understood everything that came out of my mouth and in translation it goes like this **"woman thou are**

loosed. Rejoice, today I have fully delivered you from the claws of Lucifer. Your heart was hardened and I had to circumcise it. Now in good circumcised heart you are totally free from all shackles and bondage. In total freedom go into the world and proclaim the gospel and I will be with you to the end of days".

When the interpretation came to me, I could not curtail my joy.

I started to jump up and down in so much excitement shouting I am free Jesus is Lord. I felt like calling a world press conference, say to the whole world Jesus is Lord, God is real, and I know. I know because I feel totally free and even though I could not explain this freedom I just knew I am free from something that has been compressing me all of my life.

In the 2003 experience, it was as if someone had lifted off a veil from my eyes but in this 2004 experience, it is as if my eye is not just open but I felt I am now completely free.

From this day onwards, the soft voice that I believed I heard back in 2003 became clearer in my mind and as it got louder, I became convinced without a doubt that this is the God, that the bible speaks about that is conversing with me.

I felt like an investigative reporter that has landed on the biggest scoop ever, which is that God does not just exist but he speaks and I can speak to him.

Not only was God speaking to me I find that he was prepared to answer any question that I may I have.

When I realised he was prepared to answer any questions that I may have I started to ask him the questions that have always troubled my mind and the answers he gave me were just amazing. He became my teacher and as time goes on, he said to me that I must start to write down all these things, as they are not just for me but also for the entire human race.

God said to me that the time that we are in is the end times and he has asked me to write these things for two main reasons.

First, it is to further enlighten the whole of mankind of who he is and at the same time through his enlightenment encourage the saints at heart to stay focused and faithful to the course of life to the very end.

Secondly, he said that this is to serve as his means of direct calling to all human to repent for his kingdom has come, Christ shall soon return and judgement day is near.

My entire experience with God to date is beyond what I can simply describe for God is indeed love and as love incredibly faithful as divine love.

Following my 2004 encounter, he guided me through the scriptures systematically by simply telling me to open my bible as I use to before. However, unlike before, to my surprise I will always land on a page that is full of the kind of words of promises that I went in search of in the first place back in 2003.

Through my daily experience with God, I have leant that it is by God's love that I am able to live a fulfilling life on earth and have eternal life of peace, joy and rest everlasting. I have found from my relationship with God that the love of God is my soul desire and all that I needed all along was to find his love for me. I know now that God speaks and that he is not just a generous giver and the creator of all things, but indeed the only king that is above all kings in all dimensions and dominion realms.

From my daily experience with God, I discover God love all humans so much.

Although my life from discovering God in the physical has been like hell on earth, I always find a renewed daily strength from his comforting love and in his words of encouragement to me.

With a renewed hope and strength in God, I am reassured daily of his love for me and with God by my side, I continue to rise daily above my circumstances, which I must say has been highly challenging.

Since I found God, so much upheaval has taken place in my life physically and there have been times that I had felt like giving up but in all of these things, I give thanks always to God for his love and comfort.

Through God's grace, I always have a renewed strength to go on and without his grace and mercy, it would have been impossible for me to continue in this journey of faith. God's teaching is continuous and I have been writing now for over three years on different aspects of life, and I write as he directs me.

He calls these teachings **"Revelations in Master Dominion"** and the first ever revelation lesson God gave me is about "God as the forgiver". This teaching is in many parts and is in actual conversations with God and as I continue to write as directed by him, I pray that God eternal blessings be upon all those who receive his words with an open heart. All bible references are from the normal King James Version.

CHAPTER ONE

EVERY MAN IS A SINNER

> Psalm 103: verse 3 "Who forgiveth all thine inequities;
> who healeth all thy diseases;" verse 4 "Who redeemeth thy
> life from destruction; who crowneth thee with
> lovingkindness and tender mercies".

GOD: To love the world is to die forever for the world is the world of sin. No man in the world can see without me for I the eternal God I am the light of the world through which any man can see and find his ways to high heaven. I am the Alpha and the Omega the beginning and the end. I am the Holy Trinity God and my revelation to you therefore for the record is from I God the Father, I God the Son and I God the Holy Spirit. I am the God of Abraham, Isaac and Jacob and as God of Abraham, Isaac and Jacob I am the Holy Redeemer of life.

I am the Most High God of the universe and as God of the universe the God of all nations as the creator of heaven and earth. The earth and all that is within it is mine, and as the Almighty God; I have dominion over and above all things[1] and as such, my revelation to you is for the benefit purpose of the entire human race.

---

[1] Psalm 24 verse 1

Let all those who have ears hear and let those that have eyes see in this end time that the end of for Lucifer and his followers in eternity is in the lake of fire. For all the prophetic writings in the scriptures is ahead of time already fulfilled but so that all bear record and witness in all realms I will reveal to man at the appointed time and hour that which is already fulfilled in eternity in time era.

Every man is a sinner and unless I forgive the sin of a man, his soul will perish everlasting. The starting point of my revelation to you is therefore on forgiveness for unless there is forgiveness there can be no peaceful reconciliation.

I forgive all sins and heal all infirmities for as God I am love and as love holiness everlasting. Without my forgiveness, man cannot walk in benefit of my entire perfect work.

I see you have many questions to ask and it is my promise to you that I shall answer them all for I am the one with the answer to everything.

I have asked that you have ready your bible and to begin with to note the words of Psalm 103 and in particular, the above-mentioned verses.

The bible is my very own inspirational work and as a book, the bible for man in time is their book of life that they need to navigate their way to understanding of eternal life principles. I am Word and as word, I speak.

I am a God of covenant and it is only by my own word that any man can be in covenant relationship with me.

My whole covenant of love is in blood and the bible gives knowledge of my Word to mankind so that by the blood of I AM man is in my spiritual book of life eternally to dwell in my eternal light presence.

The bible contains the whole of my word as such all-scriptural reference that I shall make in this my revelations to you shall only be from the bible. I made way for the bible to be in the world to make my entire purpose clear to man that it is eternal life for man by my own sacrificial love.

The bible is the only book that contains all answers and if the human vessels that I used to write the biblical scriptures were to send their writings today to a world book publisher, none would be interested to publish Genesis or Revelations.

The aim of the devilish man is to convince the entire human race in the end time that the earth evolves on its own and will extinct on its own to lead man to live recklessly in time and die eternally for their deadly error.

If man believes he is his own boss for he self-exists then he will see himself as unaccountable to any higher authority other than his own order. From seeing himself as unaccountable to a higher power, man will increasingly regard himself as the only universal Supreme Being that has all power, knowledge and intelligence to treat and give the meaning that he pleases to all things.

If man sees himself as the only power and order that exist then the only order that man will seek to obey is that of his own. The order of man in the flesh is evil and if man sees his evil order as universally supreme, man will only strive to carry out the works of the flesh out of his desperate mind of evil.

This is the danger for man in the end time for in the end time man's evil desire to walk in evil ways prevents him from seeing that the true consequences of his evil actions is eternal damnation of his soul.

The flesh is loyal to evil regiment and there is no peace for a man that is loyal to darkness evil. Only the truth gives peace and only in the truth is a man set free from the evil oppression of the evil deadly flesh.

I am the truth and as the truth peace.

For a man to have peace and soulful eternal rest, he must be loyal to my regime of life. My regime of life is all about sacrificial love for the manifestations purpose of my entire eternal life aims for man, which is eternal life of peace, rest and joy in everlasting regiment of goodness.

The bible is the road map to peace of mind for it is my book of revelation to man to enlighten them of my life objective purpose and if you remove the roadmap to peace no man can ever find eternal peace. The end time man is more in evil desperation for the dark fallen angels have invaded the world of flesh to have a final big feast in their death row.

In desperate mind of evil of all that man calls holy book in the world, no one book have been so heavily attacked and criticised by man like the bible.

To attack the truth is evidence of self-hatred and in self-hatred out of desperate mind to continue in sin. Man's end time attack of the bible is all in the aim to label the bible a complete total mythical lie or better still an ideology of paganism sold to the world to deceive the entire human race.

The bible is a book of revelations and it is so that man walk in mind of spiritual life purpose that I made way for man to have the scriptures in the world. to be enlightened is to be empowered and unless a man is enlightened of divine purpose of life, such man shall not embark in proper soul search to find innermost spiritual peace in me. If you throw away, your road map to peace of mind then there can be no peacefulness.

The end time agenda of the devilish man is to label the entire bible a lie and a myth. I AM THAT I AM, in my timelessness existence and if I speak to you, as the I AM in this present time then it cannot be true that the bible is all a lie. For although time will change his hand movements I that the bible speaks about as the I AM in all timely era; I am eternal in my existence and as the eternal Almighty God I am the same yesterday , today and forever.

Man seeks to take the bible out of equation in total mind of desperate wickedness. The heart of man is wicked, the ways of man is evil, and all that man is interested in is to rule the world in wicked mind of evil.

If a man accepts that I am the creator then he will seek to know my ways to have full benefit of my creations.

However when you say you are your own maker and as such you make your own heaven and hell on earth you say you are in your own right by your own power and might a god in the universe.

My emphasis on forgiveness in this part of my revelation to you is because life is all about relationship. A human being in sinful nature is always in mind to offend and if you offend each other persistently then unless there is continuous forgiveness there can be no joyfulness in the human relationships.

The answer to the problem of every man as I revealed it in the bible is in my divine loving sacrifice. The cornerstone of a joyous relationship is love, and as God, I am love. To attempt to remove love from the equation is to end up with zero profit in time and in timelessness era.

Without love, all that is left is pain, sorrow and anguish and out of their hateful relationship with the devil, all that the sinful man has in his soul is darkness from evil oppression.

The world today is full of the hateful minded and in thick layer of darkness evil man is only interested in performing the works of the axes of evil.

The evil-minded seeks to disrespect righteousness of life to promote his sinful self-righteous ways. The devil deceives a self-righteous man to lead his mind to oppress and deceive his fellow beings.

The world is a world of flesh and the world of flesh is a terrible world for the sinful nature man. Lustful spirits compresses the soul of man deeper in hell due to their increased desire to sin. The human relationship in the world worsens day by day in growth of selfishness and lustfulness in the human minds. Children hate their parents and parents oppressed by the slavery system of the world have no time for their children.

Marriage is a joke and husbands and wives when they say I do it is to say I do not immediately after. Beastly order seeks to eradicate divine ordinance for marital order in time and man in general seeks to walk against everything that is holy and divine out of evil mind of self-righteousness.
Strife is at his highest amongst brethren and the love of money and for the things of the world means, that man is no longer interested in the truth.

Life in the world is hell for many and man considers me as no longer relevant. As God, I am the author and finisher of faith and today in the world there are many movements called faith.
All of this faith speaks of love and charity and I ask if all world faith is committed to love and charity how is it that there is so much hate in the world. Faith is only possible with divine love and it does not follow that because you call yourself a Christian you are automatically of good faith.

The faith of many in the world including those that portray themselves as Christians is of vanity. Many antichrists call themselves Christians and the only one they deceive is themselves by hiding under the brand name of goodness. No man can mock or deceive me for I know all and I see all.

Many so-called Christians today are lovers of money not of Christ and only call themselves Christians to defraud many and to give the name of Christ bad publicity so that mankind is discouraged from seeking the only way to eternal life of peace, rest and joy.

Darkness is deep upon the face of man in the end time world and man is no longer interested in the truth of life for all that man is interested in is money.

No matter how crazy the idea is, so long as it is an antichrist idea with moneymaking potentials the world will embrace it with open hearts. The soul desire of a man in the world is money only and the easiest way to make money in the eyes of man is to market the idea that Christ is a liar and a fraud.

The world hates the truth and man in increased mind of sin is no longer interested in goodness respect or integrity. The human society has degenerated to bottomless pit of evil and as a result, many are only interested in doing the works of the flesh. For the heart of most human is; on world riches, the general focus is on evil and in a world full of the desperately evil mankind in general no longer see goodness as profitable.

The world market is only interested in evil commerce and in a world of evil commerce; demons from the graveyard of death feed the soul of man daily with fables.

Every man on earth is motivated to act by a spirit for all of man is a spirit and to the one you are connected is the one that you will be motivated by to carry out his works.

If you are in evil, evil will drive your mind to carry out its works and if in goodness, goodness will direct your heart for goodness sake of life.

WITHOUT DIVINE LOVE MAN HAS NO HOPE IN THE WORLD OF FLESH

The truth of life is love and beyond love, there is no higher power above love for love conquers all.

I JEHOVAH God I am love. I am the Almighty omnificent, omnipotent and omnipresent God of the universe the creator uncreated. As the God of gods I only self exist as Word.

To place mankind in consciousness of my Word I gave my whole word to man and this whole word is I Christ that I revealed as my heart of love to make man able to find forgiveness from me for goodness sake of life. From the beginning of time, I have kept man in heart of my eternal purpose as JEHOVAH God that it is love.

Through my relationship with the elect, I made my purpose clear to man in the whole of timely era that it is salvation for the soul of man by my own sacrificial love.

Man from going against the wishes of love is a criminal for the wishes of love is goodness for goodness sake. To love is to live and afford the benefit of life to others. With love, you can melt a heart made of stone for with love all things are possible.

Love is the truth and to hate the ways of love is to love the ways of hate. Only in heart of love can you create for goodness sake. Only in love is harmonious and peaceful relationship. Only in love shall you respect one another. Only in love shall you have sympathy and empathy. Only in love shall you have mercy. Only in love shall you do unto others what you wish others to do to you. Only in love is light and only in love shall you have confirmations and preservation of holiness faith in your heart.

Without love, all that is left is vanity and in heart of vanity, you can never have mercy for in mind of vanity all of man is brutal and are in wicked heart and mind of greed to grab all things to deny others from having goodness benefit of it.

No man in vanity cares about another for the love of the world is evidence of hate for yourself and fellow beings. A man in vanity heart cannot be in mind of forgiveness for in vanity mind a man is only interested in what he wants and does not care how many toes he steps on to get it.

If man is in mind of hate for their love of the world how can they see the bible as containing record and account of love and as account of love the truth.

The world is full of many ideas and most human will agree that in all of their ever-changing ideas it is still always a good idea to love another and for another to love them. To be in mind of love is to act in ways of love and if you say you love and by your actions you say you hate then it is by your actions obvious that you are a liar and a hypocrite.

To love is to be a friend of goodness and to be a friend of goodness is to have the mind of showing loving kindness to others and if you are your own enemy, you cannot be a friend of goodness.

Although most of man will agree that, it is good to love or be loved man as flesh and blood in their mortal state is demonic and a demonic flesh is incapable of love.

To love you must have loving capacity and you only become lovingly capable to love as a human being when you are a living spirit for only if you are a living spirit will you have good conscience.

A man in evil flesh that is of flesh only cannot be of good conscience and without a good conscience; you cannot have merciful eyes towards your fellow being.

A dead spirit man is full of sinful desire to continue in sinful ways to the detriment of his soul eternally. A dead spirit man full of sinful desire will pursue his self-righteous ways not just to his own detriment but also to detriment another.

Such a being in selfish mind of deadly self-righteousness cannot operate in good conscience for to be dead is to be without good conscience. Only a living soul is he able to operate in good conscience of life for the benefit of others.

A dead being is a contaminator that is always in mind to engage others in the mind to sin so that they remain sinfully infected just like him. Sin is cancer that eats the soul of man in death to remain forever dead. My entire work as I revealed it to man in full biblical context is to place man in perfect covenant relationship with me by my work of remissions so that the cancerous effect of sin, which is death to the soul of man, does not destroy their soul everlasting.

Life is all about will power and the will power of life only belongs to love. The free will of man in the flesh is to sin as his main desire and the will to sin is death to the soul eternally. The will of love is the enabling power of life. Where there is a loving will; there will always be a way no matter how high the barrier may be.

The world of flesh is a world of bad and sorrowful relationships because of wilful offensive minds and in a world of bad relationships; forgiveness is the only key to peaceful reconciliation.

Love is all about faithful sacrifice for goodness sake of life. Every divine law and prophetic purpose of life is all about love for only in love is it possible to have peaceful rest and joy in life. Divine love is all about perfect living and perfect living is only from perfect divine sacrifice.

As God that is love, I made my standards of loving sacrifice obvious to man from my own sacrifice. The standard of my divine loving standards is wilful abiding in perfect sacrifice to perfect the souls of those that are willing to abide in my own perfect sacrifice.

Love is consensual and for love is consensual, the spiritual willingness of a man to change from his sinful ways is evidence of obvious intention that he is in mind of consent to enter into eternal loving relationship with me. My sacrifice is to afford the benefit of life to man and this benefit I gave to man out of my own loving free will.

As the Most High God of the universe, I am a God of relationships and as the God of relationships the head of the pyramid of life. A man is only a living soul if in life pyramid relationship with me for all those that are not in relationship with me are dead souls and as dead souls in death regimental pyramids.

The reward of good deeds is eternal life of peaceful relationship with me the omnipotent God of the universe. To be good on deeds is to be wise for evil does not pay any goodness dividends whatsoever.

As the creator of all, I am the only one that can force a man to do anything. However, as God that is love I am all about consensual loving relationships not forceful relationships.

To allow man use of his free will is to say to man that they are not robots for a robot is only a machine with no real life potentials.

The aim of the wicked devil is to replace man with robots so that man like robotic machines is only in mind of evil programmes.

I created man to be just like me to choose between good and evil and there is no point in me giving free will to man if I will never allow them to make use of it.

No man is able to conform to divine goodness ways in time as flesh without the power of my love for man as flesh is anti goodness in their ways.

To resist evil and abide in goodness is only by power of love for only in love will a man see the eternal benefit reward of goodness ways and keep within it for the eternal goodness of his soul in everlasting life.

You can only confer benefit of life in loving free will for in evil mind use of free will all that a man is able to give another is his own condemnation in evil.

In my own free will, I gave man the benefit of eternal life so that the soul of man enjoys everlasting life of peace, joy and rest.

The only thing a man has to do to activate this eternal benefit for his soul is to enter into covenant relationship with me by my own preordained channel for eternal life relationship with me.

To enter into relationship with me by my own channel is to abide willingly and lawfully by my goodness life order and all those that lawfully abide in my will shall inherit my inheritance will, which is eternal life of joy, peace and rest

To see in the world man must enter into my divine righteousness for the perfection of his souls in loving kindness of eternal life. Love brings light and hatred places the mind in thicker darkness. No being that hate himself can love another for to love another you must first love yourself.

To give love to another you must have love in you for what you do not have you cannot give. Many although say they love themselves they know not what love is for when they behold their image in the mirror the image that their spirit sees is ugliness and in spiritual sight of their ugliness their spirit is extremely sad and sorrowful.

Love is beauty and it is only in love that you have eternal life of peace, joy and rest. Joy, rest and peace are spiritual benefits from love and hate a spiritual curse upon the hateful soul for being against the wishes of love.

To enjoy the goodness of love you must submit to the will of love and submitting to the will of love is to obey my word and in obedience follow my instructions of life for goodness sake of your soul.

Hatred leads to dead end only goodness divine love can save a man from the dead end result of hate. To be an enemy of goodness is to be a devil, and a devil is an evil doer. Whosoever is an enemy of goodness shall be just like the devil an evil doer.

To be a devil is to be a cursed demonic spirit. The reward for an evil doer is greater potion of evil and to have greater potion of evil as eternal reward is to remain in eternal damnation of pain and evil sorrowfulness.

A devil knows no mercy and as a merciless spirit incapable of forgiveness. A devil is a destroyer and does not care for the goodness of anyone for the devil is hate and hate never yield any goodness outcome. Hate is destructive and a wicked devilish man in camp hatred will always be of a wicked heart to destroy the joy of another.

The potion for the wicked is greater wickedness for what you sow you reap in greater multitude.

You do not sow a seed and harvest the same amount of seed and if a man sows the seed of evil, he will have as his reward greater potions of evil.

Most human will agree that it is wrong for a man to profit out of wrong doing and if I the God of the universe made all things is it too much to expect mankind to obey my wishes for goodness sake of life? Man from going against my wishes sold his soul to the devil and I will not allow any devil to walk through the gates of heaven to reside in heaven.

A devil as a doer of evil works will always be in mind of warfare and as such cannot have peace of mind. A demonic spirit bitterly hates himself and as such always envious and extremely jealous. A devilish minded always seeks to discredit the godly at heart through constantly trying them to react in provocation and in provocation vengeful warfare.

The devil knows that the wages of sin is death hence only interested to lead man to sin and be forever indebted to death.

Hatefulness leads the mind to oppress others in bitterness envy of hatred jealousy. No man can have joy in hatred for hatred is bitterness and in bitter resentments a man will always walk on the path of deadly evil to their own self destructive eternal end.

To be in mind of hate as a spirit being is to be a car engineered and controlled by the devil to a total crash end.

To love others you must first love yourself. Hatefulness towards others is evidence of the person's hatred for himself.

A hateful person will always seek to destroy the joy of others. To be hateful minded is to be a devilish minded being. Those that hate suffer in their hatefulness for the joy of a spirit being is in love.

Only in love do you have total peace and rest for to love is to obey the order regiment of life and all those that love will have the fullness benefit of life protective order.

The devil deceives the hateful minded in time to believe that being in hateful hell regiment in the world is heaven and for such man sees himself as already in heaven he does not bother to find the way to the real heaven.

Many in the world today are devil's agent and as agents of devils dead busy acting on devilish instructions. Every man as a spirit acts on the spiritual instruction of the spirit that he has connections with for no man is a spiritual Island. A man that connects to the devil will only be interested to promote in the world the works of his devilish master. The works of a devilish spirit is always against the objective of love for man, which is eternal life. A devil is a slave and as such only interested in enslaving the soul of a man in sin and in sin in eternal condemnation of death.

If a man connects to my Holy Spirit, I will guide his deeds performance to be in line of my divine loving order, which is eternal salvation for the soul of mankind.

A devil is chaotic minded and the instruction that a devil gives is to create chaos. A devil is a flesh eater and out of chaos, devils have plenty flesh food supply.

The world of flesh is a world of hate and in the world of hate dangerous criminals from the bottomless pits of hell leads the mind of man to carry out the works of the axes of evil.

A devilish mind is always full of wroth and a man in mind of devilish wroth will always be an enemy of peace. To have peace you must walk in divine righteousness and a man in his flesh will always in his wicked wroth seek to subject others forcefully to his wicked self-righteous ways.

To begrudge is to hate and to forgive is to love. Without forgiveness, a man cannot see in his bitterness hateful mind of the flesh and if a man cannot see the way of life, he will perish forever in death of his soul. In a world of the hateful offender, the only defence is love and forgiveness is a life objective purpose for the goodness sake of eternal peacefulness.

If you forgive one another then how will there be chaos and if there is no chaos how will there be bloodshed.

To forgive you need the power to forgive and this power is in my divine love. Forgiveness brings peaceful reconciliations but in the absence of forgiveness, all that a man has is deadly bitterness hatred.

As God I forgive all sins for if I do not then no man will be in relationship with me after the fall of the first Adam.

To hate is common to man and to forgive out of love is divine way of life.

Except a man is in heart of divine love and in divine love walk in goodness divine character of love and as part of goodness character have a forgiving heart such man cannot have the reward of eternal life.

Divine love is sacrificial and to forgive those that trespass against you is to make a sacrifice that is acceptable to me.

Man as a mortal being is selfish and no one can be in mind to sacrifice for the benefit of another in selfish mind of hatred. Salvation is a selfless act of love for only in selfless heart of love will you sacrifice to give the benefit of life to another.

To save man from eternal death of his soul I gave to the world in my own forgiveness the saints, the holy prophets and for the total remissions of sins for the goodness of my holy name I as the ultimate teacher of righteousness came in time for the sake of total perfection of man's spirit. As God, I am the everlasting Father and as the everlasting Father of all spirits I am not subject to time instead time is subject to me and even though I came in time I am in eternity forever the Trinity one God.

As Father of all spirits, I see only as my sons those that are in me and in me willingly submissive to my spiritual objectives of loving kindness. To obey my will and order is to be my son and my will and order for man is to forgive one another as I forgive them of their sins.

Only those that are by my spirit led are my son for unless you are in me established in my spiritual mind you cannot walk in my ways to serve my eternal life objective purpose.

Unless a man aligns himself with my eternal life objective purpose, he will walk in opposite objective mind order.

To be in mind of objectives that is opposite to mine is to be in mind of hate and a man that hates will only succeed in permanently destroying his own soul everlasting. The objective purpose of my goodness will is for man to have eternal total goodness of life for goodness sake of my holy name.

As God, I am good on deeds and as good on deeds; my eternal objective purpose is loving kindness. Although man says to love is good, no man in death is capable of walking in perfect faith of goodness loving standards.

Man in body of sin is his own number one enemy for all that a man in the devil does is against himself.

To hate is to enable evil to rule over you and when you enable evil to rule the mind there can be no rest or peace of mind.

By my perfect loving works of remissions, I made my objective purpose clear for man to see that it is about abiding in my divine love to walk in my divine order of life.

To have a mind of hate is to be led by evil and many so called world experts of today are agents of Lucifer for they have given their hearts to evil and unto whom you give your heart is whom you shall do his works.

To be led by the devil is to be pro evil and anti goodness.

A man that is pro evil is antichrist and today many antichrists are in the world to deceive the blind man to help them destroy their soul forever. It is foolishness to hate for hate does not produce any good seeds. Instead, hate brings about extreme darkness and sorrowful evil.

It is goodness of life to forgive for only in forgiveness is purpose of life served for the benefit of the soul of man. The world of flesh is a world of persistent evil offenders. In a world of generational offenders, there can be no peace unless man operates in mind of constant forgiveness to generate peacefulness in their relationship with one another.

If all of man as sinners constantly offends one another then only by constant forgiveness can there be peace and harmony in the human society.

If a man offends you and you choose to retaliate by offending him even more and he chooses to offend you back even more who then shall put a stop to the long line of offence where both are determined to offend one another greater than the last time?

Most human in the world are full of bitter hatred resentments and a man full of hateful resentments is only interested in harming others all in mind of vengefulness.

If all is vengeful in their mind towards each other, how then can there be peaceful relationships.

A man in heart of revenge is one with a bitter heart and a man with a bitter heart of revenge is a man blinded with fury and a man blinded with anger will never see in his hateful mind that the one he destroys is himself and it is all for nothing.

Vengeance is mine and as God, I am always just and equitable in my ways of judgement.

When a man chooses to take my universal law into his hands, he denies himself my justices and by so doing empowers evil to rule him. The book of Romans Chapter 12 from verses 19 reads **"Dearly beloved avenge not yourselves, but rather give place unto wrath; for it is written, Vengeance is mine; I will repay said the Lord".** Verse 20 **"Therefore if thine enemy hunger, feed him, if he thirst; give him drink: or in so doing thou shall heap coals of fire on his head".** Verse 21 **"Be not overcome of evil, but overcome evil with good".** I see you have a say and some questions.

ME: Yes. To be honest I believe with all my heart that you are love from my experiencing your goodness comfort.

However, since my encounter I have never known so much hatred directed towards me.

I would say life for me on the face of this earth since I had known you have become virtually and extremely more difficult than I could have ever imagined it to be.

Sometimes I wonder is it that God has become softer or what; because when you look at the God written about in the Old Testament it is as if it is not the same God written about in the New.

Your ways as God in Old Testament account is full of power manifestation and instant justice.

God as we see in the Old Testament parted the sea, brought down walls, fed his people in the wilderness and today you believe you are praying to the same God for the simplest things in life and nothing is moving or changing.

It is easy to confuse and convince a man today that there is no God or that the bible is a lie.

As evidenced by the state of the world today combined with the fact that it seems only if you follow the way of evil can you manage or survive it is no surprise that many are attracted to follow evil ways even if it is to a dead end.

Many today sees no point in believing or trusting God because they feel let down by those that they consider as savants of God.

From what their eyes have seen in their efforts and attempt to serve and be faithful to God most do not even want to hear the word God anymore because they are so burnt and due to their painful experience they feel it is better they stay clear of the whole godly business.

The church is like a joke with so much politics and corruption going on and in my experience of trying to minister to people, I see that many believe that the church is an institution that the world will be better of without it.

Many see the church as a mere political institution with many hidden dark evil secrets that has as its overall terrible agenda to deceive and defraud the poor and the vulnerable.

As for holiness and good moral standards many sees their own self believed human standard of morality higher than the church as it appears today even though they would not count themselves as godly at all.

Generally, people are discouraged from good faith and speaking to people about Christ from the attitude I have seen from people is as if I am a fool to believe in this big lie that Christ is the answer.

To believe in Christ is like enlisting yourself in camp punishment to be punished by the world and it is as if it is all for nothing.
The idea of eternal life sounds good to many. However, what about now on earth is the question in the mind of many.
This for me is the main problem because if we see you as a God that we must relate to does that not mean that whatsoever we go through on earth we should be able to rely and depend on you to relief us a little for goodness sake.

If goodness is discouraged by the fact that those that are wicked oppresses and depresses those that seeks to be godly and the evil hearted is non-stop in their bombardment of evil towards the good to push them to a break point I wonder how it is that goodness shall be seen in the world.
Today many are suffering financially and feel crippled with ongoing continuous huge debts problems.

In the midst of all this, they are not so much worried about eternal life as such but are more worried about their day-to-day problems such as paying their bills and keeping their heads from sinking deeper into the world river of never ending pain and sorrow.

Many although will appreciate the reward of eternal life however, for now in the world they are very more concerned about their daily survival.

The world is indeed a world of great evil oppression as you have said and if the cry of many to you for help is met by what seems like more oppression and greater depression how can they hold on in heart of love in the midst of what looks like a hopeless cry for help and relief. One cannot but wonder sometimes if indeed you are serving the same God that parted the sea and brought down the wall of Jericho and with Christ work of remission and all; life for the godly on earth should have become easier not made tougher and very difficult.

When I had my encounter with you, I became very interested in everything to do with Christianity and you hear many people speak about how from praying for seven or so days they had a major breakthrough.
You cannot but wonder from your own experience whether this is all rehearsed adverts or indeed fast miraculous response brought about by their power of a prayer that is greater than your own prayer.

The reality for me is like everlasting prayer and fasting and the response I seem to be getting is what appears to be greater enemy opposition and discouragement like never before.

Indeed instead of such stories encouraging me

I actually find them nowadays to be discouraging and this is because of the feeling that everyone seem to be getting answers to their prayers except you.

If everyone is getting answers to their prayers and not you then the question is what is it that you are doing wrong and everyone else is doing right. I wonder sometimes what I have done that is so bad that I cannot even have a break or a pause from what seem like constant evil bombardment.

It is lonely to have a Holy Spirit experience because to say that God speaks to you all the time and you are forever waiting on him to do the simplest thing for you is something most people cannot understand. Most especially if they do not even believe there is a God and everything as far as they are concerned is working fine for them.

If we hope to be relieved of our burden by seeking you and if with everything that I for one have been through which is as if every axes of evil there is in the universe has been empowered to torment me instead of me finding such relief.

I wonder sometimes how anyone on earth this day can hold on to their faith.

I find life in the world for me in these past years extremely difficult and worst aspect is that those that you expect to support you are the main ones that seem to go out of their ways to bring out not the best that you seek to be but the worst out of you.

I cannot as a human being understand how to keep going when it seems as if you have been punched over and over again non stop and as far as you are concerned you have surrendered to Christ because you really do not see yourself as having any other choice because everything else is seriously against you.

Even though you have surrendered and hope for the best and you are totally down with your hands up and determined to be good loving and kind it seems the enemy will not let go of his wicked punches.

I find it hard sometimes to comprehend how you provide so much comfort in midst of what to me is a severe painful situation for me to go though the pain instead of totally eradicating the pain.

If relationship with you means heavy chastisement then does it mean to be godly minded is to expect punishment on earth and eternal life of joy forever as reward for going through this things.

Sometimes I wonder if Christ died for me how then does it feel as if I am been killed over and over again non-stop.

If this is what many go through then it is no surprise to me that many end up giving up to join the band wagon of evil because it seems that it is the only way to get by in the world.

The ungodly seem to have it all in the world and seem determine to break the godly minded into pieces for wanting to be good through systematic evil oppression. The idea that there is a light at the end of the tunnel is good but what about when it seems like the tunnel has no end.

One cannot help but wonder how your God that is love allows you to go through such things that I have been through and with all his power it seems as if he does nothing to help me eradicate the whole situation instead he tells me to persevere in a situation of never ending trials and tribulations.

It does not make sense to me as a human being and sometimes I can see why many today have abandoned their godly faith in you to defect to a camp that they consider as fast and quick in responding to their cry for help. Despite having the conviction that you are love, I cannot help but understand those that wonder whether God answers prayers or whether he really cares about our human pain and sufferings.

The way I see things from a human perspective is that if out of desperation and frustration I came to you for help and now it seems I am punished severely for doing so or for finding you it begs the question what manner of help am I getting from you.

Many people today are suffering greatly for having faith in God and to be in heart of faith in God today is like to be a fool in the eyes of the world.

From my own human experience, I feel like the world is crucifying me daily and I wonder when I am likely to enjoy benefit of resurrection ascension to heaven to have eternal life of peace. I have never shed so much tears in my entire life and when I speak to people about God sometimes I ask myself what am I calling them to come to God for because judging from my own experience it is beyond my human understanding the things that I have been through all from finding God.

As much as I understand from seeing all I have seen that it is by good you overcome evil and not evil-by-evil I just like to say as a human being that it is easier said than done.

To continue in mind of goodness in a world were everything appears to be working against you just for having a desire to be good cannot be an easy thing for any human being.

It is hard to explain to anyone what you are going through and given all of my experience the worst aspect for me is you do not even know who to trust because everything and everyone seems to be against you and having to cope sometimes is like impossible.

People seem to derive joy from going out of their way to make you behave like an animal so that people can criticise and question whether you are really of God.

I understand the importance of holy character and I am desperate to walk in your holy character for goodness sake but it seems the more desperate I am the more determined are those around me to provoke me to angry reactions.

I am willing to turn the other face when someone slaps me in the other however, it would be nice if someone were to slap me on both sides and just leave me alone.

How is someone able to continue to cope when there seem to be no end to what seems like a long line of tough times and never ending chastisement and no matter what you do it feels as if everything is even more against you for wanting to be good?

For me I have no word to describe my experience and many times I have reached the point of wanting to run away somewhere even though I have no idea where to.

In all of this, I must say your support and love is indescribably incredible.

Nevertheless, I must ask how is it that those that you elect or those that seek you goes through hell on earth and it seems this hellish run has no end.

For me I feel sometimes as if I am having an experience of frying pan to fire and with those that I expect to help suddenly now appearing as my worst enemy how can one have the strength to carry on in a never changing situation.

If people in hopelessness and helplessness come to you for help how then can they continue to hold on when for coming to you, it seems they are now in the hands of their enemies severely punished by them. Although I am convinced that you are love and that, you love me like no other. I still find it difficult to understand how in your love for me you allow me to suffer what I consider as bombarded by evil beyond my human imagination.

I am sure there are people out there that will be able to relate to me in my experiences and it would be nice if you can just help me to understand these things in a way that is relative to me as a human being.

Yes, you have taught me to persevere in longsuffering and I must say you have been there to sustain and comfort me in all of these things. As such, I simply cannot thank you enough for your comfort, support and for keeping me strong and awake in times when I had simply wish to quit because I felt tired and totally fed up.

Yes, I bear record and testimony of your love and support and despite all that I have been through nothing out there can change my mind that you are love and as love the king of kings and Lord of lords forever.

Yes, I understand I am to remain good no matter what because as you have always said to me if you allow evil to break you then you have become evil.

However, despite my understanding of these things my question is when does it ever stop? Sometimes I feel like yelling out so loud because I am so much under pressure and I struggle sometimes to continue to pray for a person and forgive them when they in turn seem to be only interested and determine to destroy me no matter what.

If you try explaining to people, what you are going through the only advice they have to give is that you pray and read the word. What happens if you have prayed and prayed and it is as if your prayer is empowering your enemy to oppress you the more instead of making things better.

It is like saying to someone with a headache who has taken many pain-killing tablets to take the same tablets that they have taken repeatedly without any relief.

Indeed, from taking the tablets repeatedly they are beginning to feel that they do not just have headaches but stomachaches, leg pains and total body aches and pains.

For me this is the most frustrating part because instead of practical support all you get is someone telling you to read this psalm and fast this fast, which is exactly what you have been doing yet things instead of getting better look as if they are getting worse.

As far as you are concerned as a human being, you have prayed and fasted and you have played it all by the rules yet it looks as if your enemy instead of leaving you alone they are more determined to break you into pieces.

Sometimes it is as if you only interested to answer the prayers that you instruct and encourage me to pray for others but none pertaining to me as human being.

For me it has been one tough time to tough time without a break and it is for relief sake that I came to you in the first place.

I must say it is just too hard for any human from a practical human point to remain good, loving, kind forgiving and faithful in all of this when in your daily experiences it feels as if the whole world is against you in all aspect.

GOD: I must say you have asked very interesting questions and have made very important comments. Now before I answer your questions, I would like to ask you one question and it is this; in all that, you have been through do you still believe that it is better to be with me or without me?

ME: I had no life without you and I must say it is when I found you that I have what I can call a life and as such I say you are life and to be without you is death for when I did not know you I did not even know whether I was going or coming.

I was in complete darkness and could not see and from your opening of my eyes, life has a total different meaning to me.

The trouble for me in all of this is the fact that although finding life and the meaning of life has opened my eyes of understanding to see things in greater light I find that my discovery of life has made life in generally much harder for me to live in the world.

The reason of course is due to the things that I have had to face and keep facing for these many years. Despite all my experiences, I would not change a thing because I know I cannot live without you and nothing made sense to me until I found you.

However, if all I have seen in these many years is the story of everyone that has a godly encounter then it is like having a bitter and sweet experience kind of.

The sweet on one hand for me is that I have your support, love, encouragement, kindness and unmerited loving forgiveness. The bitter for me on the other hand is that it appears for every loving experience I have with you I suffer severe punishment in the world for it.

For me I find it hard at times to keep praying and to continue to forgive a person that seems to be determined to destroy me.

You have emphasised to me over the years never to hate no matter what because hate as you always say is to call unto evil to lead the heart to do the works of the axes of evil, which is wickedness for evil sake. I understand this fact however it must be impossible for any human to go through all that I have been through and be in mind of goodness still in the world without the help of you Holy Spirit.

Through your Holy Spirit comfort and guidance I must say my toughest days has worked out to be the best days because in every experience you always use it as a lesson point for me and as a result, I am always encouraged to hold on to what is right for it is right.

I find it overwhelmingly difficult sometimes to remain loving, kind and forgiving towards other human beings that appears to hate and despise me for no apparent reasons.

However, I find it always rewarding that no matter how hard things may get I always seem to have an unexplained innermost joy and I find in that joy that it is in itself a joyful thing to seek goodness for your fellow being no matter what.

I have no way of explaining to anyone how you have encouraged me to love those that I see to hate me. I consider this as one of the most wonderful aspect about you because if you give me such encouragement and guide me in good conscience mind to forgive then indeed you must have a greater goodness conscience and higher mind of forgiveness.

For me as a human being the most difficult aspect sometimes is in the fact that I have the burden to always forgive, love and be kind to others that are not of the same mind toward me.

This hard part is made worse by the fact that no matter what I do it is as if my oppressor is determined to provoke me to evil reaction by causing me more pain and anguish and I have to take it all in and have total perseverance instead of you preventing it from happening.

It is like being told to continue to take severe painful blow on the same spot and no matter how painful the pain gets you are always told you must take it, forgive, and forget because to even dwell on these things will mean bitterness resentment and in such mind you will be in mind of vengeance.

For me it is easier to forgive if someone ceases from hurting you after some time.

However how do you keep forgiving someone that keep hurting you repeatedly and the more you beg them to stop the more they are determine to hurt you even more than the last time.

In a situation whereby it seems your oppressor is greatly empowered to tempt you to see how much you can really take before you break apart and choose to join the evil bandwagon it becomes difficult after a while to keep your peaceful silence.

If the oppressor is determined to keep oppressing me and you continue to say I should persevere I find this hard to understand given that you are able to stop my oppressor from oppressing me further most especially given that you see all the stress and pain that the whole experience is causing me.

Despite all said, I still say to be with you is life and as life the only way for me to goodness life everlasting. Therefore, I believe it is wisdom of life to continue to obey your instructions of goodness and in doing so hold on to you no matter what I go through.

For you are to life and as life everything that is good then to be with you is what makes me to be of life.

I have also leant an important lesson from my entire experience that goodness of life is all about loving perseverance and central to the heart of love is good exercise of patience in perseverance for the sake of goodness outcome in all things.

If evil is persistently wicked then good will not be visible in the world if those in mind of goodness give up and follow the way of evil out of shear evil pressure.

If evil is desperately wicked and in such desperation does not quit from oppressive ways then the good at heart must be adamantly faithful to the ways of goodness for goodness sake of life.

From my own experience, however I think it is impossible for a human being to continue to live in harmony and in harmony have a continuous heart to love and forgive without you. Most especially in a worldly environment packed with beings that have bitter hatred for one another and everyone in mind of hate is only interested to tear each other apart.

I always see the need for you and feel that the reason why relationship has gone sour in the world is due to our lack of spiritual insight and understanding of our need of you.

Without love as you said, all we have in the world is soured relationship.

With many humans as products of bitter soured relationship, the world is packed with many beings that are full of anger, greatly distressed, depressed, confused and vengeful.

I cannot see myself to have persevered in heart of love in my experiences without the constant support and encouragement that you provide daily.

I do not see how any human can avoid not having a vengeful mind or retaliation towards someone that they see as wicked towards them without the help of your Holy Spirit.

I consider it as a miracle that through your comforting loving kindness you enable me daily to go through my experience in continuous mind of loving kindness even though I see many to be desperate to bombard me daily with so much of what I see as shear wickedness.

My encounter with you is like joy with you and sorrow from the world. In the sorrow aspect it is as if I am punished without any mercy from enjoying the love that I have from you but I still say to be with you is the whole essence of life and as such I see no hope of life whatsoever without you.

GOD: Very good answer. To start my own answers I will refer you to Psalm 73 from verses 12 and it says **"Behold, these are the ungodly, who prosper in the world; they increase in riches."** Verse 13 says

"**Verily I have cleansed my heart in vain and washed my hand in innocency.**" Verse 14 "**For all the day long have I been plagued, and chastised every morning.**" Verse 15 "**If I say I will speak thus, behold, I should offend against the generation of thy children**". Verse 16 "**When I though to know this, it was too painful for me.**" Verse 17 "**Until I went into the sanctuary of God; then I understood I their end.**" Can you relate to this Psalm?

ME: Yes.

GOD: The point I am making is that reading the psalms or the word and by that you mean the scriptures is necessary to affirm to your mind your conviction so do not see it as a waste of time or pointless to do so no matter how many times you have read it before.

THE WORD IS YOUR SPIRITUAL SWORD

The world of flesh is a world of conflict and to be flesh and engage in flesh conflicting non-spiritual ways is to be in mind of disorderliness. Life is about order and the order of life is all for perfect living.

The flesh always seeks to contaminate the spirit and man as flesh is always battling with the conflicting priorities of his flesh desires in time and his spiritual desires for eternal life.

Where there is a conflict between priorities of time and timelessness, the one of timeless existence must prevail. Time is only for a moment but eternity is everlasting and as such to focus on time is to loose sight of eternity.

Timeless existence is all about power and the highest power in all realms is love. The word of love is power and as power, the word is the sword of a spirit being.

In times of great trials and tribulations, you need to assert the word to your mind to keep walking in line of life hopefulness for when hope dies faith disappears.

Eternal hope of life is the propeller of good faith in the mind of man for when a man is in a state of eternal hopelessness all that he will pursue in time will be time related and this will only make him to loose his soul forever in eternal life.

The word as power is also living water to your soul and in time of tribulations, you need to remind yourself of the word that you believe in. This is why it is still important to keep reading the word even though you have read it before because it is by so doing that you profess and confirm your word believe to your mind.

By affirming to your mind the true word, you overcome the cripple effect of negative word of the flesh. Affirming the word to yourself will renew your strength and will enable you to rise immediately above any opposite negative word situation that you may appear to be in.

As a living spirit, you are not to fight like the dead.

For the dead wage war against themselves all to greater damage to their souls.

The living knows that he is a winner already because by my grace he knows that I have predestined him to carry out the objectives of lives to receive the total benefit of life.

The life objective desire of love is goodness for goodness sake. In light of the predestined high privilege afforded to the called predestined to have total benefit of grace reward in time and in eternal life, an elect must always have the mind to walk in divine sacrificial love to give the same benefit of life that he has to another.

A living spirit will always have full spiritual convictions that he is a life winner no matter what the case may be.

However, the aim of the evil flesh is to lead the human to confuse man to believe that evil has all the power and control.

The reason for this is to lead the human mind to walk in fleshy emotions so that in fleshy emotions the human is non-responsive to ways of good faith.

To be good on deeds is to be a winner in all dominion, dimensional realms. The confusion tactics of the devilish flesh is to make the goodness winner believe that for being in mind of goodness evil power has caged and trapped him to subject him to severe punishment.

Life is all about convictions and for every conviction you have someone has the opposite and in a world of many convictions the only way to hold on to your conviction is to be certain in your believe otherwise someone by crook or means will try to make you abandon your chosen right to partake in their chosen wrong.

There are two types of humans in the world namely builders and destroyers.

A builder is a creator and a destroyer is a wrecker. I am a creator and to be a creator like me you must have a mind of love.

I have also power to destroy for as the creator I only have power of dissolution being the Almighty God creator of heaven and earth with power that is above all principalities and powers.

A human destroyer is not operating in power of dissolution instead he is an enemy of is own spirit due to his wicked and evil ways to wreck the things of goodness.

A human destroyer is his own destroyer and such a human will only walk to dissolve his own spirit to perish in death.

A human destroyer is a slave to lies and the spirit of lies will lead such human to believe that what they do is to the disadvantage of another. This is foolishness for if you sow evil you cannot reap in goodness.

A destroyer hates a builder for the objective purpose of a destroyer is to wreck.

As the ultimate builder I did not choose you to give you to evil destruction instead I chose you to build you and enable you to build wrecked lives. You have experienced all that you have experienced because you are a builder of life temples and a builder of life temples must always have life building experience to be able to perform his objective purpose of life, which is to build wrecked lives.

To seek to build life is to be in the front line of life business to engage man in goodness ways of thinking. To be a life builder is to concentrate on what you are building for you have seen the end even before you start to lay the foundation that it is all good.

To be a builder of lives is to be wise for you know only good pays and in knowing that the entire plan of the enemy is to wreck all your efforts you remain focus in your mind to your life objectives and in your focus you do not give way to unproductive tantrums of the wicked.

Every man has a choice to make in time and every choice of man in time has eternal life consequences. I commissioned the saints in time to walk in faith of love and in faith of love enable man by perfect ministration to make the right choice in time to avoid wrongful end for their soul in eternity.

A builder at the front line of trials in the world is at the front end of blessings in the spirit for to be in the front end is to be at the forefront to give a life service. You are at the front line in the world to enable the timely disabled in my power of love for them to have a chance to rise to the front end of life to walk in their own life blessings.

When you are in the front line, it is as if you are the only main target of the evil minded.

The main objective purpose of the evil minded is to wreck the spiritual body of those that I have commissioned you in my loving power to build in time through your perfect ministrations to them.

Even though you are a winner in me in all totality, the workings of the flesh is to confuse you to believe that all arrows of the enemy targeted at those that you stand for is now directed at you battering and bruising you and this is all a lie. To be in me is to be a light and as light in me no power of darkness can prosper against you.

As a God, I am a builder and as a builder, I lay my foundations in solid rock from the precious stones of heaven. To have my spiritual sword is to be a builder, a man that builds for goodness sake of life will be my house on the rock, and no man shall be able to pull them apart. As Rock of ages, I make my house on the rock to be rock solid and whosoever tries to hit my rock in evil mind will not find fountain of life instead will be scattered into pieces.   No man can break apart that which I have built and no man can put together that which I have broken apart.

You are a spirit and my grace is sufficient for you. To have my grace is to be highly blessed and favoured and when a man finds high favour and blessing before me it is as if he has found nothing but curses judging from what he goes through in the world.

The spirit knows the truth and although it may appear as if a man has landed on greater problems instead of the solutions that he desires his spirit is aware that power of life is in his soul and as such will walk in goodness perseverance for everlasting life justifications of his soul.

By my grace, you have benefit of my forgiveness and in forgiveness justifications and as such, your trials will only work to perfect your mind in goodness faith of life not place you in wrath of my judgement at any time.

I allowed you to go through all that you have been through to assure you that you have my grace working to your advantage always.

The wages of the sin of man I paid by my grace and through my grace man is free from the sorrow of eternal damnation. If man seeks to remain in death and continue to remain indebted to death even though he has the grace of freedom then he carries his blame on his head. Through grace, I brought you to life and it is by the same grace that I sustain you in life and if I have marked you as the living, the will of death cannot prevail over you.

I placed you at the forefront of graceful life for the goodness sake of my name. For my name sake, I gave you the benefit of total victory in life as I have afforded it to you from my eternal life existence.

To be at the forefront of graceful life is to have high spiritual advantage and the trick of the devil is to deceive the advantaged that they are at a disadvantage.

To be in me is to have entire life victory and it is because you have victory in the highest order that you are in the front place to afford the same victory from the position of your standing victory to others.

No one can give victory unless they have victory for what you do not have you cannot give and when evil tries to make the front line soldier go wary by strategies of confusions it is in desperation of trying to get the front line soldier to ceasefire.

To be in the front line is to have immense fire power afforded to you by me and when the enemy tries to get you to ceasefire it is in cry for mercy but in the physical context it would seem as if you are the one under immense burning fire.

To be in me is to be fire and fire cannot burn fire. The one that is really in fire burning in severe pain from your firepower is the enemy and the game of the enemy is to get you to stop bombarding them with immense firepower.

With grace on your side, you will always shoot on target and from being on target the enemy have no choice but to let go of the prisoner that he aims to keep in burning spiritual warfare.

The power of life is the only power than can bind and loose and if I have empowered you to bind and loose whatsoever you bind on earth is bind by me in heaven and whatsoever is loosed by you is loosed by me in heaven.

The enemy from seeing the firepower authority in you will always try to deceive you to believe that every arrow you send you send to miss and that they are on target to you.

The evidence the enemy will like for you to focus on is the visible lies not the invisible yet to be visible spiritual truth.

This is so that in you focusing on the visible lies and not the spiritual truth, you start to go wary and in wariness, you start to relent your soldering life efforts.

The ways of evil is just to scare you to quit your life purpose objectives however for you are chosen for goodness sake all that evil does will only help to lead you further to your place of destination as assigned for you in life by me from eternal life.

You stay in lifeline because you know there is no profit in death and for your commitment to life; you will always have total justice of eternal life on your side.

The evil minded is always envious and jealous and envy and bitter jealousy is a mind killer.

Life is about productivity and to be evil is to be unproductive. When you have a mind to be good and productive evil will always try to deceive you to discourage you from remaining faithful to goodness line of productivity. You must understand that a wicked soul is envious of the grace you have and for they are envious, they deny their souls the benefit of the grace that is upon you.

If you have a productive line of business, you do not focus your attention on a looser for all the devil is, is a liar and a looser and just when it seems everything is getting worse be rest assured that it is all working together for your goodness.

I know this because I see all things and as God that sees all and knows all I say all things has his own time.

If you sowed in the sowing season have the assurance that you will harvest in the harvest season and your harvest shall be plentiful for every seed you sow I multiply it greatly and exceedingly.

A pregnant woman has to go through labour to bring her child to the world and the most painful time is when the child is about to be delivered.

Every labour of love brings great reward and every act that is in evil labour to achieve an evil end will always bring hard labour to the soul of the wicked labourer to suffer and lament for their evil act in eternity.

The enemy is a liar and the enemy's lie is to try to make you believe that all your goodness efforts are in vain and for nothing.

Lies may go on for two thousand years but one day the truth shall show forth itself and you will see without a doubt that the truth is power of life for only the truth shall set a man free.

There are many lies but there is only one truth and it is only when you find the truth that your eyes in the spirit will be open to see things as they are. The world is anti goodness hence to desire to be good is to be an enemy of the world and to be a friend of the world is to be my enemy.

To be my friend is to be in the world but not of the world.

When you are in the world and not of the world then you will see clearly the wickedness of the world that the world hates goodness for evil sake of the human mind.

The world is antichrist and the world is antichrist because the world is the world of flesh and the flesh is the gateway to sinfulness eternal deadly end.

All of man is a spirit being and when a spirit is a dead spirit, dead spirits tries such a spirit to be in sorrow of death but when you are awake and alive in your spirit all that is tried is your flesh and this is necessary for the total perfection of your spirit.

You said you would like me to make you understand these things in a ways that is relative to you as a human being. I say to start with, you must understand that you are a spirit being.

As a spirit being, you are an invisible being but because you are a human being on earth, you have a natural visible body.

Your main being is invisible and this invisible side of you is what matters most because that is who you really are and always will be.

To know a person for who they are you have to see them in the open eye of the spirit for a person although may appear to you as harmless sheep they can actually be a ravening wolf in sheep clothing.

If you cannot tell a sheep from a wolf then you will invite a wolf in to be your friend and a wolf is no friend to anyone because all a wolf is interested in is to steal and destroy everything you count as valuable.

The outer layer of your being, which I call the flesh, is the body of death and as body of death condemned to remain dead as the gateway to sin.

Your flesh is not your physical human body but the invisible outer layer of your human being that is of sin and as of sin of death for the wages of sin is death.

A living soul is of life even though he is flesh and the devil's aim is to try the flesh of a living being for their spirit to fail but if I am with you know for sure that the trial of your flesh is to strengthen your spirit not to destroy it.

Every man as a spirit being is invisible. The invisible spirit of man died due to the sin of the first Adam and this death is a death of the soul. Once the soul dies the human spirit being both visible and invisible is in darkness evil of death and in darkness evil in condemnation of death in all dimensions both visibly and invisibly.

The axes of evil are interested in the soul not in the outer being, which is the flesh because the flesh is in condemnation forever as the gateway of sin. If the enemy tries, what is already condemned then it means everything the enemy does will only work to your high spiritual advantage.

This is because trials to just your flesh is evidence of the fact that your spirit is by grace already justified whereas trial to your spirit is evidence of death in the soul as wages of sin.

A spiritual dead man that is undergoing trials to his spirit is not in awakening of such trials. Instead he will usually see himself as one of power and strength to do as he pleases.

Such man will always be in the mind to try others just as he is severely tried and because he is dead to the facts of his spiritual trials, he will do all things that are against the objective purpose of his soul, which is resurrection from death.

A dead spirit man will be in parallel walk to life and in such parallel walk will see himself as wise even though he is stupid.

He will see himself as rich and powerful even though he is poor and weak and he will see himself as a master even though he is a slave to the devil. If you are tried and the trial is to your flesh give thanks for your trial is for the goodness promotions of your soul.

COUNT IT ALL JOY WHEN YOU FALL INTO DIVERSE TEMPTATIONS

The book of James Chapter 1 verse 2 says, "**My brethren, count it all joy when ye fall into diverse temptations;**" Verse 3 says, "**Knowing this, that the trying of your faith worketh patience**". Verse 4 says "**But let patience have her perfect work, that ye may be perfect and entire, wanting nothing**"

Your initial trials was necessary to enable you seek in the mind of spiritual solutions and answers for only when you have spiritual solutions and answers do you have real life solutions and in real life solution completely problem free.

If for example you have not had your initial trials, you would not have seen the need to embark on any spiritual soul search at all. Hence, the saying in the book of James to count it all blessings when you face diverse temptations for out of your trials you discovered your true blessings.

The initial trial of a man that is to lead him to search for spiritual facts is indeed like been on a frying pan. However, this frying pan effect is to gear your mind to seek the truth and the truth is divine love.

A fool will in fact jump from frying pan to deeper consuming fire and for he is unwise in his decisions, he will find himself in this great spiritual deep fire and suffer serious spiritual sorrowful burns. You did not jump from frying pan to fire to be consumed or burnt by fire for in all of your trials since your encounter with me instead of you getting burnt by fire I have protected you with my firepower. As God I am fire and as fire consuming fire and be very assured that if you are in me you are fire that cannot be killed by water and as fire no weapon fashioned against you shall prosper.

You initial trials was to lead you to find your purpose in life and your follow up trials from finding your purpose is not to prevent you from serving that purpose. Instead your trials are to perfect your faith in me for goodness sake and rewards for you as a spirit being in eternal life. Life is sweetness and death is bitterness and the flesh as the body of death is always in bitterness sorrow of death but your spirit knows no bitterness once you are in me

Of course, any human being from an ordinary perspective will say how can anyone count it all joy when they fall into diverse temptations. What a crazy idea for who in their human mind will pray to fall into any temptations at all let alone diverse ones.

Also as you said how is it that your God as love allows you to go through such temptations instead of preventing it knowing very well what painful emotional reaction such temptations generates.

The answer is if you are to give usefulness and greater profitable value to gold, you must take it through the fire. Taking gold through the fire as a goldsmith is as if you hate it and given that fire is hot it is not a surprise that no human will like the idea of being taken through the fire.

However when the goldsmith finish taking the gold through the fire and it sees the perfect work of the goldsmith as it is in the end it would thank the goldsmith for all his wonderful work that has made it to be of high value and in high value utmost desired by all to have as their treasure.

An elect of mine is not elected to be punished but blessed and just like a pregnant woman, to go through the labour of love is to be assured of a joyful end by my power of deliverance through which you have victory in all circumstances to always enjoy my joyful presence everlasting.

As God, my promise to the faithful is eternal life of joy, peace and rest and if you are in me, you already are in my restful and peaceful presence. Tribulations to the spirit bring sorrow to the soul and a soul that is full of sorrow is a soul in deep spiritual pain. In joy, there is jubilation always and a soul in jubilations will not suffer the adverse effect of any flesh tribulations.

In me, you have joy in your soul in every moment and your soul testifies to the great eternal joy in you. As such, even when you feel that you are facing great trials the joy in your soul was on high increase and when your flesh is weak in tribulations, your spirit is strong in jubilations. If I have chosen you, then know that I will greatly reward you for your faithfulness to me. If just like gold I take you through the fire, know that it is not to devalue you but to enhance your value.

Know also that for the sake of my good name you will see in all of this things that as my elect you are indeed my precious treasure and so will all of mankind bear witness that you are who I have made you to be not what anyone try to deceive you to believe that you are.

Going through the fire is like going through the valley and shadow of death.

However if you get through the valley and not perish half way through and you reach your destination end stronger and more than a conqueror then it is right to say the end truly justify all the means of your entire efforts.

The book of Jeremiah Chapter 32 verse 42 says **"For thus saith the LORD; Like as I have brought all this great evil upon this people, so will I bring upon them all the good that I have promised them"**.

I am the Almighty God and as the Almighty God all powers both good and evil belongs to me. I did not create man to simply oppress and punish them but to reward them with total goodness of life out of the goodness of my loving heart and unless you are with me, you cannot have rewards from me.

For whosoever is not with me is against me and if a man is against me, he says he is a supporter of evil and as a supporter of evil against everything, which is goodness in eternal life forever. If I am to continue to be in mind of reward towards man then man by their ways must appease me by walking in mind of divine loving kindness not in evil hatred flesh to continue to provoke me by their sinful wicked ways.

It is so that I am appeased that I make the weak strong in every generation for them to serve the purpose of life for the benefit of the whole of mankind.

A child is born helpless and this child through nurturing grows to do things for himself. Nurturing is not just about doing things for the child but to enable the child to develop in right knowledge of right and wrong so that he stays in the right path and avoid the destructive wrong path.

To be my chosen for goodness sake is to understand what is right as right, and what is wrong as wrong and if you do not know evil, you cannot understand the importance of goodness.

As a spirit being, you are always of a free will and your trials are to enable you discern good from evil and in knowledgeable spiritual discernment, you will always walk in testimony of life as a witness of goodness.

If you look at things from an ordinary angle then it cannot make sense to want to be still with me if as you said you see me as a God that only allows you to go through what you see as unnecessary pain and sorrow. However because you are spiritually convinced that you are free from pain and sorrow you bear a spiritual record and testimony that all that you go through is all working to your advantage.

To walk in spiritual heart of love you must have a loving conviction that in all things love is the highest. To know that love is the highest is to always depend and be faithful to love.

When you have a love conviction, you hold on to your conviction no matter what the case may be even when everything that you go through appears as if your God that is love hates you.

Only by your love, convictions from your experiences that you will continue to see love as the highest order of life that always shall justify you in all your trials for your faithfulness to my loving ways from the beginning to the end.

Even though you tried as flesh, your soul bear testimony of my justifications for you and it is for this reason that you remain joyful and continue to rejoice in the midst of all of your diverse temptations.

The greater your test the higher your purpose and the higher your purpose the greater your reward and to be in goodness purpose mind is to always walk in total mind of divine faith. Whosoever walks in divine faithfulness mind shall be greatly rewarded and when you fall into diverse temptations be sure that it is to perfect you to receive diverse higher reward of life and in life eternal life forever.

You know that it is for the goodness of my name that I have chosen you and if I have chosen you for the goodness of my name then I could not have chosen you just to make you see things that you regard as evil from me to convince you still that I hate you.

Before you came to know me as you know me, you believed that I hate you for you do not see my goodness for what it is. Therefore, if I have chosen you it is not to affirm in your mind that I hate you but to give you a conviction different from the one you had before which is that I love you.

For what goodness is it to my name if I give you an experience to lead you to believe still that I that is love has chosen you to punish you because I hate you. It is by my loving grace that I brought you to life in your spirit and I that by my love brought you to life will not allow hate to destroy you for to hate is death to the soul and you are no use to me dead for I am a God of the living not the dead. This is the reason why I have always forbid you to hate.

If you see me to have chosen you to punish you then your previous conviction that I hate you will only be confirmed in your mind and this is not the confirmation that I raised you up to give you.

The confirmation that I raised you up for you to have is that I love you eternally and for goodness sake of life I have raised you up to be a light and a salt in the world.

It is only from seeing that in all of these things that I love you despite all that you go through that you will remain a perfect witness of me in the world. For the trick of the devil is to deceive a believer to disbelieve that his God love him or her and by such wrong believe abandon the straight line of goodness to follow the crooked means of the flesh.

Any kind of belief is a conviction and a convict either convict the mind to walk in blessing or establish the mind to partake in curses.

If a man is wrong in his convictions, such man convictions will make him a spiritual convict and as an imprisoned spiritual convict, evil hell spirits will torment his soul.

It is by your convictions and total reliance on my love for you that in all that you go through you persevere.

The enemy tries the saints to deny them eternal blessings by tempting them to believe that truth is lies and lies is truth but whosoever have a spiritual conviction of the truth cannot be deceived in their spirit to walk in blindness of the flesh.

To have total spiritual conviction is not to have a shaky faith for to have a shaky faith is to give room for the devil to manipulate the mind easily to be evil and mischievous.

To be strong in your faith of love is to always know that for I love you more than you can ever appreciate me everything you go through in goodness mind of faith is not to depreciate you but for you to see that by grace you will always be in goodness appreciation now and forevermore.

LONGSUFFERING OF THE FLESH GIVES HOLY SPIRIT EXPERIENCE OF HIGH DIVINE FAITH AND CHARACTER

The key to life success is patience and perseverance. In me is all wisdom and knowledge and to persevere in longsuffering of the flesh is divine knowledge of life.

From finding life, you have knowledge of life and in knowledge of life; you must have the mind to do all that I say is right for it is right.

To have knowledge of life is to know that those that seek to try my elect are themselves on death row to be on permanent trials of death and hellish pronouncements.

Whilst my elect have benefit of eternal life from persevering for goodness sake, eternal damnation in hell fire awaits all of those that seek evil for my elect for to be evil is to reap evil. It is for this reason that the devil always seek to try the elect to push their mind to hate and the whole essence of this is to rob them of their eternal goodness reward.

A good at heart in secret knowledge of life will always pray that I forgive his fellow being instead of retaliating for he knows that a human being in mind of hate knows not that by his hateful mind he runs a spiritual risk of eternal damnation to his soul.

I see all that you have been through before and after you came to know me as you now know me and from looking at you from a spiritual point of view I say all that you have been through has made you wiser not more foolish.

Yes it is difficult to undergo these things as a human being and yes it is even more difficult to hold your peace when someone is constantly there trying so hard to provoke you.

Yes, I know that it is difficult for a human being to always be the one to forgive someone that is mean and determine to offend.

Yes, it is difficult to stay calm when someone will not let go of his or her abusive run. However, even though I see that all this things are difficult from your human perspective it is not impossible from my Godly perspective for to be in me is to be in the heart of love and with love on your side, nothing is impossible. Good works is necessary for the manifestation of good faith and it is only in goodness faithful perseverance that you manifest the good word that is in you to afford benefit of change focus to others.

To say the right word you must in the first place know the word and I am in you as word power of life to sustain you in goodness benefit gain of life. However, to just speak the word and not act in line of the word that you speak is not to see the benefit of the word that you believe in.

No matter how much you say the word if you never take the step to walk in the line of the word that you speak nothing will change to give benefit to another.

Evil deceives the mind of man to believe that he is powerful in resistance. Perseverance is power that you need to negate this lie for good and evil must always work for goodness sake of life.

When evil appears strongly resistant it is not to work against the saint but to soften the saint mind to walk in line of perfect good faith.

To allocate benefit of spiritual forward movement progression to others you must go in power of dominion to the front line to free the spiritually enslaved.

Death is a spirit of enslavement and you cannot fear death and walk in life of good faith of life for to have divine faithful knowledge is to know that death has not power over your spirit and soul.

Moses had to take a faith step to go to front line Egypt but in fear of death, his mind was not operating in level of his allocated divine faith mission.

Even though he had the power and authority of my word in his hand, he was in fear of death and hardened to life objectives. It was to break the hardness of his heart that I hardened the mind of Pharaoh to build the confidence of Moses in divine power of faithful love.

Moses by my order and instruction had to go back to Pharaoh no matter how many times Pharaoh says no until he lets the people go. This is what faithful perseverance is all about to keep going in line of obedience to my order no matter what the case may be.

To continue to persevere is to develop spiritual confidence in me as all power. In knowledge mind that the one in you has all power hence greater than whatsoever you regard in the world as power you will walk throughout your life missions in time in total respect of life ordained ways for you are no longer afraid of death.

The wish of death is to scare a man with dead threats so that he jumps off life tracks. Evil stubbornness is a way of a goat but holy perseverance and patience is the way of a sheep.

Only in Holy perseverance shall a man complete his goodness run in missions of life.

No matter how hard you tried in a race if you drop out before completion then you cannot expect to have a position let alone hope to receive a trophy. Life is all about perseverance and to be in love and in love manifest the heart of love that is in you is to walk in opposite ways that is common to the character of man as flesh.

Perseverance in goodness heart of faith builds a spirit to be in desire mind of holy characters of life for he knows that life is all about good character and to persevere in divine holy character is to demonstrate highest strength of love.

The evidence that you are a living soul is in your unique character and this uniqueness you do not attain without experiencing diverse trials and tribulations for it is through those diverse trials that you become perfect in your faith and in faith goodness character.

To have a mind of divine love is to have unique character as a unique being in divine love.

In divine loving heart and character, it is wrong for you to react in the common ways of man since you are by my grace made to be unique in your character as someone established to dwell in my heart of divine love to walk in my divine ways.

The natural reaction of a man when someone slaps his face is to slap that someone back harder not just once but many times so that they never again make the mistake of slapping them on the face.

It is natural thing for a man to panic and in panic, emotionally wrecked when he faces diverse trials and tribulations. It is also natural for a man to react in anger when provoked however as the elect I have revealed the supernatural ways of life to you so that you walk in the supernatural not in the common natural ways of man.

When you are strong in divine patience and perseverance, it is as if you are weak and foolish in the eyes of man.

It is supernatural demonstration of wisdom and strength to turn the other face when someone slaps the other for the spiritually wise knows not to fight like those in the flesh that are blind in their spirit.

A spiritually blind man cannot see in the supernatural and if a man cannot see in the supernatural, such man will be a devil's puppet.

The flesh is weak and no man in the flesh without total focus in their spirit can walk in spiritual strength for they will be as you have said, pushed to the limit. If you run out of patience because you feel you are unjustly pushed, you are bound to react in the wroth of the flesh, which is wrong and unacceptable to me by my own standards.

Every man is a sinner hence no man is perfect in his own right.

The power of life is love. It is divine wisdom glorify the power of the love that is in you by goodness character for to glorify love in time, is to abide in the glory of love in everlasting life.

The real power that you have in heart of love is goodness character. Your real power manifestations in the world of the provocative flesh is in your meek and gentle character for even if you demonstrate powers that no man has ever witnessed before if your character is devilish then they will say you are certainly not of God.

Even if you are meek and gentle for envy and jealousy they will accuse you still of all sorts and the whole idea behind such accusations is to discredit you so that no one sees you as Godly and good hearted.

The entire game of the enemy is to raise doubt to your credibility and to play into the enemy's hand is foolishness. You control the enemy by goodness character for all the enemy is after is to control man through deceiving them to believe that in bad character walk they are in absolute control.

As my elect, you are witness of good and you stay in good witness walk in demonstration of holy character of life. To be out of control as a witness is to play into the enemy's hand.

The aim of the enemy is to taint the witness so that no one believes the witness good testimony for once the witness appears stained the witness will no longer look and appear credible.

All of this I have explained to you in this many years to place you in understanding of goodness faith walk. To be good at heart is to be of goodness character for by your character shall you be a sheep not a goat and as a sheep, I am your Shepherd and as your Shepherd, I will always shield and protect you from all harm. A sheep is to my right and a goat is on the left.

Those that are on my right I make to operate in my firepower and protect them with my fire but my consuming fire consumes all on the left for they are stubborn goats.

Your trials are necessary to make you a sheep in time to reside with me as a lion and enjoy the benefit of I the lion king in eternity.

For all of man born of the flesh is a devilish stubborn goat and as stubborn goats, evil in character and no goat can enjoy any benefit of eternal life.

If a man is tried after he found me it is not to make him worst in his character but to open his eyes to see the ugly character of the flesh and by so doing seek to walk in goodness character of my Spirit always for goodness sake of my name.

To know whether you have patience, you must put your patience to the test. If no one has ever tried your patience, how can you say you have patience? If you say, you are a calm person and you have never met anyone to try to make you act in calamity how can you say for sure that you do not have a calamity hot temperamental problem.

To know whether you have a forgiving heart, someone must offend you and to understand the importance of walking in perfect character you must understand the wicked ways of the devil from your experiences.

The devil is a foolish pest that is always in mind of bad jokes and without good experience, a man will easily fall for the devils' tricks and will appear foolish in the eyes of mankind instead of the wise that he is made to be. To be of good character is honor and to remain calm in humility walk of character is to always maintain yourself in high honorary standard of life.

To make your faith and ways perfect towards me I made you to see beyond the ordinary to the extraordinary ways of life through allowing your experiences to take place. Experience perfects faith and it is to perfect your faith in divine life that you had to have your experiences. Only in good faith will a man have benefit of total life victory. Faith is necessary to complete your life missions and only a fool in time will abandon his eternal life faith missions.

The wise knows that by my good faith all my life missions I have made possible in eternal life to give man the benefit of life in eternity. A man that walks in good faith is a man insured to have eternal victory for even if he were to die in line of faith he will rise to eternal life glory out of my own faithfulness.

A saint in time is by my Holy Spirit eternal life knowledge assured that they are forever in victory and for they know they have victory eternally, they are always ready to take a stand in good faith.

By their faithful stance, their record in life is that of one that overcame the objectives of the devilish world of flesh by good faith of divine loving hearts and as such forever entitled to rewards of eternal life. The objective of the devilish world of flesh is to present good faith as a lie and lie as the truth.

A saint knows the truth as I have revealed it to his spirit and his soul in light of my glory always bears record and witness that I am the way, the truth and life. From having the total spiritual convictions that I am the truth, a saint is by the knowledge and convictions of his soulful heart assured that I am the truth enlightened. In spiritual enlightenment empowered and always willing to perform all his missionary faithful works to the glory of my goodness name. To stand in goodness is to see that I your God is indeed the Almighty and the devil as a looser is a liar.

The enemy knows that the fear of man in the flesh is of death and the game of death is to keep the mind of man in fear of death so that they do not walk in goodness faith. The enemy knows human weaknesses and does not wish for a man to act in spiritual strength in his trials but in the weaknesses of the flesh to be in total disorientation. The game of the enemy is always to use your natural human weakness against you so that you do not see the point of good faith. The entire enemy tempting attempts is to focus your mind on your flesh weaknesses not the spiritual strength that you have in me as life.

If the enemy sees that hot temperament is a major weakness that you have then he will always taunt you to get an angry reaction from you. The whole essence of this is to discredit you in the public eyes of man so that no one sees you in light of your spiritual accreditation.

As you have discovered by experience you will find that once you show any kind of angry reaction the chiefs amongst devils will be quick to levy all manner of criticism at you and not so much at the one that provoked you into anger reaction.

As an elect the spotlight focus is on you so is the onus of good behavior and this is my teachings to you that you remain supernaturally calm always to avoid natural chaotic attitudes and behaviors in every situation no matter how provoking the circumstance. You will remain clam always if you walk in mind of humility for only in humility do you silence the arrogant ways of the flesh, which, is the usual root cause for wanting to operate in flesh self defense.

To fight in the flesh is to shoot blanks and this is the entire game of the enemy to provoke arrogance to lead the mind so that in flesh arrogant ways a man humiliates himself for not operating in spiritual humility.

The entire game of the enemy is to make a saint appear as a devil in the natural open eyes of man and once you know that this is the devil's trick it is pointless for you to keep blowing hot steam all for nothing.

The enemy does not seek that you have a good shinning life experience so that no one sees the shinning spiritual spotlight on you. The enemy intention in its entire provocation attempts is to put a saint in bad spot in public eyes of the world through provoking strategies. This is geared at entrapping the saint to act publicly in ways and manner that will lead every man to question whether he is indeed a real saint or in fact a devil in disguise. This is aimed at preventing the rest of man from seeing that the saint is shinning light.

To be of good faith is to know that life is all about love and that with love all things are possible. To be in heart and mind of divine love is to have a doubt free mind towards love. For if you see love as a deceiver then you say I your God I am a liar and if you see me as a liar how can you trust me enough to obey my goodness instructions.

Your faith and patience in goodness is due to your conviction that goodness is the way to eternal life and it is only in goodness, that you have a good conscience. To have sympathy you must have a good conscience.

To have empathy with another you must experience what the other has experienced. If you have not walked in the shoes of the one that you are to sympathize with, their pain and suffering would mean nothing to you and for their pain mean nothing to you, you cannot be in any mind of mercy.

If you cannot understand, what a person is going through you cannot sympathize with them and as God, that is love, I am always in my heart of love for mankind sympathetic and empathetic. If you say you are of good faith and you are not sure of what you believe in then how is that your faith good. Faith as I said is all about your own convictions. If you believe in something, know for sure that someone in the world has a theory or an idea to say your beliefs is a total nonsense lie.

If therefore you are not fully convinced about your faith you will be easily fooled to abandon it. When it comes to faith what matters is what you believe not what others says your believe is or should be. Even though you believe, you have had a godly encounter and this encounter has led you to write these things some will say you are suffering from some kind of illusion or paranoid delusional problems.

Many would consider your believe in a God that they say does not exist as foolish. However, to say that the God that many say does not exist speaks to you and you speak to him many will say that is total insanity and some will call it blasphemy.

Therefore, my point to you is if you are to be in total mind of faith, you must see the ways of the world of flesh that it is anti goodness and for it is anti-goodness, always hateful towards those that are on the side of goodness.

THE DEVIL IS A MAN'S HOPE AND VISION KILLER

To have a calling is to have a vision of life and to maintain your focus in your life visions you must walk in line of positive vibrations and not allow the devil negative vibes to distract you.

The entire aim of the devil is to replace good hope of vision materializations with hopeless frustrations through his attempts to focus the mind on negative lies.

To have a high good vision is to undergo diverse temptations from the enemy. The whole essence of those temptations is to try and make you loose focus of your believe in your true life visions and start to believe that it is all a lie and it will never happen. If a man is frustrated and hopeless by trials and temptations then he will no longer see in light of good visions and such a man will start to walk in blind darkness mind of evil to a dead end.

The vision of man in the world is from the darkness blind spot of evil. My vision to you is from my total sight of everything.

Once you have an invisible life vision everything in the natural will appear as if it is impossible for you to move ahead to reach your vision manifestations predestined destination.

A man with a vision of life must understand that for the visible manifestation of his visions to take place he must stay focused and dedicated to his life objective aims despite everything in the natural appearing as if all his efforts to move ahead is futile. Frustrations and hopelessness build high negative barriers in the mind and it disables a man from good movement to the finish line of his predestined destination.

However, good focus on the perfect end result and in goodness focus continuous walk in goodness mind of divine faith enables forward progressive movement in swift locomotion might without any unnecessary delays to the finish line.

A person that moves swiftly in line of good faith will soon find that all that he sees is falsehood appearing as real that is all intended to deceive him to believe that his reality expectations is all unreal.

If I showed you the end from the beginning then know that I already see the end from the beginning and continuous trust in me is demonstration of divine wisdom for if you say you do not trust me that is truth, then you say your trust is in the lies appearing as the truth. If I give you a vision objective and you say you believe in it then you do not demonstrate your believe by abandoning the vision missionary objectives.

The world is a world of darkness and my purpose of faith mission for a man is to shine him as my light so that as shinning light others see their way to the shinning light that is in him. The aim of a world devil is to deceive mankind not to see the light of heaven.

If a man quits from light into darkness then the darkness that will cover his eyes will be much thicker so that he would not see any point of returning to light.

The aim of darkness evil in attempts to erect darkness barrier in the world is to prevent a man from shinning as light in the world and to be the wise is to know that light is the supernatural power of life and natural darkness can never prevent the supernatural light of life from shinning.

To focus your mind on the shinning invisible light that is in you is to eventually see visibly the visible good change and difference that the invisible supernatural light has made for you to benefit and enjoy not just in the limited visible time era but eternally in presence of my immortal invisible existence.

Darkness submits to light without arguments for when light comes darkness simply disappears.

If a man proclaims light from his mouth and by his actions walks in ways of darkness then he says that his real spiritual intention is to submit to darkness and not to light. The ruler of the mind of such man will be darkness and a man that submits to rulers of darkness will partake in the spiritual sorrow of the darkness rulers that masterminds his mind to carry out their evil works.

Good faith is to know that every negative world barrier that appears as strong is already down by my supernatural power and it is only appearing as holding strong to greater engage your mind with the one that is all strong and mighty which is I the I AM the Almighty author and finisher of your faith.

Goodness faith is of the supernatural and a man that walks in good faith will find that by his goodness step of faith every negative world barrier is only working together to fully establish him in lifetime divine faith rewards.

To hope in the visible is to loose sight of invisible good faith. A man of good faith will have his hope in the supernatural goodness of life and as such, he will not allow natural evil to prevent him from line of supernatural good movement.

The natural middle ground barrier between vision and manifestation is to build your faith in the supernatural and if by seeing this natural middle ground barrier you loose faith and trust in my supernatural power then you cannot say you believed in me as the Almighty supernatural power of life and death in the first place.

You are either a believer or unbeliever and to keep believing in the supernatural truth you must keep your supernatural eyes focused in the supernatural eternal goodness that awaits you at the completion of your entire faith journey in time. If after your supernatural awakening you continue to focus only on the natural then you say you still do not believe in my supernaturalism.

My entire aim is to super-naturalize you to become a heavenly citizen and no man that is world focus can pass the eligibility exams of right of abode in heaven.

If I give you a promise and everything happens immediately in the visible as I say, it would happen, as you will expect that it happens so quickly then you will not need to have faith. Faith is necessary to materialize the invisible yet to be visible goodness promise that I have made to you.

This is why as an enemy of good faith; the devil is always in mind to deceive the faithful to abandon their line of good faith so that they will not see the manifestations of my promises as already fulfilled by my own goodness divine faithfulness.

As God, I am wisdom and to keep walking in line of supernatural good faith despite the negative sights of things in the natural is to be wise just as I am and only the wise shall inherit my kingdom.

The devil perished for his betrayer of good faith for as God that is love I am always faithful and only those that walks in good faith in line with my eternal goodness ordinances shall be ordained by me from the beginning to the end to have eternal life rewards.

To abandon line of good faith is foolishness for good faith of life gives a lifetime reward but to abandon the line of faith is to perish everlasting for being a quitter.

No one gets the result that they desire from quitting and if a man can have a mind to commit to his flesh selfish world ambitions with a strong determined mind to attain his desired ambitious world result then it is no excuse for any man to say he cannot dedicate himself to eternal life aims. A man that dedicates himself to his worldly objectives do so out of his mind of self gain and if a man is only dedicated to gain the world then he cannot expect to gain his soul for to gain the world of flesh is to loose your soul in the real world.

The trials you go through after you have a divine vision of life is to build your faith in divine life for my vision to you is not for you to hope in vanity but in divine ways of eternal life. To hope in vanity is to hope in death and all that hopes in death is zeroed out of life and shall gain nothing for all that death gives is zero end results and you cannot add zero to zero and get anything.

To see the materialization of your goodness vision, you must keep in line of your life vision for the aim of man is to kill your vision so that you will not see. You keep your vision alive when you keep your hope and believe of eternal life alive and in your believe you walk in total perseverance.

To persevere in line of true hope of life is to be more than a conqueror all that persevere I sustain in my power of love for them to gain and inherit my kingdom life rewards everlasting.

Everything that has a beginning has also an end and as God that sees the end from the beginning my vision revelations to you is to put you in awareness of the perfect end result from the very beginning. Through perseverance and patience, you will see that no one trades with me and ends up at a loss.

Patience is a divine virtue and to be of good virtue you must go though the fire on the left to become fire in the right. The one thing that you will notice in all that you have been through is that you are never in want of your needs for as your God I am always there to supply all of your needs according to the richness of my goodness glory.

Divine faith is wisdom and wisdom is to know that the one that called you for his mission knows already the end from the beginning and has made everything from beginning to the end to work together for your goodness.

To be wise is to see the inside for what it is and in knowing that all things work for your goodness sake you are much able to go through your faith perfection run in greater joy of the higher hope of the eternal life you have everlasting.

To persevere in longsuffering is to have conquered the lies of the devil that your God hates you and if you have conquered lies then know that your spirit is in full liberation by the power of my love.

For love is the truth and by trusting in love that is the truth you will remain sustained in life to walk in the truth and for abiding in the truth you will always prevail over lies in all situations.

The aim of lies is to make you believe that truth is lies and lies is truth and when you hold on to truth no matter what then you show that your faith is not of vanity but of divine love and to have divine heart of love is to be forever blessed.

As God, I am a spiritual goldsmith and whosoever chooses to give me their heart for me to perfect is my precious golden treasure.

If what you know as gold in the world is able to speak, it would of course protest to a world goldsmith not to take it through the fire. However, if the whole essence of you going through the fire is to give you greater value then is it not better that you go through that fire most especially given that it would not burn your spirit no matter how hot it is.

Isaiah 43 says you will go through the fire and it will not burn you and through the river and it will not overflow you.

By grace of my love, I made you a living soul and as the one that made you a living soul to perform life objectives I am not blind to your human struggles, plights, objectives, desires, goals and total aspirations in life.

In fact, my total spiritual objective for you and for the entire humans' race is to make each and everyone of you successful spirits in every aspect of life. For you to be as successful as I desire for you, you must have the kind of experience that you have had to have a good understanding of life. Life is all about good faith and good faith is only possible in perfect heart of love. The faith of a man in flesh in the world is of vanity and faith in vanity only leads to a mystery Babylonian dead end.

It is experience that perfects faith and faith is all about good works for as written in the book of James chapter 2 verse 17 faith without works is dead. Your trials as I said are necessary to perfect your understanding of faith for although you had a godly encounter you had no faithful experience.

In the stories of men like Abraham, Isaac and Job, you will find that they had to walk in line of good faith to stay within the line of manifestations of fulfilment of my promises to them. Acting on my instructions is wisdom for to obey my word is to make acceptable sacrifice to me.

My perfect sacrifice is out of my own divine faith and if man makes a sacrifice in heart of my divine faith then he will receive the benefit of my promises, which I fulfilled in time from my timelessness existence out of my own divine faith.

Longsuffering of the flesh is necessary to build the spiritual mind to be in good hope of eternal life for only in good hope of eternal life will a man in time walk in perfect divine faith of life.

Faith is visible by actions and to be in mind of perfect faith you must see the necessity to be of good faith in your entire actions.

Life is all about goodness actions and the one thing the devil is after is for man to have negative spiritual reactions to partake in deadly actions in the world to the detriment of their spiritual souls.

MYSTERY BABYLONIAN FAITH IS VANITY FAITH OF THE DEAD

The essence of good faith is to carry out good works so to say that you have faith and not carry out good works is to say that you have no understanding of divine faith. Faith is the way of love and it is only by divine good faith of life that you will relief the evilly burdened and oppressed. The problem as you have identified is that many act in opposite mind of love and not in line with the loving standards, they openly declare with their mouth.

It is good to say to someone read the word and pray the prayer. However, it is devilish to see a person in need of help and support and just send them away to go and pray still when you are able to provide the help and support that they have been praying to have.

The world is mystery Babylon and as mystery Babylon, the world is loyal to the image of the beast.

Many of the so-called church that you see in the world are mostly church of Babylon and all that church of Babylon is about is to take from the needy to give to the greedy.

The church of Babylon is antichrist and as antichrist full of hypocrisy. There is more evil inside the so call church today than outside for many devils hides under the goodness brand name of the church to deceive their fellow men that they are saints.

This is foolishness for if you are in mind of deceiving know that you are greatly deceived by your worst enemy to self-destruct yourself. Freedom from mystery Babylonian lies is through divine faith for in divine faith you will clearly see that although the fire is raging and burning in mystery Babylon it will not burn to harm you because the Lion of Judah is on your side.

I the Lion of Judah I am fire and by my super firepower I have made a saint holy fire and holy water. Fire does not burn in fire and water does not discomfort water but the dead beast in mystery Babylon has no choice but to succumb and surrender to holy fire and holy water power of life for the heat from the burning fire alone has sufficiently melt him down to nothing.

I always aim for relief for humankind and my desire for man is to enable and empower their spirit to walk in the protective shield of my fire so that they do not perish in the burning fire of mystery Babylon.

You cannot enable or empower others if you are in mind of hate for the whole objective of hate is to disable others from goodness movement not enable or empower for goodness sake.

The whole purpose of the evil hearted in their trials of the elect is to disable the elect from goodness progressive movement.

However for an elect is predestined to serve the purpose of goodness for goodness sake such trials is turned round for their spiritual advantage with the total outcome being goodness enablement of their spirit.

Instead of such trials working to the disabling of their spirit as intended by the evil, it works against the flesh to prevent it from antagonising or contaminating the spirit and as such, your spirit flourishes to continue in goodness development and growth of life.

To grow and mature in goodness heart of faith your trials are necessary and it is by those trials that your faith in goodness becomes perfect. Yes I agree that going through this things was hard for you as a human being but look at it this way I know it is far much worse for your spirit to be compressed in eternal death hence by my own faithful works I gave you the grace to place your spirit in total benefit of life justifications.

My entire spiritual objective for man is to resurrect the soul of man from death to be in total spiritual freedom and this I have done by my total works of remissions.

I understand that many have bills to pay and that they are depressed from all manners of trials and tribulations that they go through but to focus on the surface problems and not care about the eternal positioning of your spirit is to be a fool.

You are a spirit being and if you say you do not care about your spirit then you say you do not care about yourself at all.

I know all about the world as the one that has all wisdom and knowledge and my desire is to reveal the secret of the world to you so that you do not feel oppressed or compressed by anything that you go through.

The one thing a devil does not want a man to know is world secrets for if you know the world secrets you will no longer be in mind of fear and all that the world is about is to generate fear in the minds and by fear create great confusion.

As the all knowing I know that the system of the world is greatly unjust, corrupt and debt ridden and from knowing this as your God I am there to enrich your mind, body, spirit and soul with entire goodness rewards to free you from all debts.

I can see in your mind that you are thinking it is all right for me talk this way after all I am God and I do not understand what it feels like for mystery Babylonian loan shacks to hound a person.

However, I want you to know that to give me your heart is to be my friend and if you are my friend then whatsoever concerns you concerns me.

I know perfectly well how you feel because if you are with me everything you go through I am there with you to take you through it. I am there with you to encourage you in positive mind of life to take you through all challenges as one that is victorious in life.

I allow you to go through all that you go through because I know that you will come out on the other side not the way you were before going through it but like a shinning precious stone for your goodness perseverance in your going through it.

As your God that is your friend I am there to perfect you and from sustaining you to be in mind of goodness perfection as you go through all that you go through your understanding increases for goodness sake of life.

You will agree that if you had not gone through all that you have been through that you will not understand things as you do today.

If as written in your favourite Psalm which is 23 you go through the valleys and shadow of death and you come out on the other side more alive and well then without a doubt in your mind you will know that you have overcome death by grace of my love for you.

Only if a person perishes as they try to go through the valley of trials can you say they are a looser but if a person goes through their valley of trials and come out at other side stronger than when they started their journey then they are a champion in life.

The relief that the foolish man seeks in his pilgrimage to earth is to his flesh and any man that seeks relief to his flesh will greatly discomfort his spirit to achieve his flesh objectives.

The flesh is incapable of relief for the flesh is the body of death and to seek to relief that which is not relievable is to perish everlastingly in death. A wise man on earth will pursue spiritual relief for he knows that if he has relief in his spirit then he is fully relieved no matter what the circumstances might appear to be in the visible.

To have spiritual relief is to be joyful in your soul in every moment of life hence the reason why you continued to have joy irrespective of the circumstances. If I am in you then your soul shall be full of joy in every moment and my joy in you will always be your strength.

The devil as an enemy of man does not seek for the spirit of any man to have relief from the sorrow burden of death instead; the devil's main objective is to lead a man to sin to place them in wrath of my judgement.

I gave my graceful benefit to man out of the love of my heart and placed the devil in eternal disgrace for his wickedness.

The entire evil game of the devil upon man is to prevent man from having the benefit of grace. The devil's aim for man is to deceive man to partake in his disgraceful curses through leading them to continue in their walk of rebellious mind of sinfulness against the true objective desires of their souls.

The devil is a tempting spirit and he tries the goodness at heart to discourage them from progressive walk in goodness faithful actions and to confuse them so that they make a hateful choices and by so doing become rejected by goodness not accepted and rewarded as the diligently faithful.

The devil knows that if you attempt to hate you provoke me to wrath judgement for no one in mind of hate can be up to any good. All the devil is after is to lead man to sin against me for the devil, as the first and last guilty accused knows that the wages of sin is death.

I know the tricks of the devil and by allowing you to go through all that you have been through it is to reveal all the devil's tricks to you for I am your friend.
This is so that in goodness spiritual understanding the devil will not fool or discourage you in the world by cunning ways and means.
A devil is never up to no good. A devilish-minded man will always be evil orientated and the orientation of the evil minded will always be

directed at disheartening the good hearted from taking goodness faithful steps.

For I have made you for goodness sake of my name then know for sure that, I will be in greater mind of faithfulness to enable you to be all that I have made you to be.

MY INTEREST FOR MAN IS TO FREE HIM FROM DEADLY SPIRITUAL HIGH INTEREST BAD DEBT

The devil is in wrath of my judgment everlasting. The wrath of my judgment is death and the devil as the dead is not able to pay the wages of his sin for he already has my final judgment and in that final judgment he is by me pronounced dead forever.

A man in sin is indebted to death for the wages of sin is death and no man is able to pay the wages of his sin in death. The wages of the sin of man I paid by my grace and through my grace man is free from the sorrow of eternal sorrowful damnation.

If man seeks to remain in death and continue to remain indebted to death even though he has the grace of freedom then he carries his blame on his head.

The question a man must ask himself as a sinner is; is he still indebted to death even though grace of redemption and in redemption resurrection from death is available to him. If a man is still indebted to death when the trumpet sound then he will have no means of redeeming his soul from death ever again and it is with his soul that he will pay his debt to death everlasting.

I know all about the struggles that a man faces in time for as God I know all things that is of time from my timelessness existence.

As Word, I remain the same everlasting and my eternal aim is always goodness for goodness sake of life. A blind man in time will allow the changing tides of time to affect his life priorities for he sees himself as a time master planner. However, the wise in the end time will concentrate more on achieving his life priorities for he knows that the time given to him by the real master in all dominion realms will soon run out.

The life priority for a man is salvation for his soul and this remains the soulful spiritual aim of a man from the beginning to the end.

In the changing tides of time the priorities of the flesh human remains to pursue his sin more as a right and in mind of sinfulness the only order that man aims to be his driving force on earth is evil.

To effect this high sinful order which man sees as his priority, the end time man is more into evil robotic illogical spiritual reasoning to lace the human spirits even more with evil drug poison so that in evil drug poison the world is in global darkness of evil.

This is backward thinking and to walk in backwardness is to end up forever dead for the goal of a man must be to move ahead to find eternal life and no man that is in evil compression is able to rise and walk let alone move ahead.

My priority for man in all generation of time is to enable man in time to walk in goodness hope of eternal life. To have hope of eternal life is to stay within the line of salvation for if a man hope is only consecrated in time then he only hopes in death for to hope in time is to end up with high level of disappointments.

To have a spiritual encounter with me in time is to appear mad before the ayes of man. However, insanity in the eyes of man is sanity and sanity they see as insanity and the only hope of man is not in what he sees as his own sanity but the sanity ways of life, which is my goodness love.

As God, I aim to give to man total spiritual debt free solutions. To be indebted to death is to suffer oppression, depression, compression and suppression from wicked dead demonic spirits.

Dead spirits are wicked soul destroyers and as demonic satanic agents, they know no mercy and show no mercy. You will find in the world that the world debt collectors have no mercy whatsoever and whosoever borrow from the world the world will seek to make them pay many times over.

A world creditor only has one thing in mind and that is to collect from the debtor not just what he borrowed from him but everything else that he owns. I say all this to you so that you know that I know all that you know and all that you do not know.

I placed you in my Holy Spirit to fellowship with you to impart my divine knowledge and wisdom to you to upgrade your reasoning capacity to my level of spiritual standard.

I know that the world system is a system of high interest debt and this is so that it is not easy for the debtor to pay of his debts and be free from the hands of his world creditor.

When the debtor can no longer afford payment for obvious reasons, the world creditor is fully prepared to take everything that the debtor holds as valuable as payment for his debts.

The more they see that you have that is valuable the less they are prepared to negotiate with you to come back another day for they know that you have something of a high value which they cannot wait to get their hands on as payment for your debt.

The world is a market place and the real object of trading is souls and as the creator uncreated ultimate soul redeemer of life I am the legitimate owner of every man souls. If a man engages in the illegal trade marketing of his souls to the devil then such man trade with the devil to gain death as his eternal reward and will loose everything that is of life rewards everlasting.

The devil is after the soul for the soul of a man is his value in life and if a person owes the devil through their selling of their souls to him, they cannot negotiate to pay with anything else but their souls.

A person indebted to the devil cannot negotiate for the devil to write off his spiritual debts for the devil knows no mercy and as such unable to show mercy.

The sinful man became indebted to the devil due to sinful fall and my interest for man is to write of his bad spiritual debts and this I have done by my own perfect spiritual sacrifice. All that a man needs to do is to walk in perfect mind of sacrifice to enter in holy covenant with me and if a man is in covenant with me he is free from all debts.

No matter how hard the struggle is for man in the world a man must understand that his spirit faces a greater eternal struggle if he quits the good line.

A man quest for answers and solutions must always be a spiritual one for every problem of man is rooted in the spiritual. If you focus on your trials as you see them to be on the surface then the solution you will seek will all be surface solutions.

As God, I am not blind to human suffering and it is to free mankind from sufferings that I made my word flesh for the perfection of the spirit of man.

To see things, as they are you must look at it from inside out and inside out means from the invisible to the visible.

To see things just from the visible is to be greatly deceived for a thing that looks bad to the ordinary eyes is not always the bad that it appears. Also just because something appears good does not mean it is good. If you do not see a problem, you will not seek a solution and the trial of any man is to lead his mind to be in mind search of spiritual answers.

The problem with man is that the answers that he seeks are always to his outward problems and today in the world, much profession has emerged from the many problems faced by man. Many seek solutions to their problems from the world cults and for they look in the wrong places instead of finding spiritual solutions, they find greater spiritual problems.

If the world of flesh is anti goodness life then looking for answers from the world is like asking the devil to help you get through the gates of heaven for you to reside their joyfully ever after.

The devil I everlastingly condemned to eternal hell fire and man cannot expect the devil as the condemned heavenly outcast to show them the way to heaven let alone help them to get in and reside there joyfully ever after.

What a devil does not have he does not want any man to have. As such, the devil as an enemy of man is always pretending to be a friend of man to lead him to believe that I God I am the enemy and this is to cause the soul of man maximum eternal damage.

Every problem of man is rooted in the spirit and so is every solution to those problems in the spirit.

Out of total confusion and blindness, man sees his problems more and more as only physical and when you have a spiritual problem and you seek to apply physical prescriptions, it will not work.

The first thing is to accurately diagnose the problem for only in accurate diagnosis shall you apply the right prescription.

What appears as a huge problem is not always, what it seems and whether a thing is good or bad it is all a matter of the spirit.

The question that a man must ask himself and by man I mean all of mankind is; is his trial just to his flesh or his spirit?. If the trials he faces is to make obvious to him the trials faced by his spirit then such man should give thanks for his surface trials for if he is wise in his solution search he will find spiritual answers and in answers total life solutions.

Life is all about wisdom. It is wisdom for a man facing any kind of trials to embark on a soul search for spiritual answers.

However, such man will be stupid if out of desperation for what he consider quick fixes causes his spirit greater pain and sorrow by making the grave mistake of selling his soul forever to the devil. Through your initial trials, for instance you found the answers to the question of what is your purpose in life.

This is because you sought in the right mind for the right reasons, which means if a man seeks, he shall find. To find something different you must do something different.

If a man keeps seeking for nothing he will continue to find nothing but when a man seek to find what is, was and always shall he will find himself in me.

To discover true spiritual blessings a man must seek in the right mind and knock at the right door otherwise the devil shall give lies to such man and he will treat it as ultimate solutions.

Many in the world are in the bottomless pits of hell yet they regard themselves as the rich and powerful in the world and for they see themselves as having it all they see no reason to seek for their lost souls. If you believe you are already in heaven you will not look for heaven and if you are tried it is for you to learn from those trials not perish in them.

Every man is on earth to make a choice between good and evil and only the wise shall be in mind of spiritual soul search to find goodness eternal profit.

If a man finds life through his soul search then he says that he is wise. If however, as the dead a man sells his soul to evil and ends up destroyed permanently then that man says he is a fool by submitting to evil to rule him forever just for what he sees as a momentary gain in time.

To gain the whole world and loose your soul is to gain nothing for all of man came to the world naked and naked they shall leave.

If as a human being you believe everything you see with your ordinary eyes is exactly the way it appears then you say you are blind because the ordinary eyes is blind to realities of life.

It is not everything that glitters that is gold and it is not everything that appears rotten that is bad.

Out of rotten seeds, comes a new life from the ground and if you do not open your eyes and see things as they are you will throw away something of high value for you cannot see the high value potential because of the way it looks in the ordinary.

Only if your eyes are open in the spirit shall you see things as they are.

YOUR EXPERIENCE IS NECESSARY TO PERFECT YOU IN HOLY SPIRITUAL LAWFUL ABIDING

What I seek for man is deliverance of his soul from death and unless you know that, you are dead how is it that you will think to seek to live. If you know that you were once dead and now you are alive you will always see the need to hold on to life because your soul knows very well that there is no joy in death no matter how diverse the trials you face in the world from finding life.

Once you become a living soul, your flesh only is tried and to face diverse trials as flesh is to step into diverse blessings as a spirit. The trials of the flesh will work together for the total goodness perfection of your spirit. Your trials are necessary for you to see that by my grace you are justified and if you are by grace justified your trials will only place you in entire goodness prospects of eternal life reward.

From my Holy Spirit perspective, you must always see all things as working together for your goodness. Everything that appears negative is to give you a positive mind of goodness. For if, you are in my Holy Spirit led to be in heart of goodness for goodness sake of life all that is negative is to focus your mind not on the negatives but the positive aspects of life.

In my Holy Spirit is entire goodness of life and for a man to have my Holy Spirit goodness everlastingly he must obey my entire word and I Christ is this entire word revealed. Obedience to life is wisdom for all those that obey the will of life shall inherit my kingdom will of eternal life of peace, rest and joy for their soul everlasting. Your trials is to perfect your mind in faithful obedience and holy lawful abiding so that you walk always in benefit of my divine faithful work.

Good faith is a sign of courage of life. Only in divine courage mind will a man be faithful to perform his goodness life ministerial objectives.

This is why as a spirit being it is always important to listen and obey my instructions because as the creator of all things, I always know best and as one that knows best I will never mislead or misguide you.

The entire game of the devil is to discourage you from obeying my holy rules for he knows that disobeying my rules is sin and the wages of sin is death.

I placed you in my Holy Spirit to make my rules clear to you and to enable you obey them easily. It is important that you obey my rules for my rules are my royal command for the interest benefit of all of man. I gave my rules to man to enable them walk in total goodness of life.

To disobey my rules is to walk in the ways of the devil and all that a devil is after is to lead man to sin to deny them of their true eternal inheritance.

Even though you are fully awake in the spirit, you are still flesh.

As such, I am not surprised that you see it as difficult in seeing things from the human flesh perspective to stay calm and not react in anger in situations whereby you feel you have been provoked.

It is because I know this that I afforded you the benefit of my Holy spiritual presence in time so that you can walk in my perfect goodness divine order of eternal goodness to inherit my kingdom everlasting.

I placed you in my Holy Spirit so that you do not walk in the ways of the flesh for to walk in the flesh is to demote your own spirit and this is the aim of the devil to demote the promoted.

Even though as flesh you are weak; in my Holy Spirit of life, you are strong. To focus on me is to see the strength that you have in me whereas to focus on your flesh is to feel weakened and frustrated and in frustration unable to move in the goodness promotion that I have established your spirit being in.

I promote the elect to sustain them in goodness promotional walk and as their promoter, I am aware of their flesh weakness. As such, I am gracefully generous towards them so that they continue to rest and abide in my Holy Spirit presence.

In my Holy Spirit comfort and preservation of their spirit in my eternal life existence, they continue to remain eligible for total rewards of life according to the will of my grace. To preserve the life of man in eternal life rewards I am always generous in my heart of forgiveness towards man for without my generous forgiving hearts no man shall see in light of my glory. Whether a person has overcome is a spiritual matter and not a question of physical stance or position.

I can assure you if anyone is in my Holy Spirit; they have overcome every world barriers.

All barriers of the world are to stop you from ever being in my Holy Spirit covenant of life. To be in my Holy Spirit is to be a living soul and the objective purpose of the world of flesh is to deceive man to remain in his soul a slave to death so that death can oppress his spirit to remain in sorrowfulness everlasting. For you to have made it to be in my Holy Spirit against all the odds and the lies that there is no God you have nothing to fear.

You have overcome the darkness world for you are in me because given all said and done; you are still standing strong to walk in good mind of faith. As evidenced by the answers you gave to my question it is clear that the devil has not fooled with his tricks because you know that to stay within the protectiveness of love is to walk in meaningful protection of life.

What I would say then to you for the things that you have been through is to always be thankful for you know now that by my enabling grace you will always overcome for goodness sake of life.

In mind of thankfulness, you confirm always that you are victorious and in victory proclamation by your thanksgiving, you will always be of a good courage and cheers.

Know that by my Holy Spirit I have overcome all evil for you for goodness sake of your soul. Always have faith in my overcoming power and put your mind in total rest in my peaceful assurances that no one can be against you for I am with you as you will find written in Romans chapter 8.

If I am in you and you are in me then you have overcome your enemy, which is death, for if I am with you the entire wicked will of death will work always to your advantage.

The devil as a demonic spiritual is a spiritual accuser and an abuser of those that he accuses.

The trick of the devil in his attempts to deceive the very elect is to try to con even the very elect into believing that he the devil is all-powerful as evidenced by the external factors and I God by the same evidence has no power.

The essence of this is to lure the elect away from the protective shield of his God so that he can accuse them of sin and continue to abuse their spirit. A man that falls for such tricks cannot say he is just like me good on deeds for to be good on deeds is to be a wise man. and how can any man say he is wise if he is easily fooled by a common spiritual demonic criminal?

If a person is not able to see that a demon is nothing but a looser that is in mind of big hype to confuse and deceive to make believe that he is all power then such a person will abandon the course of goodness and jump in the band wagon of death to crash at a dead end.

Every man on earth is subject to trials as flesh. The initial flesh trial is to jumpstart a man to seek spiritual answers and if a man rises in his spirit then even though his flesh will continue to be tried his spirit will be in line of justifications for eternal life rewards. .

It is in trials of his flesh that the risen man becomes confident in power of life. For by standing in good faith to overcome his entire trial situations he is able to walk in testimony of the truth that the devil is a looser and I his God is the Almighty power of life. From knowing that your God is everything that is power of victory, you know very well not to waste your valuable time on a pest that is only interested in distracting you from performing the good business objectives of your God.

THERE IS GOOD PRECEDENCE FOR YOU EXPERIENCE SO BE OF A GOOD CHEER

The devil as a deceitful liar seeks to make humankind trade to loose their soul everlasting through his entire deceitfulness attempts towards man. When you go through the bible, you will see that there is precedence for the experiences that you have had since your becoming a living soul in me. The book of Matthew Chapter 5 verses 12 says **"Rejoice and be exceedingly glad: for great is your reward in heaven: for so persecuted they the prophets which were before you"**. A divine supernatural precedence is binding on the natural law for all that is in the natural is subject to my supernatural rule of law. An obvious supernatural precedence as documented in the scripture is that good will always prevail over evil and whereby a man goes though persecutions or trials for goodness sake he will have great reward of heaven.

A clear example of this precedence at work is in the story of Job and from the story of Job it is apparent that trials to the flesh only necessary to promote you in spiritual life.

I am the Holy Redeemer of life and as life Holy Redeemer, if I have favored you highly then the devil will not wish to try you if he can have his way. As you will find in the story of Job, the devil in his worldly wondering escapades did not see Job as a trial candidate. This is because he knows that if my glory is upon a man then any trials attempt of that man will only work to help the man to serve his purpose of life to be in my glorious presence everlasting.

The devil is after the soul not the flesh and the devil is after the soul to destroy it for as a spirit the soul of the devil is eternally condemned to be in eternal damnation of sorrow.

If the devil can only try the flesh and cannot touch the soul, as you will find in the story of Job then the trial will only work to promote the tried spirit to see beyond and above the realm of flesh.

The realms of flesh is the realms of darkness evil curses and to rise above the darkness world of flesh is to land in my holy divine territory to walk in goodness multiplication of blessings of life in my divine presence as the divine Father of life.

Job was a wise man and as a wise man, he knew that his Redeemer is all power. As all power, Job knew that his redeemer has perfectly arranged his momentary timely test to place him in reward of lasting blessings. Job; for he was a wise man knew that if you are in me the Holy Redeemer then you have my binding principle of life working to your favor.

My binding principle as I reveal it throughout the scriptural precedence is that a man that stays loyal to love life long objectives in goodness heart of perseverance will have total goodness of life in eternal life.

Job persevered because he knows that his Redeemer lives and if his redeemer is all power in life and as such the only one with power to bind death then he was in his mind certain that no deadly power fashioned against him can prosper.

To go through a test and exams of life and pass it is to have a graceful testimony.

The entire game plan of the devil is to deceive man to remain in sin and in sin be an obstructer of his graceful salvation to the detriment of his own soul. Your testimony in life as a goodness witness from all that you have been through and overcome by my power of love is that your Redeemer lives and for he lives no principalities power of death can prosper against you everlastingly.

Your testimony in life is that you have been able to overcome all barriers of evil in the power of love and not by your will and power but by my Spirit.

For you know that you have overcome all barriers of evil by the power of your Holy Redeemer you know that your Redeemer that man says is dead lives. For if, your redeemer is dead then he shall not be able to take you through the rivers or the fire without you perishing in it.

If you have been through the river and fire and you are still standing stronger than ever then know that you are more than a conqueror and know also that greater is he that is in you than that which is in the world.

If your enemy tries you to lead you to your destinations of goodness rewards then you are the winner the enemy is the looser for although he tried you in mind that you loose he actually has helped you to have all goodness reward of life by those trials. If your spirit has overcome death then your soul is automatically in joy of life. If your souls is in joy of life then that joy of life that is in your soul is your strength and in me you are always able to overcome any barrier for goodness sake of life.

True deliverance is of the spirit. My total agenda for man in time as the eternal everlasting God is to free the soul of man from death and in total spiritual freedom man is to be in mind and heart of love and in such mind of the heart of good faith. This agenda objective of mine I have fully performed by my finished works so it is now up to man whether he desire to be free from death or stay buried in graveyard of death.

The world is the way that it is because man is desperately evil and wicked and to be a wicked is to be in the valley of dry bones.

I will not rain manner from heaven in this day for the children of Israel eat manner in the wilderness and still died for they could not see my spiritual propose for them that it is spiritual deliverance from sin to walk in liberty freedom of life in eternal life. I came down as manner from heaven so that man can see that the purpose of life is spiritual not flesh and whosoever eat of me even though shall die as flesh, yet he shall live for I shall raise him up.

Out of ignorance, man seeks for deliverance on the outside however, what is the use of physical freedom if the spirit is imprisoned and the heavy laden of death compresses the soul. In the days of Moses, it was physically necessary for me to path the Red Sea so that Israel can cross over to reach their visible destination.

However, the same Israel that crossed the Red Sea went back into captivity and this is all because the flesh is rebellious to the ways of love. Today you fly over the red sea in an aeroplane to get to your destination so I say no need for me to path the seas for you to cross on foot to prove that I am the same God today, yesterday and forever.

However, man still has a Red Sea problem today and this Red Sea problem is an invisible spiritual one.

Many today are lost souls and as lost souls wanderers and unless they are free in their spirit they will wonder to the end of days never reaching their soul destination, which is high heavens. At the sound of the trumpet, it will be too late to cry wolf when the head is already off.

The devil as a heavenly outcast is a wondering spirit of hell. As such for a man in flesh to have peace in his mind he must arrest and bind the devil for if a man freely allows the devil to rule his mind it would be to compress it in great darkness. A man that walks in line of my binding principles will have my power of arrest to operate and use it against the devils of the world.

The world is full of devilish dead spirits and unless a man has my power of arrest, the devil will keep them under spiritual arrest to compress their souls in unrest. Those that have my power of arrest will arrest and bind the devil in power manifestation of life but the unwise spiritual man will stay in the unrest of the devil and in the devil's unrest will not have spiritual development.

Spiritual life is all about power and the power of a saint is from his knowledge of divine life rules and principles. To know divine life is to have power for divine life is secret and those that are not in knowledgeable secret of life are food for the devil.

Life sets precedents to reassure follow up saints that all those that walks in holy precedence will abide in my eternal restfulness.

To have this knowledge of life is to have open eyes in the spirit and it is in open eyes of the spirit that a saint performs his life objectives to the entire shame of the devil and the glory of I his God.

You will see in the biblical precedence that goodness always prevail. For goodness is light and evil is darkness and when light comes darkness must disappear.

The precedence of life is set in the supernatural. Just as I gave Michael the archangel of goodness victory over Lucifer the archangel of evil so is it that a man that stands for goodness will always have victory over evil.

Even though men in one generation may treat a saint like a robber and a thief in one generation, all of man from generation to generation will esteem such saint for whether you are good or evil is not a matter of your timely existence but by order of my eternal certifications.

The divinely knowledgeable knows that goodness always prevail over evil so he is not so much afraid of any evil mind against him.

Instead, he serves his life purpose to the very end, which is to pray for mercy for the soul of the wicked man that is persistently wicked against him from the very beginning to the very end due to total lack of wisdom.

The wise knows that a man in darkness evil does not understand the true consequences of his evil ways and it is for this reason that the wise always pray for mercy for the wicked for he knows that the potion for the wicked is greater potion of wickedness.

You will find in biblical precedence that many prophets were stoned to death, many saints beheaded, and in all of these things, they prayed for those evil-minded beings for they know that terrible punishment lies in wait for those wicked souls in eternity. Many prophets as you will find in the biblical precedents wept for their nation and those that they wept for ended up killing them.

I myself the king of kings the devil tried me in the world of flesh and I was crucified by man for the purpose of sinful remissions. Yet in line with lying traditions of the devils and to keep the mind of man still in disbelieve and in disbelieve an enemy of goodness many devilish agents today say such things as my crucifixion and resurrection never took place let alone my ascension to heaven.

I as your God have walked in your shoes so I understand exactly how you feel.

I see you all the time and as such, what no one can ever understand I understand because I am always there with you and in my perfect understanding of your feelings know that according to my precedence of life all that will preside over you in eternal life is goodness everlastingly.

A saint has my holy spiritual living water in them and as such understands the merciful grace of I Christ for he knows that without me he will be dry in his soul and in dryness thirsty in death.

Hence, a saintly-hearted will always be in mind of holy mercifulness towards thirst. Only in holy merciful walk is a man able to pray for those that stone him.

The focus of a saint is eternal life reward and from understanding divine holy precedence they know that it is not possible for them to stand for goodness in time and for goodness not to back and support them in eternity. In that knowledge of life, they stand always against evil in their knowledge of spiritual victory in eternal life forever.

A man that has benefit of life in his soul has overcome evil for the aim of evil is for the soul to be evil and wicked so that it perishes in the eternal lake fire of death forever. As such if man experiences trials when he is in life of life hearted and goodness minded to serve life purpose and aims, let him rejoice indeed.

For once you are in life and in life of goodness heart of faith all good and evil shall work together for your goodness.

The good at heart through experience I make to see the secret of the devil. The devil's secret is that he is a pest and as a pest always in mind to distract the elect from focusing on and performing their goodness life missions. To be in mind of divine wisdom is to put the devil in its place and the place for the devil is bottomless pits of hell. For you know that the devil is in hell to burn everlasting you will not allow yourself to be troubled by its antics and evil tantrums that is aimed at distracting you from serving your heavenly purpose of life.

The world of flesh is the world of darkness and in darkness, no man can see.

If it were not for my gracefulness perfect works of remissions and the affording of my grace to the saints for the perfection of the spirit of mankind no light shall be seen in the world.

To be subject to attack in your spirit is what is real tribulations and in all that you have been through since your encounter I can assure you that it is all to your flesh like in the case of job for your total spiritual advantage.

Those external factors you see is not to blindfold you but to open your eyes of the spirit so that you walk in mind of internal perfect good faith. For only in mind of good faith are you able to have sympathy and empathy for your fellow beings.

If you have not walked in a man's shoes, you cannot relate to his experiences. If you have not had a debt problem, you cannot understand the feelings of a person that is experiencing pounding and hounding from devilish merciless loan sharks.

A loan shack is not just interested in getting back that which he has borrowed the debtor but determined to steal all debtors' joy for having the stupid mind of borrowing from him in the first place. If you cannot understand how a person that is having relationship problems feels for you have never experienced any kind of relationships problems as far as you are concerned you cannot mentor such a person.

The trials of man are diverse in nature and you have had diverse trials to open the eyes of your understanding so that in that understanding you see the purpose for good works for goodness sake of life.

It is by my finished works and the good works efforts of the saints that I make my goodness visibly preserved in the world so that man continues to have benefit of graceful light. For without my perfect sacrifice and the sacrifice of saints through my alignment of their steps with my footsteps no man in the world will ever see the light of goodness.

The devil by his cunning ways deceives man in the world to lead them to the wrong conclusion that total power belongs to the evil and the wicked man and as such, it is profitless and pointless to be good.

A central character of darkness evil is greediness and this is a problem that, men have in the wicked world. A devilish man will always seek to feed his flesh and by seeking to feed his flesh his soul will forever starve to death and will remain everlastingly in death due to lack of good spiritual soul food. The more mind set a man is on vanity the more devilishly greedy he is and a devilish man out of greediness will always greedily feed his flesh to deny his spirit spiritual soul food.

The problem in the world is evidence of the preferred choice of man that it is evil not goodness. There is surplus in the world but the trouble is the greedy and the wicked men all in the mind of oppressing the needy are always in mind of keeping such surplus to themselves.

However as you have found in Psalm 73 the final end for such being is eternal death. The more you have to give and you refuse to give for goodness sake the more you shall be held accountable for denying those that are in need of what is in your hands which of course is mine for naked came man to earth and naked he shall live.

Those that I elect for goodness have the reward of goodness by the fact that by grace they are my chosen for goodness sake of life.

Many are elected by evil for evil purposes and such beings in the world see their evil purpose as a must serve hence extremely dedicated and committed to their evil objectives all to the detriment of their soul.

To be a chosen by goodness is to be at the heart of the goodness regiment of life and any being that is in goodness regiment is not a weakling.

Even though they may appear as if they are foolish and stupid because of their meekness and goodness gentility character they know they are not stupid. For by experience they know the game of the wicked and they know the end for the wicked is greater potion of their wickedness.

To be evil is to have an ugly mind and when in awakenings of life the ugly face of evil I reveal to you, it is for you to know that you have defeated the evil and wicked forever. The day the eyes see evil for what it is, is the day you bury evil in its graveyard. Evil is a secret and evil does not want its secret revealed to man. This is because if you know the secret of evil then you know that evil is desperately wicked and if you are wise you will not be in mind to be part of a desperate wicked force for evil does not pay.

The world of flesh is a world of the desperate evil minded and anyone in the world that is in their heart good on deeds must be very faithful to their chosen line of goodness for without total faithfulness no man will complete the good run of life.

To deliver goodness you must conceive goodness and a man that is faithful to evil is a man deceived to conceive evil as his objective purpose.

Such man will never know the joy of spiritual deliverance. For in mind of wicked objectives, the devils will try his spirit to perish everlasting. The goodness hearted as my elect is always a winner for by my grace he is justified to be a spiritual winner in all his trials that he faces as flesh.

The trial to the soul is the real trial for when a soul is in darkness and tried, that soul in deadly compression will not be conscious to his trials and as such will perish in evil darkness sorrow of his trials. A soul that is justified will be in fullness of joy no matter what the trial is to the flesh for even though you lament as a human being for what you go through your spirit rejoices for all that you go through is to your own spiritual advantage.

I understand that it is difficult for any man to understand these things in ordinary sense. However, from the answer you gave me when I asked if you feel you are better off with me or without me it is obvious that you do not see things simply from an ordinary mind perspectives anymore but from a spiritual angle.

If you look at things from an ordinary angle then it cannot make any sense to want to be with me still if as you said you see me as a God that only allows you to go through what you see as unnecessary pain and sorrow.

However because you are spiritually convinced that you are free from pain and sorrow you bear a spiritual record and testimony that all that you go through is all working to your advantage. It is for this reason that you remain joyful and continue to rejoice in the midst of all of your diverse temptations.

The wicked in the world appears as strong lion but this is all to trick every man including the very elect itself that it is in evil you have all the power. A man in evil is a slave to death. To be slave to death is to carry mark of the beast and the mark of the beast is the mark of death and as such eternal curse upon the soul.

To be in my Holy Spirit is to have my shield and total protection of life from me as the eternal God that is of eternal life.

By my Holy Spirit, I sustain your spirit in time in me to be of eternal life hope. In hope of eternal life; you have willingness to persevere in your trials and overcome them and by so doing remain in covenant relationship with my Holy Spirit of life in eternal life everlasting.

The devil knows that if you are a living being he cannot abuse your spirit and all that you go through is to your flesh and your flesh of course is an enemy of your spirit. The devil also knows that because you are a human being you cannot always see everything for what they are for in the ordinary what looks bad is really good and what looks really good is really bad.

I have made by my own word flesh for the benefit fulfilment purpose of man's salvation. Good deeds in the realms of flesh appear evil and evil appears good. To continue in line of goodness when all that you see directed at you appear as evil is to be a good on deeds for to be good on deeds is to be good no matter what you see as evil.

To continue to rely and depend on me to fulfil my promises even when the external factors makes things all appear as if I am lying to you is to remain in line of entire life rewards from I the Greatest On Deeds.

My entire promise to man is fulfilled in the giving of my Holy Spirit for if you have my Holy Spirit you have total benefit of life. To be disengaged from me is to be dead and to be dead is to be eternally dammed and sorrowfully condemned.

The greater your test the higher your purpose and the higher your purpose the greater your reward and for being in goodness purpose mind you will always be in goodness mind of divine faith.

Whosoever walks in divine faithful mind shall be greatly rewarded and when you fall into diverse temptations be sure that it is to perfect you to receive diverse higher reward of life and in life eternal life forever.

Your spirit is the main being and if in me, there is nothing like having hell in time and heaven forever for if I am in you and you are in me then your spirit is no longer subject to hellish sorrow. Instead all good and evil work together for your total advantage spiritual promotions in life. If sorrow last for a night and joy comes in the morning then you must get through the night to see the joy that awaits you in the morning. Therefore for anyone that is going through diverse temptations for goodness sake I say to them just as I always say to you, persevere for there is indeed a light at the end of the tunnel. In addition, I say do not see things from an ordinary perceptive for the ordinary eye is blind to spiritual facts.

Always see all of your trials in the world as the night and know that to persevere for goodness sake is to see the joy of light that your spirit sees in me as the Morning Star everlasting. Give thanks for your trials and seek spiritual solutions not the physical answers the devil wish that you go around chasing to frustrate your mind further. Find the truth in spiritual mind and from finding the truth, always be in mind of total commitment to truthfulness of life. Remember my word daily and stay convinced in my word not in the negative lies.

As I said in gospel of John Chapter 16 verses 33 **"These things I have spoken unto you, that in me ye might have peace. In the world ye shall have tribulation: but be of good cheer; I have overcome the world"**.

Know that under the banner of grace, my armoured shield covers your spirit and as such, you are in perfect spiritual defence hence no weapon fashioned against you can prosper.

Also, know that for you are in my Holy Spirit your spirit shall always walk in success of my victory in all circumstances and in total shield of your spirit in my presence be rest assured by your spiritual joy always, that goodness is upon your soul by my grace to you.

Only in such perseverance shall you see that there is an end to the tunnel and at the end, there is in fact light. I am still the same God of Abraham, Isaac and Jacob and I am not asleep nor do I slumber. I am a God of divine justice and the rule of divine justice is simple what you sow is what you reap. If you are good at heart, be good still for the good-hearted will never loose out in anything that is of goodness in my universal order of life.

I have not elected for the world of darkness to continue to influence you. Instead, I have elected you to be a light to the world and as light walk in perfect faith to shine as a light in the world so others can see the goodness of life that is in you.

If you say because a person has made life difficult for you and you seek to retaliate then how can you say you are unique and different from that person? If a person is desperately wicked, you know that their wickedness is to themselves for the potion of the wicked as written in the book of Job is greater potion of wickedness.

All that persevere shall be a continuous shining light and as light the darkness of the world shall not overcome them.

Whosoever is in the world of the world, is in thick darkness and in thick darkness night shall not see and if a man cannot see in the world then that man shall be tried to fail.

The night of the world cannot deceive the light that is in your spirit and it is to sustain you in light of my glory that I placed you under the protective banner of my Holy Spirit. A spirit in me is a light and I the I AM, I am the light of the universe.

To be a light in the world in time is to have my eternal reward of eternal life everlasting for I as the Alpha and Omega I am the Morning Star and when the Morning Star shines on you, darkness has no power whatsoever to oppose you in any way for when light shines darkness must disappear.

Therefore, I say rejoice and be of good cheer always for all things is working together for your spiritual goodness. If you face trials for goodness, sake of life then know that all is well. I say unto all that are of good faith and are facing any kind of trials to persevere for your trials is only against your already guilty flesh to keep your spirit continuously justified in eternal lifetime justifications.

Stay joyfully strong in knowledge of the fact that it is necessary for your flesh to experience such trials to subdue it from contaminating your newborn beautiful spirit so that you remain in continuous promotions of life in eternal life.

My peace to all the saints at heart and be assured oh ye saintly hearted that no man trades with goodness and loose and if you are in goodness serving the purpose of life know that in all dominion dimensional realm you are more than a conqueror. I see you are satisfied with my answer.

ME: Yes thank you very much.

GOD: You are welcome. I will continue my revelation on forgiveness in chapter two for now remain in good cheer and know that I have conquered the world for you.

ME: Thank again

GOD: You are welcome again.

CHAPTER TWO

TO FORGIVE IS DIVINE

> St. Matthew Chapter 5: verse 43 "Ye have heard that it hath been said, Thou shalt love thine enemy". Verse 44 "But I say unto you, love your enemies, bless them that curse you, do good to them that hate you, and pray for them which despitefully use you, and persecute you". Verse 45 "That ye may be the children of your Father which is in heaven: for he maketh the sun to rise on the evil and on the good, and sendeth rain on the just and the unjust".

GOD: To forgive is divine and without my divine act of forgiveness, no man shall be in perfect reconciliations with me. To love those that hate you and bless those that curse you is divine life. No man in the flesh of sin will be willing to pray for those that curse him or love his enemies.

To love your enemies and pray for those that curse you is to have peace on earth always. If you hate those that hate you and curse those that curse you then you will be just like them full of hate and a child of mine must never operate in mind of hate for to hate is to walk in heart and mind of wickedness towards another.

To be wicked is to have the potion of the wicked for a mind that is wicked will be evil oriented and to be in evil orientation is to be desperately vengeful.

To bless those that hate you is to be a unique being for every man will want to curse those that curse them. To live on earth according to my divine principles is to have my backing and support in all things. If you bless those that curse you and pray for those that curse you then you say you leave your battle for me and everyone that abide by my royal law will always have my divine justifications.

To follow my divine law is to walk in righteousness and whosoever abides by my righteous rule shall never be without defense of life.

If a man does not bless those that curse him or pray for his despiteful user then he will deny himself divine justice.

For every man that is flesh is demonic in his flesh and the way of a demon is to offend persistently. The only way to correct a wrong is by doing what is right.

A child of mine must live by goodness example and it is good example to do what I say is right for it is right. Good examples bring positive life changes whilst bad ways of the flesh influences the mind to be loyal only to sin.

Every man is a sinner and in a world of persistent sinners, the only way to remain justified is to walk in divine heart of love and it is divine love to love your enemy.

If you are, in mind to only love, those that you believe love you then you will be full hatred for those that you expect to love you most are the ones you feel hurt by the most.

For every man is a sinner, if I do not forgive all sins and heal all infirmities as you read in Psalm 103, then no man will ever make heaven. David the instrumental vessel that wrote Psalm 103 was a sinner like every man.

However even though he was a sinner he was a man after my heart because he was always in genuine mind of repentance and anyone that is in genuine mind of repentance will find the forgiveness goodness of my heart.

The wages of sin is death, no man is able to forgive his own sins, and as long as the sin of a man remains and he continue to walk in that sin so will his unrighteousness grow.

All that come to me come unto me always first as sinners for no man is righteous by his own makings.

All those who repent I shall forgive them of their sins, and out of forgiveness, I will heal them of all of their infirmities.

A sinner that does not repent walks in self-guilt and in self-guilt self-condemnation and in self-condemnation self-destruction.

Those who are wise shall repent for sin is infirmity to the soul.

A man that lives in sin carries the wages of death, and no man is able to pay the wages of his sin in death. I only can forgive all sins. I only can heal all infirmities and if man in their heart comes to me with a heart full of repentance, I shall forgive them all of their sins.

The issue is not just about coming to me but it is in what spiritual nature mind you come unto me. If you come with arrogance and pride, you would not have come with a good heart but if you come with a submissive heart, you would have demonstrated repentance just from your heart.

As a God, I seek to make the heart faithful so all that come with a little faith in their heart I shall forgive them of their sins and heal them of their infirmities.

I do not only heal those with high faith or forgive those whose faith is on a high level. My dealings are in accordance to the level of your spiritual maturity to bring you up to a level of my high spiritual reasoning.

However there must first in any event be believe for faith is all about believing and those who in their little faith believe that I can forgive all their sins and heal all their infirmities shall be set free from the curse of unbelief and in freedom they shall be made to grow and mature spiritually.

Unbelief is out of fleshy arrogance and ignorance. Those that are ignorant are arrogant fools because in their arrogance mind they are blind for believing that they can see all things.

Life is about responsibility and accountability and no man shall respond to his true spiritual ability if he is not in account of life.

To be in account of life is to submit your will and desire to life to be led by I the Holy Spirit of life for goodness sake of eternal life.

The consequences of sin remain punishment by death in eternity, and salvation of souls through forgiveness by my grace remains the only way to eternal life in me.

As long as man is of flesh, he remains a sinner but by grace of my remission works such man sin remains accounted to his flesh not his spirit.

Hence, by my grace sin will not contaminate the spirit of such man for by grace I have accredited to his spirit holiness divine justification for goodness sake.

TO BE FORGIVEN BY ME IS TO BE JUSTIFIED

By my remission works man is by me justified to be in reconciliations with me for eternity. To be justified by me is to appear before me pure and perfect just as if you have never sinned.

Through my justifications, sin that is a terminal cancer is by my blood of remission disabled from causing terminal eternal death in the spirit to the spirit of man.

By grace, a man covered with my blood even though is a sinner still in time does not appear before me any longer dirty.

As such it is no longer necessary for me to disengage myself for by covering the spirit of a man with my blood I afford to him by grace the gift of life and such man even though is a sinner still in time remains pure and clean before me. Such spirit through continuous walk in repentance will grow and mature and it is for this maturity to take place that you must not knowingly commit sins.

Man as flesh must understand that they are sinners and in such knowledge resist knowingly committal of sins through spiritual discipline.

To walk in spiritual discipline is to lead a healthy spiritual life at all times. This involves fellowship with me to have spiritual knowledge and wisdom.

A man will continue to grow and mature in me as a spirit when he in willingness engage constantly in effective fasting and prayer life to seek things of the spirit not of the flesh. In so doing a man as a spirit makes obvious to his soul the objectives of his spiritual free will that it is to operate in discernment power of life to resist further sin so as to be in perfect walk of divine righteousness for goodness sake of life.

To be spiritually undisciplined is for a man to invite the desire of sin to rule the mind. When the desire to sin propels the mind of a man, death rules such a man to walk in the flesh to carry out the works of the flesh.

The desire to sin makes a man a puppet of death ruled and controlled by death to walk in the opposite of life. Man in desire to sin is against the things of life for in sin the desire of man is of death to remain dead hence man in death mainly seek things that is of death which is not the objective desire of his soul.

In sinful desire, man walks against the objective desire of his soul not yielding or responding to his soul cry for awakening from pain and sorrow of death.

Sin enslaves man to death and death to continue to compress the soul of man in death deceives man to walk in self-justifications.

The devil leads a mind bent on sinning to justify sin as a right thing to do and even when man sees sin as wrong, his strong desire for sin leads him to walk in manner that is to take evil advantage of my forgiveness loving kindness due to his lack of spiritual maturity.

Many justify their continuous walk in sin by saying God will always forgive them but although I will always forgive, the problem for the continuous sinner is lack of spiritual growth and development. Each time a man by his free will chooses to walk in sin, he suffers a blow that sends him back to the beginning and such a man by consciously walking in sin shall be in up and down spiritual trend many times with the ultimate danger of eternal condemnation to his soul out of immaturity.

A sower is only interested to harvest the matured crops.

For if a crop is immature on the day of harvest you have no need for it and it is for this reason that man must not walk in wicked mind of sin just because I am able to forgive all sins and heal all infirmities.

Many knowingly go back to sin repeatedly after I had forgiven them and out of self-condemnation, they loose their soul. They reach a point and they start to pre-determine what I might do or might not do out of self-guilt. For they have knowingly sinned many times they conclude that God shall not forgive them so in guilt they continue in sin and in sin ends up succeeding in ultimate destruction of their souls.

This is the worst mistake man can make and this is what David knew.

David as man after my heart knew that although he is not a perfect being as flesh he knew that as a God, I make perfect the imperfect and as a God, I forgive all sins and heal all infirmities.

When I forgive all your sins, it is as if you have never sinned so you have a clean slate. Does that then mean that you should over and over sin knowing that I shall always forgive?

The answer is no. The whole idea behind repentance is to have willingness to change and remain in heart and mind to continue to change from your sinful ways because you are aware of the deadly spiritual consequential effects of sin.

Every human that is flesh, is subject to temptation and you resist such temptation by spiritual matured wisdom and knowledge of the truth.

To repent is equivalent to saying sorry based upon the fact that you have realized your wrong and in this realization, you are willing to remain in my line of perfections in your ways not walk the walk that you use to before your realization.

If you then say sorry and you continue to tempt me with continuous mind to sin then all you do is subject yourself to greater temptations and in greater temptations greater spiritual punishment of sin. I see you have a question

ME: Yes. What you are saying about sin is it not equivalent to someone hurting you repeatedly and says sorry each time only to do the same thing to you continuously.

GOD: It is equivalent to that so to speak. So do you say that you should not continue to forgive such a person for they appear to be taking advantage of your forgiving kindness?

ME: I say although is a good thing to always forgive is it not the case that if you do not put your foot down the person will continue to take advantage of your good heart of forgiveness.

GOD: By putting your foot down I see you mean not to allow yourself to be hurt again by the person so do you also say this means not forgiving or do you say forgive but stay away from the person so that they hurt you no more.

ME: I say forgive but stay away from the person because unless you stay away they might not even appreciate what they are doing to you.

GOD: The book of Matthew chapter 18 from verses 21 reads **"Then came Peter to him, and said, Lord how oft shall my brother sin against me, and I forgive him? Till seven times?"** Verse 22 **"Jesus saith unto him, I say not unto thee, Until seven times: but, Until seventy times seven"**. Bearing in mind, this verses, I ask you this, if it is natural way of man to offend one another to the point of considering separation necessary, do you think most consider separation necessary to effect a change in the person that wronged them or is it that they want separation out of hate.

ME: I would say most people must seek separation because they no longer find it desirable to stay connected for whatever reasons.
Everyone I am sure will have their own story and for some it could be because they believe they no longer love the person.
For some it could be because they want their freedom for example in parent child relationship and for others it could be to effect a change

because despite all efforts the person has refused to change their ways towards you.

In any relationship, I say when you love someone you really do not want to break your ties with them but is it not also the saying that if you love someone, you should let them go and if they are meant to be with you, they will come back.

GOD: With love, all things are possible for love conquers all.

The problems faced by humankind in their relationships with one another lies within their lack of real love in their hearts for one another.

Real love is spiritual and as written in 1 John chapter 4 verses 8, I JEHOVAH God the I AM, I am love.

To love you must have experienced love for without experience there can be no practical understanding. If you have a theoretical knowledge with no practical understanding it is like believing that you know all that there is to know when you do not really know what it is that you know.

Theory of the flesh and real love divine practice are two worlds apart because what you believe you know is different from the way things are in real life.

Only in love can you have a heart to forgive. With love all things are possible and only in true love can you serve the divine purpose of life. No man can have a heart of forgiveness except in divine love.

Knowledge of love is knowledge of life and when man speaks of love in the flesh it is lust they mean and a relationship of lust is like candle in the wind and for it is like a candle in the wind it does not last.

Theoretical knowledge of the flesh does not give spiritual understanding of life.

Only by practical applications do you understand the goodness ways of love.

Love is all about positive practical actions and it is only in practical positive spiritual actions do you have total spiritual solutions in life.

A man says he loves with his mouth but for he hates in his heart his practical actions will show the negativity of his mind not the positive love proclamations that he makes with his mouth.

To understand my spiritual love you must have practical experience of my love for you. To have experience of my love for you, you must be in relationship with me as a spirit for as God I am a Spirit and only a living soul can be with me for I am a God of the living not the dead.

You do not generate positive attitudes from an empty mind word that is full of negativity for a mind full of negativity will only speak positively to deceive and to give false hope. A positive action must follow a positive word.

The action of many humans towards one another even though they claim to love each other so much is of deep hatred. When negative and negative meets, what you have is fireballs and in many fire balls there would be so much heat and in so much heat all will be seeking some kind of cooling off period.

To love you must be alive for if a spirit is dead then even though he speaks of love all his ways will be against love.

Such a being for he is dead will be very spiritually dissatisfied and in spiritual dissatisfaction, such a man will be in mind of confusions and in mind of confusions will not know what he is looking for.

If he finds from someone anything that he sees as love, he will hate that someone and seek to punish them for their loving him through seeking to always take evil advantage of their loving kindness.

If he finds someone that, he sees as uncaring and hateful towards him he will hate them still.

This is the dilemma of a dead spirit and this is the reason why mankind is always in mind to hurt one another. For they are dissatisfied in their souls they hurt each other so much and from hurting each other so much bitterness pain and sorrowfulness increases deeply in their souls.

To be in the flesh is to be in heavy laden sorrow of death and instead of the relief that man seeks from jumping from one relationship to the other he finds more pain for he lacks practical knowledge of real spiritual life.

Every man on earth is seeking for my spiritual love and only in my spiritual love shall a man be satisfied for unless a man is alive and well in his soul he will be totally void no matter high up in the world ladder he sees himself to be.

Experiencing love brings peace of mind to the soul but when you do not have spiritual experience of love all your saying shall be in theory knowledge of the flesh and the flesh for it is anti love will frustrate you in those theories.

It is only through practical life experience that knowledge makes practical sense to your mind, it is in mind of practical sense, and understanding of real love that you become confident and rest assured that your knowledge is good for you see the goodness outcomes that it brings.

Most human although speaks of love they are incapable of loving or even appreciating divine loving standards for a dead spirit hates any kind of loving gesture towards him and cries when he is chastised by hatred.

A dead spirit does not know or understand love and as such cannot give love.

You give what you have and when man seeks love from one another it is like seeking to take from each other what they do not have to give.

A human gives to take more than he is capable of giving and when you give and get nothing you will not be in mind to continue giving but take back all you believe you have given out of your annoyance towards the one that you see to be taking evil advantage of your goodness gesture.

With love, you are able to overcome any kind of barrier but where there is no love the barrier itself is the lack of love and the root of all of human problems is their deep mind of hatred for each other.

A spiritually dead human being is in thick darkness and in thick darkness; deep hatred presses down the soul of such man to walk in evil mind of deep hatred.

In hatred, a man is a thorn in the flesh of his fellow beings and if you are a thorn in each others flesh all you will be in mind of is were to find relief.

A human being in mind search of relief is always in the promiscuous mind of jumping from one relationship to the other hoping that he will find the kind of loving relief that he is seeking for in another relationship. Most jump from one bad relationship to the other and each time you engage in an oppressive relationship you add more sorrow to the sorrow that is already there.

TO BE BLAME FOCUS IS TO BE VICTIMIZED BY EVIL SPIRITS

To change you must stop blaming for as long as you blame you cannot see your own faults to take steps and amend them. To be blame minded is to self recommend yourself that you are perfect. Blame is a barrier to change and to change the barrier of blame must come down from the human mind.

A blame minded being will see himself as a victim and as a victim bitter and highly resentful. Such person will be empty on the inside and in emptiness dead spirits will fill them up with wickedness and a wicked mind can never know peace. A dead spirit is a void hearted being and in void heart always in mind search of fulfillment.

To seek fulfillment physically as a spirit being is to be foolish minded for to be full and filled in your spirit you must be a living soul.

Only as a living soul shall rivers of life flow in your belly and no man is a living soul unless made to be by my divine love.

Human beings are like masquerades and as masquerades you never can tell what you will find when you lift up the veil cover from the masquerades face.

Human relationship is like entering a relationship with someone that is heavily masked and well into the relationship you suddenly realize as you begin to unmask one another that the one beneath the mask is not as good looking as you thought they were initially.

A human being as flesh is defensive in his ways of offensiveness towards another and this is the most frustrating aspect of human life. When you allege that someone has offended you and instead of saying sorry and promise to change they allege that you have offended them even more, unless you both admit that you have wronged one another equally the same and for peace sake apologize with the mind of changing your ways towards one another there can be no peace.

Human as flesh are always in mind of blame and when you are in mind of blame, you cannot be in mind to change and amend your ways.

To change you must realize the impact of your offensive ways on the complainer and if you meet, a complaint with counter complaint instead of redress then the result will be great frustration and it is in this frustration that many seek to be apart from one another. To understand the impact of your offensive ways on another you must see the impact of your actions as it affects the other for if you cannot see the hurt as painful as it is then you cannot understand the need to change.

Most human will do unto others what they will not want others to do unto them and most human will defend their wrong by blaming the one they have wronged.

It is common for a human being to counter an allegation by saying whatsoever they have done wrong the person alleging that they are wrong is the one that made them to be as they are and as such if anyone needs to change it is not them.

Human relationship is painful and sorrowful because for every offence you defend the offence instead of admit the wrong and change for goodness sake.

If it is common for humans to defend their wrong instead of admitting it and change then unless you have a forgiving heart towards those that offends you, your mind will always be full of hatred.

In the book of Matthew 18 from verses 21 to 20 you saw that Peter, a disciple of I the Son asked whether it is enough to forgive seven times before as you said put your foot down.

The answer that I gave of course is that you must forgive not seven times but seventy times seven, meaning countless times.

I am a God that gives coded meanings to numbers and the key number here is seven for zero is not an active number.

Seven is the number of grace and grace is unmerited favor out of the goodness of my own forgiving heart. If by grace, I forgive you countless times then you must forgive those that offend you countless times just as you would like me to forgive you.

Matthew chapter 6 verse 14: says "For if you forgive men their trespasses, your heavenly Father will also forgive you". Verse 15: "But if you forgive not men their trespasses neither will your heavenly Father forgive your trespasses".

To forgive is to show appreciations for grace. For it is by grace that I forgive your sins and whosoever appreciates, my grace will always abide in my graceful justifications.

It is necessary to forgive countless times because in a world of defensive offenders, you will be offended countless times and if in most times instead of the person saying sorry and promise never to offend you again they will blame you to offend you even more then to be blame free yourself you must always forgive.

To take the blame even when you know you are blameless is to be Christ like for I the sinless blameless took the blame for man to set man free from the evil compression of death.

If a man walks in Christ like nature then he is a Christ in me and to be a Christ in me is to be my living sacrifice and son. All of man as flesh is in the nature of the devil. A man in the devil of the flesh will only walk in mind of abominations and will perish in death for promoting his devilish master abominations. For a man to inherit my kingdom of eternal life peace, joy and rest must abort dead end missions and engage in life missions as a Christ in me for goodness sake of his soul in eternal life.

For only the Christ like natured is my son and if a man is in Christ he is no longer subject to the ruler of darkness for I Christ I am light and as light the power that is above all powers of darkness principalities.

To forgive a person even when you believe they have wronged you is to take the blame for the situation and to do such a thing is to have automatically benefit of my Christ faith justifications, which is high life promotions in regiment of life.

The problem in human relationship is mostly on the fact that no one is prepared to take the blame and make peace in any situation.

To take the blame is to take the responsibility for making and ensuring peace.

To be a peacemaker is to be blameless in my eyes for if you take the blame to ensure peace then blessed you are always in my courtyard for your holy act of peace.

It is a holy thing to be a peacemaker for a devil is always in mind of making wars and keeping the minds at battle to distract the attention from focusing on real life objectives.

A devil is a thief and a robber and as a thief and robber totally against peace because in peaceful unity you will unite to defend your territory but when you are against each other the devil is busy stealing whilst you are busy fighting one another.

No man is able to take the blame for peace sake except in spiritual maturity for unless you see yourself as justified you cannot see the need for you to be just in your mind for peace sake towards someone that you believe to have offended you.

Spiritual maturity takes place through good spiritual understanding of life of the ways of love.

To love is to hold the one that you love dear to you heart.

You do not fall in and out of love for love is not like a clothing garment that you put on one minute and take off the next to exchange for another.

Love is eternal, it is everlasting, and as love, I say love is a matter of the heart. When you love someone your heart follows them wherever they go and because your heart follow them wherever they go you will not want to let go off them totally from your heart but pray that they change and be, as you desire for them.

Love is always in mind of reconciliations for when you love you will always want to be with the one you love and there can be no such reconciliations unless there is peaceful sacrifice for goodness sake.

If you believe, someone has wronged you and that someone believes you have wronged them even more neither of you shall seek to make any peace offering towards one another.

To make a peaceful offering you must take your mind off the offence and focus it on the peace that you seek to prevail.

If you focus your mind on the offence you will only get angrier and the angrier, you get the more you will not see the need for peaceful unity.

Only from a spiritual angle shall you be able to forgive countless times for in the flesh man is not in heart of love but lust and in lust there is only hurt and pain in the mind and no forgiveness can be found in the heart of a bitter painful resentful being.

Human beings have no understanding of divine loving ways and for they have no such understanding, they walk in blindness of the flesh.

Divine love is all about perfect sacrifice and no man is in mind of sacrificing for the benefit of another in selfish mind of the flesh.

To put your anger aside and seek to be at peace with someone that has aggrieved you is evidence that you have divine understanding of purpose of life that is loving kindness for goodness sake.

A man as flesh is always full of arrogance and in arrogance will not be in mind of admitting his wrong let alone apologize for them even when it is blatantly clear that he is very wrong.

To love someone is to do everything to please him or her and when you start to find that such person's main interest is to displease you then you certainly will not see such person as loving you and for you do not see love from the person, you will not feel comfortable being around them.

To love is comforting and in the comfort of love, there is always joy, peace and total rest of mind. A human relationship does not last because in every relationship each person always seeks to change the other from attitudes or behaviors that they see as inappropriate or unacceptable.

If every complaint you make against one another the other sees it genuine for what it is and amend their ways by not doing what you complain about again then all of man will be at peace with each other.

The problem is if instead of changing you continue to offend one another then there can be no peaceful relationships in the human society.

This is because when you offend to the point of seeing the need of going your separate ways it is not often to fly away and come back in realization that you love each other so much rather it is to tear each other apart in your separations in greater mind of hatred. I see you have a say.

ME: Yes. Are you saying from what you have said so far that one should not be in mind of physical separation in any circumstances?

GOD: My point so far is to highlight the reason why human seek to separate from one another and this reason as I have said is in their lack of love for one another.

Love is not physical and as such, whether you hate or love someone is not a question of you being with them physically.

PHYSICAL SEPARATION DOES NOT MEAN SPIRITUAL DETACHMENT

In terms of physical separation, it is right to say that in certain situations staying away physically from someone that keep hurting you is necessary however you must understand that staying away physically does not mean not forgiving them.

Separating from someone physically does not mean end to the spiritual relationship and if a man is in relationship with a dead spirit in death regiment then separating from the regimental vessel does not mean freedom from the darkness regiment of hate.

The only way to break free from the curse of hate is to walk in heart and mind of divine love.

Forgiving someone is necessary to set yourself free from the burden of hatred mindfulness.

If you merely separate physically from a person and hate them in your heart for whatsoever they have done to you then simply separating from them physically will not relief your mind from the pain and hurt that the darkness regimental force behind the broken vessel body of hate have caused you.

In a human society of allegations and counter allegations, what you have is many depressed, oppressed and aggrieved heavily laden souls with a mind of deep hatred.

To be free from the heavy laden of hate you must forgive. When you forgive, you proclaim by your act of forgiveness that you are of divine life with a heart that is of divine love.

You show that you have a divine heart by your divine actions to take spiritual responsibility for peacemaking and in mind of peacemaking, you say that you seek relief for the burdened not help any spiritual darkness regiment to further burden the burdened by being hatred mind.

Hatred is a heavy spiritual burden and when you hate you burden your heart with hate and a heart of hate is a heart that is always deep in sadness and sorrow.

To forgive someone that has caused you great hurt is a wonderful divine act of love and you cannot be in a mind of such divine act if you are not in appreciation of graceful walk of my loving kindness.

To forgive and forget you have to be in heart of appreciation and daily remembrance of the works of my graceful works through which you have a clean slate of your own sin. Remembering and appreciating my good works cancels out the hurt and from being in mind of appreciations joy increases daily in you for your goodness actions of good faith.

Every time you are in memory of the hurt a person caused you out of bitterness and anger, the bitter memory will make the wrong feel like freshly deep cut wound with much non-stop heavy bleeding.

Bitter memory and mind of hate gives a debilitating effect and if hate weighs down a person due to their mind of bitter memory, they will not be able to make any positive movement.

Forgiveness is a positive action that counters the negative effects of bitterness and if a person does not engage in the positive action of forgiveness, they cause their spirit greater harm from their being unforgiving.

I understand it is difficult for humans to get over their hurt especially if the person responsible for that hurt refuses to admit their fault and apologize for it but with me all things becomes easily done.

Most human would say that in most cases what the person that has been hurt needs is a remorseful apology to help them get past their hurtful feelings.

The problem is in most cases the person that is responsible for the hurt is also claiming to have suffered hurtfulness from the hands of the claimant.

If the one you complaint against counter complain that you have hurt them even more how will the person ever reach the point of making a remorseful apology to you. If you wait on a person that believe you have hurt them to come and remorsefully apologize to you then you will have very long to wait for just as you are waiting so are they waiting that you come and apologize to them.

To get over your hurt you must look beyond the one that you see to have hurt you because the one that has hurt you in most cases will hurt you even more by denying they have hurt you and will anger you even more by their defensive attitude and ways.

If someone hurts you, you cannot find relief from their being unapologetic or in their denial of the hurt, which they have caused you. This is why in most cases when humans as flesh gather to talk things over they end up in serious fights because what you get is blame and counter blames. I see you have a say.

ME: Everything you are saying from my own experience is true. My question at this point is on getting together to talk things over and as you said this normally ends in disaster.

Therefore, what is the way forward because if for example, you do not want to physically separate and you wish to talk things over for peace sake without it ending up in a shouting match like this things normally do what is the best way of going about it.

GOD: When a human being takes the initiative to talk things over in the human context, it is usually in mind of attempting to make the other person see their wrong still.

The talk will go well if you state the case and the other simply says guilty as charged but so long as the other is in defensive mind to give a defensive offensive talk there can be no way forward.

Defensive flesh communications will only build a higher barrier. The right way is not in the flesh and it is important you understand everything from this perspective.

In the mind of the spirit, you take the blame for the situation not because the other person does not have any blame to take.

However, you must understand that in the flesh nobody sees the point of any other but his own.

No matter how wrong a person is so long as they believe they are right you cannot make them see their wrong simply by insisting they are wrong and you are right. It is common human saying that two wrongs does not make a right.

I say if two that are wrong believe they are right then they will only bring greater wrong upon themselves.

To make a person see their wrong it is not just, from your talking it is more from your actions.

A person that is blind in their spirit cannot see and if you as a living soul is to help them to see it cannot be from acting in the same way they are acting.

When you call a person to make them to admit their wrong, knowing that they will insist that you are more wrong then what is the point in long fruitless talks.

Defensive flesh communications builds barriers and to talk and progress you must lay down your flesh defenses and pick up spiritual swords.

Your spiritual sword is my word and you use my word as a living spirit that is in my full armored protection. If I have afforded you all protection then you need not fight to defend yourself like a fool. To wage war in the flesh is to fight like a fool and I have opened your eyes so that see you see and you need to see to know what is right and do what is right

A person that is offensive in their communication is a person that is not in knowledgeable wisdom of divine life for the good in their spirit shall always be in mind to give comfort in their communications.

To give comfort you must have comfort and to give peace is to acknowledge that you have peace in me for I am peace.

To have peace is to be in mind to make peace always.

A peaceful minded person will always follow through his word by peaceful actions to achieve the peace that is in his mind for only by such peaceful actions shall it be clear that you have a genuine peaceful intention.

To be a peaceful maker is to walk in line of righteousness in your ways for no man that is against peace can walk in any manner of my spiritual righteousness I see you have another saying.

ME: My God, this is hard. If someone does not see their wrong let alone admit, it and you always have to make peace how then can they see their wrong.

GOD: You are still asking the same question in a round about way. Now here is a question for you. Is a person able to see their wrong because you do what is right or what is wrong just like them?

ME: Maybe if they have a taste of their wrongdoing they may appreciate that it is wrong to be wrong and not admit it.

GOD: By that, you mean hate and in hate, revenge and I totally forbid that for you.

To be in mind of revenge is to take the laws into your own hands and anyone that takes universal law into their own hands automatically have lost their case before me.

VENGEANCE IS MINE

Vengeance is mine and if you want justice, you come to the incorruptible judge that will always give you perfect good justice.

You do not perform the role of the judge when you are a defendant.

Every man is a sinner and for all man is a sinner, it is against my order of life for a man to seek to take his own revenge.

Roman 12 from verses 19, which I have before referred you says you do not counter evil with evil but evil with good.

It is impossible for a human in the flesh as flesh to make peace with someone that is unwilling to accept their wrong but it is easy for you to do so as a spirit being in my heart of divine love. To take matters into your hands is to make matters worse.

To make peace is a matter of a good heart. A good heart is not all evident from you taking the initiative to talk things over with the offender defender for if your primary intention for summoning the person is to make them admit their wrong then the person that you summon will only be in mind of counter allegations and not peaceful resolutions.

If you call a man to allege that he has wronged you and you already, know that he will allege that you have wronged him even more what is the whole point in long talks if you are unwilling to take the blame for you are in mind of peace to make peace.

To have what you want is to focus your mind on achieving it.

Effective communication breaks barriers whilst offensive talks builds higher barriers and to talk with someone in mind of making peace is to be willing to do what is necessary to have peace.

If you call someone in mind of peace making to talk to them to have peaceful reunion who is to say that they are not in mind of war to ensure that you do not have that peace of mind and joy from achieving your peaceful objectives.

If you see the point in peace making then it is no point of trying to make them see their wrong through offensive talks because the starting point of peace making is to take the blame and be blameless in your heart.

From taking the blame in high mind of spiritual maturity you have showed already that, you have a peaceful mind and those that are in mind of peace will always have peace in their minds.

If you have called, someone that will not admit they are wrong to make them admit their wrong then your calling on the person is for them to come and provoke you further.

The best way to deal with a tantrum child is not be like the child.

To bring a situation under control you must be willing to be on the side of spiritual maturity. As a living soul you know that when you take the blame for a situation for peace sake you are blameless in every situation because as your God I am not blind and vengeance for is mine I will always avenge you for goodness sake of life.

To have a mind of forgiveness is to always obey my royal law for you cannot say you love someone when you cannot have the mind to forgive them and no man can have peace unless in heart and mind of divine love.

My royal commandment is that you love me as your God with all your heart, mind body and spirit and that from loving me you love your neighbor according to yourself.

No one that loves himself would want to be at war with himself and to go against my loving commandments is to make war with the inner self.

To take a spiritual mature step and apologize even when you believe the other person is wrong is to say you do all that you do for my name sake.

If you offend me, out of your stubbornness in trying to prove that, you are right and the other person is wrong then do you not say you do not care for your soul whether it lives or die knowing very well that the wages of sin is death.

Whatever punishment you can give to a person it is nothing compared to what they will get from me if they have indeed wronged you.

To wrong my elect is to be my enemy and no enemy of mine can have rest. If you as my friend says you care more about your ego as human being more than pleasing me how is that wisdom for to displease me is to see the redness of my eyes.

If I am willing to take the blame for you always then know that taking the blame in a situation for peace sake is to show by example that you are Christ like in your ways.

You cannot loose sight of the spiritual facts and the spiritual fact is that the entire aim of the enemy is for you to reach the point that you will decide to take matters into your own hands.

The enemy knows that once you choose to do that you have chosen evil and if you choose evil once you know goodness and the benefit of goodness it is far worse than before you came to know goodness because the pain of spiritual self-guilt will be terrible for the soul.

No matter what the case may be, deciding to give anyone the taste of their wrongdoing and by that choosing to retaliate is out of the question.

That is my job and as the judge, I will always give the potion of the wicked to the wicked. All you have to do is what is right for it is right and this is to be an example to others always in heart of love.

In love, all things are easy for nothing is impossible for love.

When you perform a love action, for my name sake, I recompense you with abundant blessings always and to have a mind to make peace is to have my peace in your soul always.

The main reason for a man not admitting his wrong or apologize for it is his ego and human ego is a spiritual eternal killer of their soul.

The spiritually mature will always humble himself before me and those that humble themselves before me will have my total respect and in total respect my entire blessings.

I always count it as great act of humility before me when a man shames his flesh to the goodness promotion of his spirit by being in mind of peace and in such mind take responsibility for peacemaking for goodness sake of life.

I see you have another saying.

ME: Yes. Are you saying no matter what the spiritually matured must always say sorry?

GOD: What I am saying is that no matter what, the spiritually matured must never act in the immature way of the non-mature flesh being.

Making peace is a divine way of life and if you see my own act of peace making to bring you into reconciliations with me then nothing will be too difficult for you to do for my name sake.

Peace making is not just a matter of spoken word. When you look at things in the way that you are looking at it, which is say sorry no matter what, then you say all that is necessary to make peace is to say sorry. Everything you do is a matter of the heart so even though someone may say sorry it does not mean they mean their sorry.

In fact saying sorry could anger you in some situations because if someone as you said keep hurting you only to say sorry it would reach a point that their sorry would mean nothing to you and instead of you, feeling appeased by their sorry it would cause you deep serious anger.

When I say, take responsibility for peace it is not just in matter of saying sorry by word of mouth and holding grudge in your heart.

To be in mind of peace is to have a clear conscience and to have a clear conscience is to forgive the other person from your heart and in greater mind of peace intercede for them in prayer and in addition take the bold step towards reconciliations.

You must remember in all of this things that just as I see all that you do I see also the other person in all that they do for as love I am not blind.

Love is all about your inwardness so is hate as such if someone hurts you then you do not seek for solution for that hurt from the outside but from the love that is inside you. This way only shall you counter the hate that is from within pushing you from the inside to oppress your mind to hate those that you see on the outside that you believe to be hateful.

When you look on the inside, you will always find me and by obeying my commandment, you do yourself a great favor.

What you must always bear in mind is that what matter most is what you do.

If you are to love only those who love you then you will never love anyone because those that profess to love you most are the ones that you see as hurting you most.

If those that say they love you dearly are those that you account your hurt feelings to then how can you be in mind to love anyone if you see those that you trust so much as those that hurt you so deeply.

To see things from my point of view which is a clear spiritual view you must not dwell on the wrong from the person but the right that you see from me and it is only from seeing my right towards you that you will find total peace of mind.

A person that carries the burden of hate is a very sad person and if you have a clear conscience you will do all that is necessary for the peace of your soul.

The actions of peace that you take in good spiritual conscience is not in mind of proving the person wrong for if you are both in any mind of strife then whether or not you both admit it you are both wrong.

To take a step from goodness conscience is to take steps that I have rightly ordained for goodness sake of your soul and by following those steps, you show without being in any mind of proving any point that you truly are a peaceful champion.

A human being in the flesh due to ego problems will find it difficult to seek to do what is necessary to make peace even when he knows he is wrong. For such a being even though they know they are wrong due to their ego will be too foolish to admit their wrong, shame their flesh and be set free from the spirit of deadly compressive arrogance.

To be egoistic is to be self-destructive for out of stupid ego a person will infuriate a situation to a point of no resolution when in fact what he seeks for is resolution.

A living soul will not entertain strife for strife will only drive the mind to be malicious. A wise being does not keep malice in his heart for his soul will not let him rest and keeping malice is not a matter of not talking to a person.

You may be smiling and laughing with a person embracing and kissing them and hold a terrible grudge against them and you may not say a word to someone yet you fast and pray for them for goodness benefit of their soul.

To understand my sayings correctly, you must look beyond physical actions to the mind. The physical steps of a person can be very deceiving but if a person takes any step in goodness heart of spiritual conscience, it would yield a goodness outcome result.

Your actions must always be spiritual for although man cannot see your goodness intercessory spiritual actions I see it all and for I am your witness, you stay justified before me no matter what man says to condemn you.

Spiritual actions are what matters and when you forgive as a spirit, you do so from your innermost heart.

You could easily say sorry to someone but that does not mean you mean that sorry. You could call someone to talk things over with them but that does not mean you are willing to admit your own wrong and by your admittance ready to change for peace sake.

You could apologize to someone over and over again that does not mean that they will be satisfied with your apology if by your actions you continue to say you are not sorry for what you have done even though you say sorry by your words.

You may plead with someone to forgive you that does not mean it is from you realizing your wrong it could all be a way of you gaining their trust again so that you hurt them still.

To forgive is a life positive action and positive actions that are invisible to man will always generate positive visible results.

The way to have understanding is to look at everything from invisible to visible. Forgiveness is from the heart and so is the mind to make peace.

When you have a spiritual mind of peace and by this spiritual mind you forgive from the heart, you will be in mind of peaceful rest in your soul.

To forgive is for your own peace of mind because the one that you forgive in your heart will not necessarily be in desire of peace for you in their mind.

Just because you have a mind of peace towards someone does not mean they will be in the same mind that you have towards them.

However, making peace in your mind with a person is to release yourself from the burden you carry from your feeling of hurt for which you believe they are responsible.

In addition, if you realize that you have hurt someone and seek that they forgive you and they refuse, if you are truly repentant and in repentance, you have found my own forgiveness then know that you are forgiven.

Understanding spiritual life means you always must see yourself as the responsible one and as the one that is responsible the one that must always carry the torch of goodness. To carry the torch of goodness is to have a mind of positive action always and this means be ready and willing to do whatsoever is right for goodness sake of my name.

If you see all that you do that it is for my name sake then everything that is difficult in the ordinary sense becomes very easy because you know that as your God I will always compensate you for all that you do that is for the glory of my name.

I see you are satisfied with my answer so far.

ME: Yes. Thanks. As you said if it is for your name sake then it becomes so easy to do for, as I know, you know best and whatsoever you say do, I have found that it is always for my interest.

Just one last thing, does that mean anyone can just take liberty because they know you cannot but forgive because they see you are always in peaceful mind to make peace.

GOD: No one can take liberty of any kind for unless I liberate a man any attempt to take any form of liberty will further deepen the soul in darkness captivity of evil.

Always know that whosoever is devilish in their mind towards a saintly-hearted being will never find any kind of liberty.

To be at liberty is to have soul liberation and no man is in any liberation from the oppressive and depressive heavy hand of death in evil heart of hatred towards another.

This is why to believe that it is liberty to harm another in evil mind is total foolishness for to do evil is to have the reward of evil, which is eternal pain and sorrow.

If a person walks in goodness, they will have reward that is of greater good and if it is evil, it would be greater reward of evil.

It is for this reason that you must never seek to retaliate evil with evil for a person that retaliates evil with evil shall have the reward of greater evil poured as hot coals of fire to his soul. It is by standing firm in goodness always that you say you are more than a conqueror.

As someone that is more than a conqueror, you do not operate in common emotional character but in precious character of love.

In precious character of love you show by your mature spiritual actions that you are not by any means compressed by your human emotions instead you rise above and on top of them for you are at liberty of free will of my goodness and in that liberty of my free will all things works together always for your goodness.

Always bear in mind that I see all and know all and I will always avenge my elect as the universal God of life in my all power and for the entire goodness of my name. I see by your smile that you are very satisfied with my answers so far.

ME: Yes thank you.

GOD: You are welcome. A question for you, from all that I have said can you see why a human being nurses the same pain year after year even when they have separated physically from the person.

ME: Yes like you said it is because of the fact that you keep begrudging the person for what they have done to you and unless as you said we let go the pain remains fresh no matter how many years has gone by.

GOD: Physical separation does not eradicate the spiritual burden of a darkness relationship.

The actual act of hurt could be for a few minutes in time but the lasting spiritual emotional bitterness that it leaves behind in the mouth is what is difficult to get rid of. The worst kind of hurt for a human being to get over is emotional hurt and pain.

EMOTIONAL PAIN IS CAUSED BY DEEP SPIRITUAL INNERMOST WOUND

Emotional hurt and pain is hidden to others and obvious to the one that is hurt and how deep the wound is on the inside is not obvious to anyone but to the one that is hurt. Most human are deeply hurt emotionally and from such hurt they make hurting others their personal business and my say is, no one profit from hurting anyone.

To get over your hurt totally you must forgive and forget the one that you see to have hurt you and to forgive and forget is not a thing that a human being is capable of doing in their highly emotional flesh.

To forgive as I said is divine and to lead a divine life you must be awake in the spirit and to be awake in the spirit is to forgive and plead the course of the one you have forgiven before me for goodness sake of life.

If you not only forgive them but pray that they repent to have benefit of my own forgiveness then you say you are not a common human being but a unique being that is centered in the regimental heart of love for goodness sake of life.

Although as you said physical separation in some situations may be necessary however as I have emphasized, if you do not forgive physical separation makes no difference to pain and hurt.

By not forgiving, hatred will eat up the heart and a person eaten up by hate will be bitter and more resentful whether the person that caused the pain now resides a million miles away from them.

If what you really desire from a person that you love is not to separate from them but to make them to stop hurting you, then separating from someone that has hurt you alone will not get you the result you require. I see you have another saying.

ME: Yes. I understand that physical separation will not heal the hurt from all you have said. However could physical separation help give breathing space that a person needs for them to think of forgiveness.

If people stay together in a high level, tensed environment is it not possible for things to get worse particularly given that there is limit to human endurance.

If staying with someone that keeps hurting you could make things worse is it not better to just separate for a short while if not permanently for the sake of some form of healing process to take place.

GOD: Healing comes from within your spirit being because the person that created the problem is unlikely to see the dept of your hurt let alone be in mind of healing your wounds.

The healing that you need is to your spiritual being for the flesh is forever hurt and damaged as gateway to sin and when a person is hurt on the surface their surface hurt is nothing compared to their internal wound if they are in mind of hatred and it is this internal bleeding that causes great resentment.

To allow internal hurt to grow is to give room for hatred to grow and when hatred grows in the mind the pain and suffering of the spirit is terrible for the soul to bear.

Whatsoever a person goes through that they consider as hurt; the pain and sorrow that their spirit undergoes is beyond their human imaginations and comprehensions if they are hateful and dead as a spirit being.

Spiritual pain and sorrow is like deep invisible emotional wound that is unseen by no other but greatly painful for the emotionally wounded to bear.

A person that hates due to emotional hurt carries the burden of his emotional hurt in his heart and because no other human can see the dept of the emotional wound, no human is able to understand the cry of the emotional wounded in the agony of their emotional suffering.

No human is able to say the extent that a person is hurt emotionally because it is hidden hurt and no matter what the emotional wounded say to try to make another human understand the dept of their hurt they cannot see it for what it is.

A person that suffers from physical wounds is more likely to have the sympathy of his fellow beings for his wounds are obvious to the ordinary eyes.

However when a person is emotionally wounded they are more likely to end up bitter and resentful from lack of support or understanding of the dept of their hurt from their fellow beings.

Those that the emotionally hurt seeks understanding from often accuse the one that is hurt of playing emotional games to obtain sympathy. Due to lack of support combined with the accusations that they are playing emotional games, such a person will only go further into their shell to suffer their hurt in silence.

An emotional cry is a cry for help and when a human believe that despite many cries they do not get the help that they need they end up being very bitter and resentful.

The help that a human needs is in the spirit not on the outside for the abuser is a spirit and to seek to free yourself from a spiritual hurt by physical mechanisms is to indulge yourself in futile efforts.

To overcome a spiritual hurt you must walk in spiritual loving strength and power that is above all powers and principalities.

The cure for emotional hurt is in divine love. In the world of flesh many are emotional wrecks for the ones that they seek healing from is by death commissioned to wreck and depress their mind further in painful sorrow.

The ways of the devil is to get the emotional hurt on their own to ruin their mind completely and in so doing place them in complete mind of hate and in hate total hopelessness and in hopelessness be an evil robotic being with the devil holding the remote control to control the mind to manifest evil and wicked works.

A devil is an oppressive abuser and as an abuser, the accuser of the one he abuses and if your oppressor is your accuser to make you carry the blame in all aspect then unless you are free from the burden of the blame then the spirit will remain heavily laden.

In cases of emotional hurt which as I said is the most common of human experiences you will find that the person that caused you the pain will also most likely be alleging that you have hurt them and whereby you have two counter offensive defenses what you have is deep pain and resentment from both sides.

Healing for spiritual hurt is by love spiritual medicine and if a person is oppressively hurt in their spirit then staying physically away from who they see as their abuser does not automatically free them from the spiritual abuse that is from the abuser and accuser of their soul.

Physical separation as I said does not cure emotional pain and just like pretending you are holy does not make you holy so also separating from someone does not free you from the burden of hatred you have towards them. Love endures and perseveres in every situation for a goodness outcome and the endurance and perseverance of love is in the heart of true love.

Being with someone physically is no indication that you love them so is being away from them physically is no indication that you hate them. Whether you love someone or hate them is all a matter of the heart and if you love someone you will persevere in your heart of love for goodness outcome and forgiving a person that has wronged you as many times as necessary is a supernatural act of love.

In enduring divine love, all things are possible. The natural ways of man is to be against one another and when you are against one another you cannot be in peaceful relationships to endure anything together in heart of love for goodness sake of life. Divine love is eternal enduring love and for it is enduring, there will always be a way where there is no way.

I know all about human endurance that it is very limited indeed and I as God understands why a human with such limited endurance will desire to part physically from someone that they see as constantly tormenting them.

An abuser of any kind is a devil and I as love will not encourage any human to remain in an abusive devilish situation.

There is for example so much abuse going on in the so called church today and many so called church are silent on this things for those that are meant to act in good faith are the perpetrators of devilish ways.

By day, they say they are Christians and by night, they are in the devils cults bowing their heads to the beast. I say they are fools for no man can mock me for what no man sees I see all.

The church of the end times as I said is a church of mystery Babylon that is full of devils.

Whether you stay with a person or you separate from them so long as you have a mind of hatred and resentment towards them, it would be as if they are still there with you hurting you even more no matter how far apart physically you live.

A devilish abuser as I said is a being that hates himself and no one in heart of love would seek to abuse another for in love you seek always to give joy and relief not pain and sorrow.

You will find that common to many devilish abusers particularly within the church environment is to use the scriptures to justify their abuse and this is extreme wickedness for to use the scripture to justify evil is to be extreme in mind of wickedness evil.

I understand that it is difficult and a terrible thing for a human being to undergo any kind of abuse however to begrudge your human abuser or seek to retaliate or not have a heart of forgiveness towards your human tormentor is to cause yourself even greater torment and harm in your soul.

This is because if you choose not to forgive them then the memory of their abuse will lead you to have great bitter resentment and in bitter resentments, hate will eat you up on the inside even if you move to another country.

Behind every human abuser is a devilish abusive spirit. The one that you need to destroy its yolk is the slimy devil cunning abuser that lurks in the mind of a human abuser to lead them to abuse just as the devil in them is greatly abusing them.

To stay always above hate you must always operate in heart of divine love.

As God that is love, I understand why a human would seek to have separation from another human being that they see as tormenting them.

I say understand because I myself separated from man due to their sins.

In sin, man became a demonic being and as a demonic being wicked and evil oriented. Also in the parable of the prodigal son, which for example you will find in Luke Chapter 15 from verse 11 to the end, you will see that the father allowed the son to go.

The father allowed the son to go not because he hates the son but because the son needed to learn his lessons and once he has learned his lesson and willing to return to be a good son to his father the father gladly accepted him back.

This is just to say to you that I understand your point about if you love someone you let them go if they insist on leaving you and as you said if they are yours, they will return to you.

However even if you let the person you love go your love for them will remain in your heart and for the sake of the love you have for them you will not begrudge them for leaving you instead you pray that they realize their wrong and return home where they belong with you.

The sin of man as I said made me to separate from them however even though I separated from man I always see man as a prodigal son and have in my mind the desire to intercede and intervene for them to return back to me to have eternal reward of life everlasting.

If you separate from someone and you are resentful and hateful to that person for whatever reason then they will continue to make you bitter and angry.

This is the problem with the world today because today in soured relationships many human daily seek to separate from one another like never before to hate each other even more from afar in their mind of high resentments.

Separation does not eradicate resentment instead it makes it worse and from physically separating from one another most humans are more in mind to tear each other into pieces in deep mind of hatred.

Hatred gives way to the devil to rule the mind.

When a person allows the devil to rule his mind he allows the devil to steal his joy for the devil as a looser is a thief.

The way to counter hatred is not to hate but to operate in mind of divine enduring love. Love gives lifetime solutions whilst hate creates eternal problems.

Love intercedes to effect change as such; a life intercessor is a spiritual change champion. With love, you can melt a stony heart and to melt a stony heart you do not do so just from separation but from loving intercessory prayers.

There is goodness potential in every man just as there is evil and a man in hate cannot see his goodness potential for the hatred of his heart has blinded his eyes. Hate compresses the heat in darkness to harden the mind to walk in greater dept of sinfulness and the only way to break the hard stone of hatred on the heart is through intercessory love.

If such man eyes were to be opened to see you will be surprised to find just how much good is in him even though he has been all along wicked.

This is why you always have to have mind of forgiveness and in forgiveness a mind of prayer intercessions instead of just being in mind of physical separations.

Yes, I would say in some situations it is not ideal to stay in the same physical environment with the person. However, as a person in spiritual awakening you must understand that physical separation on its own does not break spiritual ties and if a person is linked in their spirit to hate it matters not were they live they will still not just be a thorn on each others flesh but on each others spirits.

To stop a person from being a thorn in your spirit you must always have the mind to forgive them no matter what the case may be just as I will always forgive you of your sins no matter how many times you sin against me.

Without forgiveness there can be no reconciliations after separations and if reconciliations is to take place it cannot be in mind of hate but of love. I see you have another question.

ME: Yes. You mentioned intercessory prayers but if you see all that, a person goes through and it is unto you they will pray to for you to intervene why is it that you require the victim to engage in further prayer of intercessions to you given that from their pain alone it is obvious that they need help.

GOD: I promise to answer all your questions and my answers to all your questions will always be a spiritual one for I am a Spirit and so are you.

Only when a man has spiritual answers and as such, in true knowledge and wisdom of life shall he be far from being a victim in any dimensional dominion realms.

To start my answer, I say, why you ought to have asked was it necessary for me to allow my only begotten Son to go through pain and suffering to set man free when I can simply say to man "thou are all forgiven" and that is it.

Why is it necessary to sacrifice my Son to me and how is the Son the same as the Father and the Father and Son the same I the Holy Spirit.

Why if I see all that is in your mind do I allow you to speak at all either by prayer or in conversations with me?

You could say given that I see all the objective desires of your heart why allow you to go through the trouble of asking me to do what is in your heart for you if I already can see it for what it is and it is my wish that you have them.

You could say because I am God and I see everything you should only pray to me in the following manner; "God you see all that is in my heart so no point in me saying anything further so be God that you are and do the things that are necessary as you see them in my heart".

Many from looking at things from an ordinary perspective will say the whole idea of the Trinity is madness. As God, I am extraordinarily over and above all things hence for a man to understand me he must reject his ordinary thinking mind to see in light of my divine reasoning.

The point I am making is if you look at things from ordinary eyes, nothing will make sense to you but if you look at things from my spiritual objective sense of view then you will see the sense in everything.

I am God to the intercessors for every objective of divine life I have fulfilled through my intercessory works of life.

The aim of the wicked is to intercept the mind to control it to sin and in sin lead the heart to be pro evil dead works and anti life goodness and no man profit in sin for the wages of sin is death.

My loving aim and desires for man is to free their mind from sinful oppression by my divine sacrificial intercessory interventions so that they have true benefit of life in eternal life.

To answer your question therefore, I say yes it is unto me you will pray and yes it is I that will answer those prayers and yes still I see all things either spoken or unspoken.

As God, I am a God of purpose and I do not instruct you to do anything unless there is a purpose for it.

It is for goodness purpose that I perfect you in my good faith and a very central aspect of faith is intercessory work.

To be an intercessor is to advocate in my presence for others and for you to advocate for others before me I myself must give you the right to do so.

No other can afford you the right of audience to be before me and if I give you, the right of audience to be before me it is for a goodness reason.

As God I am king of the universe and as king the utmost judge and if you see me as the king and judge of the universe you will see the sense in me saying you cannot just cut corners to be in my presence.

To have an audience before an earthly human judge sitting at the highest court of the land you cannot just appear in court and insist that the judge gives you a right of audience.

To have a right of audience you must have the right credentials and qualifications. Besides your qualifications or school credentials you must have had years of experience as an advocate of higher standing before you can acquire the privilege of having a right of audience before a judge sitting at the highest court of the land.

If this is the case in the world sense it must not come as a surprise to you that I the king of kings and Lord of lords expect a spirit to have the right spiritual credentials and be also a spiritual advocate of a higher standing to have the privilege of an audience before me.

The right spiritual credentials is a faithful anointed heart and this I give by my grace for no man is capable of a good heart of faithfulness towards me by his own ways independent of me.

You become an advocate of higher spiritual standing through faithful experience and this experiences you acquire from your diverse trials in life.

To promote goodness you must see the importance in doing so and if you do not see the desperate ugly mind of evil that it is to eradicate all things that is good for evil sake you cannot see the point in promoting goodness.

No man is empowered or enabled by evil for all that evil gives is a crippling effect and this crippling effect is through fear.

Fear is an evil offensive weapon and the counter defense to this offensive weapon is courage of life in operative divine power of life.

It is so that you have such goodness courage of life that you had to go through all that you have been through to build your courage and faith in goodness for total goodness sake of life.

To have this courage and perfect you in goodness faith I anointed you and to be the anointed means to be made able to perform an objective goodness purpose of life and the objective goodness purpose of life as I have revealed it to you is spiritual relief for the oppressed.

Unless you are able, you cannot enable another and as God, I am all-able.

As the all able only I can enable the unable man to serve a goodness purpose of life and as the Almighty only I can make a way for you where there is no way.

I make able the unable to be able to serve a good purpose of life for goodness sake of my name.

I as the enabler being your master and creator will place you always in all things in goodness protective walk to keep you continuously enabled for the total goodness performance of my entire missionary objectives that I have enabled you to be able to perform.

To enable you to be a good advocate for the benefit of your fellow beings I as the king advocate have trained you through placing you in faithful walk to have the true understanding of good faith.

Good faith is all about intercessions and intercession is necessary to afford the benefit of eternal life that you have unto those who otherwise will have no chance of having such benefit of life.

Faith is at the heart of love and no man can say he is operating in divine love without a heart full of loving kindness. Intercessory work is highest-level manifestation of divine love for love is all about relief and it is by intercession that you give relief to the spiritually oppressed.

The evidence of your faith is in your faithful actions. Good faith is to act in reliance to the truthful word that you have heard and for you know it is the truth, you know that it is wisdom to believe in it and to continue to act in line of the truthful word.

No man is capable of having a divine faith of love in the flesh by his own self for the faith of man in flesh is of vanity and to be a good advocate you cannot have a heart of vanity.

For you to be a good advocate it is necessary for me to perfect your faith in goodness by allowing you to have necessary life experiences to focus your mind on my purpose which as I said is to give relief to the oppressed and the depressed in their souls.

All of man as sinners is advocating for something and for someone.

A man that is a devil's advocate is always in mind to tempt another not to offer them relief of any kind.

An intercessor is a good advocate and a change champion as such will have lifetime benefit of goodness inheritance rewards

To advocate in life you must have authority and power of life. It is by power of life that you arrest the devil to release and develop the captive spiritual slave in the ways of life and no man is able to release the spiritually dead from the land of the dead unless equipped with the power and authority to bind death.

This is the power that I have given to a life intercessor to bind death and loose the captive.

A devil's advocate is a looser and as a looser, a tempting spirit that is always in mind of accusations. Every man as flesh is a persistent sinners and devil's advocates are always in mind of blaming others for their wrongs. A devilish man loves to sin but hates the punishment for his sinfulness.

Devilish spirits are accusers of men and the purpose of accusations is to place man in judgment of sin so that they can compress their soul in deeper in death. A devilish man will be in operative mind to blame just like his devilish master and for a man to be blame minded towards another is to carry own blame and the blame of his devilish master accuser wish is great pain and sorrow in death.

If all man is a sinner then as sinners in mind of blame towards one another instead of repentance and change then how can they have my forgiveness?

To repent is to say you have realized your wrong and as such, you are willing to change for goodness sake.

The question then is if a man is not able to realize his wrong let alone be in mind to turn over a new life how can he ever find forgiveness from me.

I am love and the heart of love is always full of forgiveness. Divine intercessory work in goodness heart of faith is necessary to afford benefit of forgiveness to the blind sinner.

Sin activates death and repentance activates benefit of my forgiving heart. If a man does not see himself as wrong how can he see the need to repent from his wrongful doings and if a man continue to walk in the wrong then he continues to activate death to rule and oppress his soul.

When you say sorry and that you are willing to change, you appease the one that you have wronged and the problem with man in sinful death is that instead of appeasing me they offend me the more by their desperate and wicked self-righteous defensive ways of sinfulness.

If man is always in mind to offend me, how shall they have the benefit of my forgiving heart even though my heart is full of forgiveness for them?

It is to give man the benefit of my forgiveness that by my own intercessory sacrificial works I made way for man to have the benefit of forgiveness so that they do not continue to suffer in death being the punishment for sinful disobedience.

Through my own intercessory sacrificial works, I also open the channel for man as a creature to be in good advocacy mind towards one another instead of in mind of blame and accusations like the devil.

As the king advocate and judge, I enable a man to be just like me and to be just like me is to be in mind to perform my life goodness objectives which as you know by now is centered in goodness intercessory works for the benefit relief of others.

A man as a sinner is his own enemy and as his own enemy does not see the need for repentance.

Therefore, if it were not for my own works of intercession no man will have the benefit of the forgiving heart that I have towards man.

If every man is a devil unto one another then all they will seek to do is accuse one another to remain condemned.

If all man is wicked unto one another then no man will have any kind of relief mind towards another as their objective purpose and if my business objective purpose is to give relief to man then as God, I must enable others to be in same mind of relief as I AM.

I self-exist as life and as life eternal life forever. As the self-existing eternal God I am the only one man must worship and sacrifice unto for his soul to have eternal life of peace, rest and joy.

I made man to be a living sacrifice unto me but man in sin became demonic and as demonic beings began to slay themselves needlessly to feed wicked fallen angles that are flesh eaters.

A man appease me to receive from me great life rewards of eternal life by being a perfect living holy sacrifice unto me and you are unto me a perfect holy sacrifice when you are in goodness heart of faithful obedience towards me.

Through enabling the elect to be in goodness advocacy, their sacrificial prayers continuously appease me.

An intercessor appeases me by their prayers for their prayer is perfect and acceptable sacrifice before me. It is by the continuous faithful walk of the saint at heart that my objective purpose remains seen for what it is by man on earth from generation to generation that it is spiritual deliverance and salvation for the soul of man.

The world of flesh is the world of the desperate wicked and evil.

Man in sin is against my soulful objective, which is salvation for their souls for they are devil's advocates and this is to their own soul disadvantage. To be in mind of goodness purpose of life is to be a living soul and no man as a sinner can have the benefit of resurrection to life from death except by my grace.

Man in wages of sin is further compressed in death because of their evil and wicked desire to continue to sin.

If man is faithfully committed in his mind to sin, for he is wicked, as a spirit then such a man will not have the benefit of my forgiving heart to the very end.

For man are desperate sinners, if at any particular time there is no man on earth in goodness heart of perfect sacrifice to continue to appease me still then mankind as generational sinners will only see my wrath and not my gracefulness. Although the world is full of sins today mankind as whole continue to have still the benefit of my graceful forgiveness heart and this is all due to the fact that I elect in every generation saints that I enable to continue to carry forward the sacrificial torch of goodness for goodness sake of life.

Through the works of this elected saints as I enable them to perform it, my objective purpose continues to remain seen in the world to the very end that it is salvation for man from the beginning to the end for goodness sake of my holy name.

As I am always appeased from the sacrificial prayers of my elect I am always in mind to give benefit of merciful forgiveness unto sinners and it in this mind of mercy that I make the unable able.

Without the sacrificial prayers of saints, sinners in the world will not be able to continue to have the benefit of my forgiving heart for if all by their sin provokes me with no one to appease me then all that man will have from me like I said in the world is my wrath.

If all that man sees from me is wrath then no man shall be able to testify to my goodness in the world.

As the highest God of gods, I am good on deeds always and no man compressed in sorrow of death is able to see me as love and as love eternally good on deeds forever.

 It is important for goodness sake of my name to enable man to see my objectives purpose that as love I am not just in mind to punish and compress the soul of man in death.

Rather, my entire objective purpose as life is to relief man from his painful and sorrowful death.

By my grace, I promote the repentant to be at the heart of goodness regiment of life to be in total benefit of life so that by their testimony of life all others that darkness has covered their eyes can see in light of my glory to walk in line of resurrection of life.

If man as a generational sinner is desperate to sin and in sin provokes me into wrath judgment then if no man at a given time is walking in the footsteps of my perfect appeasement sacrifice the soul of all man will be in complete darkness and in darkness in greater mind of evil.

The world of flesh is a wicked world of generational evil full of many depressed and compressed souls that are loyal to the devil and as devil friends, the world of devilish minded is full of the extremely wicked, minded.

INTERCESSORY WORK AFFORDS GRACEFUL MERCY TO THE SINNER

As love, I always have mercy in my heart to release the sinner from his sinfulness sorrowful pain out of the goodness of my heart.

It is for this reason that I always elect to enable and from generation to generation I am always willing to listen to the sacrificial cry of forgiveness from my elect for the sinner for goodness sake of my name.

Through my perfect intercessory work and the continuous faithful works of the saint's humankind continue to have my mercy and by my enabling, the saints to remain faithful to my universal goodness objective purpose of life, man remain in line to continue to have full benefit of my entire good works of my intercession to the very end of days.

A sinner does not appreciate his wrongdoing and in desperate mind to continue sinning, a sinner is blind always to the true consequences of his wrongful actions.

I do not want the death of the already dead sinner but for them to repent and have the benefit of my forgiveness so that by my forgiving them I bring them back to life to be a living soul.

A dead soul is a destroyer and as a destroyer counterproductive whereas a living soul is a life builder thus a productive being.

I am as a creator in mind of life productivity not destruction for evil sake and although as you have read in the bible that I destroyed the earth with flood water and will destroy the world still with fire at the end of days in time it is all for goodness sake of life.

I made the earth for goodness sake not for evil and all spirit that had the benefit of my creations on earth is accountable towards me as the creator of heaven and earth and as a God that rewards I say nothing goes unrewarded.

If you are an evil destroyer, you will have the reward of evil.

If you are good in your heart and in heart of goodness in mind to preserve goodness ways for goodness sake of heaven to be seen on earth then know that you have eternal life reward of goodness from me for your faithful ways towards life goodness objectives. A devil is not in mind of life preservations but in mind of destruction of anything associated with goodness out of bitterness hatred.

As the creator of man, I do not seek for their destruction but for them to remain sustained in life to have total rewards of life for goodness sake of life. As God, I am a Spirit and man is a spirit being also.

The sacrifice of an intercessor places the sinful man in line of graceful benefits. To know me for who I am you must be in relationship with me as a living spirit and only a living spirit have any manner of advocacy audience before me.

Dead spirits does nor hear me so they say God does nor speak.

If I am word, which I am, it is foolishness to say that I that made the tongue and the mouth speak not.

Spiritual life is all about orderliness and to have an audience before me you must subscribe to my orderly ways of life by your goodness heart of faithful obedience. Mankind in sinful fall lost their right of audience before me and to give back to man this right of audience there must be an obedient sacrifice and as God, no one can fully please me in loving obedience but me.

This is because my standard is the highest order and to satisfy the standards of my highest order you must be just like me hence it was necessary to sacrifice the Son to me I the Father.

This sacrifice is also necessary to place mankind back in my Holy Spirit to remain a perfect living sacrifice for unless a man is a perfect holy sacrifice he is not acceptable to me.

A dead soul is not able to see me in light of my glory so when many say there is no God it is because they are dead spirit beings and as God I am a God to the living not the dead. Only the living can know me as I AM and as I said it is to afford the gift of life to the whole of mankind that I elect some to perfect in my faithful run to make them eligible to have the right of audience before me. Before a saint became a saint he was once all devilish and it is to make him see the necessity to abstain from devilish ways that a saint is taken through the fire to be made precious shinning gold.

I listen to the cry of a saint for as the judge that is also the prosecutor and the king advocate I have made the saint to have a shining golden heart so that he performs the objective purpose of my business to the full joy of my heart.

The objective purpose of my business as I said is salvations and deliverance and without sacrificial intercessory work there can be no deliverance.

Intercessory work is necessary in time to reveal the upholding eternal life principles of life for what it is in all dominion dimensional realms I can simply say to the whole of mankind that they are forgiven being their creator and the Almighty but as God I am a God of principles and for goodness sake of life I abide by my own principles for it is the right thing to do.

A devil is into death principalities and not life principles.

Principalities are doctrines generated by dead spirits aimed at confusing the mind of man to subject them to rule of evil forces and deadly spiritual powers that is beyond the comprehensions of mankind.

Eternal life is all about life principles and no man can escape from principalities oppressions when they walk in opposite side of my life principles.

To have an audience before me you must abide by my principles and it is to make those principles clear to you that you are by me trained in faithful abiding walk for goodness sake of life.

If after I had trained you to be in mind and heart of goodness you now see no point in goodness advocacy, it is like being a king and seeing yourself as a slave still.

To be in mind of goodness advocacy is to be a king in goodness regiment of life and to be a king in goodness regiment of life is to be in heart and mind for love to rule in the hearts for total goodness to be the outcome in everything.

Prayer is communication with me and the word that you speak as a saint in intercessory prayer that I show mercy to the unappreciative sinner is acceptable sacrifice before me.

It is by that perfect sacrifice that a sinner continues to have chances of resurrection, which is the total benefit of my forgiving heart.

A man in desperate mind of sin and in tormenting mind towards another is a mad man for he does not appreciate the consequences of his action at all.

Unless another intercedes for him that man perishes forever in his mind of wicked sins.

As I have said, life is about goodness orderliness. Before any other and for the sake of goodness order of life to prevail in all dominion dimensional realms; I made my binding rules all in my goodness order dominion mind.

All of my rules are for love sake and even though you will find many rules in the bible, all of my rules are to focus the mind of man on the ultimate rule of life, which is loving kindness being my perfect order of life in eternal life.

An established binding rule that I have made for goodness sake of life before I created man is that every soul that sin must die. As a result, when Adam the first man sinned all of man as descendant of Adam became subject to death just like Adam.

The other established rule of life that I also made before I created man is that unless there is the shedding of blood there is no remission of sins.

This means unless there is a perfect sacrifice the curse of death, which of course is punishment to the soul of man I will not revoke

This is because before man became subject to death I pronounced the rebellious angels as first sinners dead for their rebellious acts.

If as God I did not spare the angels then it would be unjust for me to depart from my universal rule of divine rule and justice.

For I pronounced the angels dead for their sins, it would be unjust for me to simply spare man without performing the rights that are necessary to spare them from eternal death punishment.

Out of my love, I gave man the grace of resurrection from death by my own remission works.

Although my work is finished man must repent to have the benefit of my finished works. If man is to have, the benefit of my finished work from beginning to the end all souls of man in every generation must have the benefit of grace manifested to them.

It is for this reason that I elect and enable saints to be in mind of intercessory prayers so that man continues to have the benefit of grace in every generation all the way to the very end.

A devil cannot remit his sins for to remit sins the remission sacrifice must be perfect and untainted.

All of man through the sin of the first Adam became by implication sinners and as a sinner just like a devil unable to remit their own sins and as they are not able to remit their own sin they became their very own enemy.

A man as a sinner is only interested in committing more sin and man in heart and mind of sinful committal became very hardened in his heart against all that is good and in stony heart a terrible spiritual criminal that is only in perpetual mind to continue to re-offend.

Adam as a dead spirit could not give birth to living souls for the dead can only have dead children and as such all children of the first Adam are dead souls.

Out of my loving kindness I gave my own flesh to remit the sin of man and this is the grace that I gave to man to resurrect their soul back to life by performing the necessary sacrifice to make them a living soul.

No other is able to remit the sin of man for man in death is a demonic being and it is for this reason that by my own works of goodness faith I saved man from soulful eternal death through affording him the grace of resurrection.

I enable a man to be a saint and as king of the saint, I open the eyes of their understanding to be in knowledge of these things.

This is the knowledge of life and many perish for the lack of this knowledge.

Knowledge of life is what the bible is all about and this is why the devils hate the bible because the secrets of the devils is contained in bible text and when a man seek me in goodness mind of faith I will open his eyes to have a better understanding of those secrets.

The aim of the devil in the end time as I said before is to say the entire bible as a holy book is a lie. That way you cannot refer to the bible as point of reference for if it is widely accepted that the bible is a lie then quoting the bible as a reference will make you look like a total fool.

A saint at heart with knowledge and understanding of life aims and purposes must always be in mind to sacrifice for another as appreciations of the grace that I have given unto him.

A man becomes a saint out of my gracefulness to afford the benefit of grace to other men. No man is a saint by his own right and I have not made any man a saint to be wicked and selfish.

To be a saint is to be meek and gentle even though you are a spiritual lion for you are in me.

To be a saint is always to see the need to sacrifice for the benefit of others and it is so that you see the need that I allow you to go through all manner of diverse trials to perfect your mind to be in confidence of life in goodness faith of life.

Without grace of remissions, man will only be in mind of killing one another in mind of extreme evil towards one another.

In sin, man is always in offensive mind of hate to offend one another to great wroth and in wroth all you have is battle minefield.

No man in death of his soul is in heart of peace and if you are to intercede for another, you cannot be the one to accuse that other for when you are in mind of accusations you cannot be in mind of intercessions.

To be in mind of intercessions for benefit of another is to say that you understand and appreciate the benefit of forgiveness you have by grace of my loving kindness. Every man is a sinner except I the Son the sinless slain and unless I by grace place your own sins in remissions you cannot be in a position to intercede for another as a sinner in death.

As a saint, you show your appreciation towards my graceful love by being in mind to love your fellow beings.

To be a saint is to have the benefit of life and a saint does not have the benefit of life by his own might but by my own Spirit.

A saint in knowledge of life knows that even though he is a sinner he has the gift of life out of the goodness of my heart.

In this mind of knowledge, a saint in his heart of loving-kindness will intercede always for another out of his appreciation of my love.

In loving appreciations a saintly hearted that is in mind of good conscience will always desire by his constant intercessory forgiveness prayers for his fellow being to have the same benefit of my merciful abundant forgiveness that he enjoys.

A saint in spiritual mind of understanding knows that a devilish man in death is subject to extreme oppressive rule of death.

In oppressive and total compressive death rule of their souls, such a being is an enemy of his own spirit for in death he will only be in desire to continue to sin and in continuous sinful nature will be in total detrimental walk against his soul desires for life.

SPIRITUAL FREEDOM IS THROUGH PERFECT SACRIFICIAL ATONEMENT FOR THE REMISSIONS OF SINS

For every actions of hatred by man, there is a spirit behind it and unless they are free from that spirit of hatred, they cannot link their mind to goodness ways of life.

A spirit cannot be free from death unless as I said by atonement sacrifice and no man is able to atone his own sin.

Perfect atonement is by my own sacrificial Lamb and this sacrificial Lamb is I Christ the Son made flesh by the Father to atone perfectly the sin of man so that man in perfect atonement can have back their audience before the Father.

Only a living spirit can have audience before me for as God, I am fire. My fire protects a living spirit but consumes a dead spirit for their wickedness.

My atonement sacrifice was necessary to remit the sin of man for without my atonement sacrifice the spirit of man could not enter the gates of heaven again.

For in death the dead man walking saw himself as the living and because the walking dead saw himself as alive his only main desire is to rule the world in his dead evil body of sin and not resurrection of his soul from death.

If a man does not even see that he is dead in his soul he cannot see the sense in resurrection of his soul.

The world is full of dead souls and dead souls are spiritual criminals led by spirits of hell to manifest the works of axes of evil in the world.

A spirit that carries out the works of a devil is in line to partake in punishment of the devil.

For a saint appreciates the spiritual freedom afforded to him by my loving grace he will always have spiritual empathy and sympathy for his fellow beings and will always intercede for them to be free from heavy laden of death.

Hence, when the devilish at heart stones a saint in the hope of silencing him from speaking the truth, the saint weeps and prays still for the devilish hearted as they are stoning him for he knows that without my merciful forgiveness the punishment that awaits the souls of those responsible for stoning him in eternity is extremely immense.

As God of the universe, I make my intercessory objectives clear by my own sacrifice that it is perfect sacrifice from a good clear mind of holy conscience.

A saint in understanding of this spiritual fact must always be in mind of goodness conscience and in good heart of spiritual conscience and appreciation of grace must always see the need to pray and intercede for another.

Most human beings are not able to pray for themselves let alone for another and if a man is given the grace to carry the sword of the spirit which is fluid powerful word of prayer such man must not be selfish in his use of that spiritual sword that is given to him by grace.

If everyman is able to understand as a spirit being that they cause themselves great harm then they will immediately seek to repent and for a man is in the spirit by the iron curtain of evil blinded, a spiritual dead man cannot see that he is killing himself more with hatred.

A hateful minded being is a spiritual criminal and as a spiritual criminal needs a good advocate to advocate on his behalf for the devil that is in him leading him to be in mind of wickedness is his number one accuser.

Without a saintly advocate, a dead soul will not find spiritual mercy.

It is so that all of man benefit from grace and in grace mercy in every generation that I made some apostles prophets, pastors, teachers for the perfection of human souls on earth for heaven sake of life.

I make saints to be an advocate of goodness in heart of love. For a saint to ask why he must pray for another is like a qualified criminal lawyer saying he sees no point in practicing the criminal law that he had so many years trained for to obtain a certificate of practice now that he finally has the practicing certificate.

Life is about love and to love you must appreciate the goodness sacrifice that I as love made for you and it is always in this appreciation and in the understanding of all of these things, I have said that you will always see the need to love those that you see as hating you.

To be free and in freedom in walking liberation in my dominion regiment of life is to be hated deeply by the world.

The world of flesh is a world of many dead sinners.

The ways of a sinner is antichrist and an antichrist is an agent of Lucifer the disgraced fallen angel. A repentant man has benefit of my grace but the devil hearted is a walking dead man that daily partakes in the disgrace of Lucifer.

The world hates light for all that the devilish man is interested in is to remain in deadly darkness camp of the rebellious devil to commit sin as a matter of right.

Sin is spiritual wrongfulness and the punishment of a spiritual wrong is spiritual death. No man that is a dead soul can see his way out from the heavy-laden graveyard of death. The spiritually dead are hateful minded and when you walk in light as light in the world, the spiritually dead will attempt to lure you away from light back into darkness.

However for a saint has my grace, every attempt of the dead will only work for the benefit purpose of the saint. For all good and evil must work for goodness sake and this is my predetermined order of life that no man can change.

If a man hates you know that they hate you because of me for if you are in me you are light and as light hated by darkness for when light comes darkness must disappear.

The one thing darkness does not want is for light to show up and when you become a living soul you were greatly tried by the world of flesh and it is all for the sake of discouraging you from being a goodness witness.

It is also because the darkness world is afraid of you as light and as a spirit in light awakenings, it is normal for you in the natural to see certain people particularly those that are close to you suddenly become even more terrible towards you.

This is because once you are made light every spirit of the world in enmity mind of evil will seek to discourage you so that you disengage from light and who can best get at you but that which is naturally close to you.

A spirit of light in the world is an enabling spirit to enable another.

As I said the aim of the wicked is to disable and to oppress and if suddenly you are now in mind to help another to be in awakening it is no surprise that the world spirit sees you as their enemy because your mission is to destroy their objective which is always to do with evil oppression.

My answers to you is knowledge of life and knowledge of life is power to the soul

The knowledge that I give you in my answers to your questions is so that you have detail clear mind of understanding for knowledge is power and my word is never void of power.

Only by detail clear mind of understanding shall you always see the need to forgive and plead for me to forgive others like you just as I forgive you daily.

If I do not forgive you daily then I would have had to separate my spirit from yours from time to time given that you have sinned against me since you became a living soul uncountable times which means if by grace I have not forgiven you all your sins, one minute you will be dead the next alive.

As flesh, you are a sinner still even though I have made you to be a living soul by my grace. If I do not forgive you your entire sins past, present and future I would have disengaged my Holy Spirit from your spirit countless of times due to the fact that as flesh you sin against me still.

Through my heart of gracefulness towards you and for goodness sake of life purpose, I continue to have a mind of forgiveness towards you to place you in continuous total perfect engagement with my Holy Spirit.

Disengagement from my Holy Spirit is death for unless a man is my Spirit of life to fellowship with me such man will be a fellow in evil satanic being and to be a fellow in Satan is to partake in deadly evil fellowship and perish eternally.

A man to live must separate from death and engage with my spirit of life to have eternal life. It is necessary for every man to separate from dead spirits and this separation is not a physical one but a spiritual one. For if a dead man physically separate from another that is dead their physical separation does not end their deadly spiritual relationship.

Intercession enables a dead spirit to separate from death to for perfect life rehabilitations. A separation that is necessary for every man is separation from death. Although physical separation as I said in some situations may be appropriate to give you a physical space from one that you see as physically tormenting you, you must not be in mind of such separation in heart of hatred or bitterness anger resentment.

To remain bitterly resentful towards the one that you have separated from is to continue to maintain a deadly relationship with the evil spirits that is in their flesh and it is for this reason that you must never entertain any notion of hatred.

Only with total heart and mind of forgiveness towards others will a man continue to walk in line of my perfect spiritual faith and it is for this very reason that I always say you must forgive no matter what.

Once you start to nurse hatred, you will be vengeful in your mind because to be hateful is to seek to offend me by being in mind of retaliation towards those that you see to have offended you.

Hatred debilitates whereas love rehabilitates and it is for spiritual rehabilitation purposes of the criminal man that I make the weak strong for goodness sake of life.

To have a hateful mind is to loose focus of your rehabilitative purpose in life and to loose focus of your purpose is to start to operate in mind of confusions.

I elect a saint for goodness to be smart not stupid and a saint remain smart by total focus on his objective purpose in life.

The central purpose objective of a saint is to intercede for others and no one can be in mind of intercession for anyone whatsoever in hatred mind.

It is stupidity to loose focus of your goodness purpose in life for to serve a good purpose is to have from me great eternal life reward forever.

Anyone that is in mind of retaliation or vengeance will by their heart of hatred call upon evil to lead their mind and a mind that is led by evil cannot be of the heart to perform a saintly objectives.

A mind of hate is a mind bent on self-destruction and if a person is committed to self-destroying himself or herself how shall such person be able to help another from destroying themselves. This is wisdom and this divine knowledge. This is wisdom, that the darkness world wishes you not to have and this is so that you do not see things for what they are in the real sense.

Life I say again is about love and although ordinarily it is impossible to endure any situations that you find as trying nothing is impossible with love for love conquers all. My saying therefore to anyone in the world that sees themselves as a product or subject of any kind of abuse from the hands of their fellow beings is forgive from your heart if you want my own forgiveness and be fully liberated from deadly compressive spirits.

For by not forgiving you engage your spirit deeper in greater harm of evil and sorrow and in evil sorrowfulness, you compress your soul more in heavy laden of death out of not forgiving those that trespass against you.

If you come to me for forgiveness then you must be prepared just as you want me to forgive you, to forgive also those that offend you.

Vengeance as I said is mine and as God know that, I am just always.

If you do not seek to take revenge for yourself in any situation but for you trust me to afford you justice, you leave everything to me for you know that I know best then you say to the world that you are different and unique in your character.

A good at heart is a precious stone of Zion and it is a precious way of life to forgive and intercede for the weak hearted.

To be a shinning precious stone always you must never allow the ugly mind of hate to taint your beautiful loving hearts and in appreciation of love, you must always see the need to intercede for others to afford them the benefit of the grace that you have from me. I see that you are satisfied with my answers with your smiles.

ME: Yes thank you. I pray that I always have the mind to forgive and intercede for others to have the benefit of the forgiveness that I always have from you out of the grace of your love for me for the entire goodness sake of your holy name.

GOD: I say so shall it be. Now do you see how fast I answer your prayers?

ME: (Laughter) Yes, thank you. I know you answer prayers but is just that is hard sometimes from a human perspectives having to go through all this things that we go through in the world.

GOD: I know and this is why I made my Holy Spirit available to the whole of mankind for goodness sake of life and as I said if anyone is in my Holy Spirit all of their prayer is already answered for whosoever is in covenant relationship with my Holy Spirit is blessed forever.

Now, that you are smiling with so much manifested spiritual joy I see that you see the joy of being in my Holy Spirit. For perfect reassurance I say, as your Father in heaven know that I am not in mind to see my child fail so to give you even bigger smiles know that if I am with you all things shall always work to give you successful returns.

ME: Amen.

GOD: I say so shall it be and so it is. So shall it be, by the way is another way of saying Amen. The master will continue with more revelations to you after you have had much rest in my restfulness but I see that you still have a question.

ME: Yes. I was just going to say may I just ask you one more question God sir.

GOD: You may so ask says I in my royal highest nest
ME: (laughter). You know you are much fun to talk to than I could ever have imagined yet many say you do not exist.
One of the main reasons often stated for saying that you do not exist is that there is no evidence that you exist.
My question is if you want us to see that you love mankind and you see the heart of man that despite everything you have done they seek evidence still of your existence what is the evidence that you see in the mind of man that they need to have for them to be satisfied that you exist.

GOD: Besides opening the skies and say in a loud voice to the world at the same time that I AM THAT I AM, repent for my kingdom has come and by my voice send the whole earth into a tremor nothing else will do.

ME: So why do you not just do that to put an end to all this debate?

GOD: I knew that is what you have in mind and it is so that you know that I know that I see all that is in your mind that I stated it to you so that you know that I know. Now that you know that, I know I will proceed to answer your question.

To say there is no evidence that I exist is a devilish man way of saying he has no evidence whatsoever to say I do not exist for a devil knows without a doubt that I the Alpha and Omega God I am Word and as Word self existing everlasting.

Life is all about divine wisdom and it is only in divine wisdom that a man will be in spiritual locomotion.

The carnal mind of the carnal flesh man is only interested in the doctorial of death and for the doctorial of death is the mind interest of the dead man; his mind aim will only be to propagate evil doctrines of death. The main principalities unspiritual idealism, which is that there no God, is to keep the soul of man oppressed in evil darkness so that they continue to oppress and rule the soul of man to an eternal dead end. As God I am love and to say there is no love is to say all there is in existence is hate and a man that say only hate exist says he hates himself.

No man that hates himself can love another for to love another you must first love yourself. Life is eternal and life is only worth living in love for if eternal life is all about hate then what is the point? Man suffered spiritual amnesia in the fall of man into sinful death and in such sinful death man became time conscious and in time consciousness man became unconscious of the state of his eternal soulful existence.

To have eternal life in me is by true knowledge and wisdom and I say as the omnipotent God that the intelligence of the world is carnal. The knowledge of man for it is carnal is of death and as knowledge of death only leads man away from true knowledge of life.

Those who have knowledge and wisdom that I as God I Am, is, and ever shall be shall seek not in the natural for supernatural answers. A common question that man has asked over and over again is, is there life after death? The question that all man must ask to find the answer to this question is, "who am I before birth into the world". If you do not know where you come from how shall you even begin to think of were you shall return. If you come from death and you do not choose life in time then you return to eternal death.

If you come from death and you choose life then even though you shall die in the body of sin I shall raise you up to walk in my eternal body of glory.

If I am in you only are you in life for if you are not in me and I in you all you shall see shall be death. To find the way all of man must trace their footsteps.

All trees has a root and if you cut the branch off from the tree then you have disconnected that branch from the root of his feeding and such branch shall wither without proper nourishment.

All of man is a descendant of Adam and Adam is the forefather of the genesis of sin. To ask for forgiveness you must first accept that you are of sin as a decedent of Adam.

To embark on a soul search you must first admit that your soul is lost.

If you think you know then you are foolish but when you admit you do not know and seek in the spirit to know then you say you are wise.

If you see yourself as a descendant of Adam then it is easy to see how you as a descendant of Adam are a partaker of Adam's sin.

If however, you say, you evolve from some animalistic evolutionary age and by age, developmental process you became who you are then you say all that you are is a beast and as a beast one, that carries the mark of a beast forever in death.

Those that see me as the creator of all and demonstrate the willingness to change by repentance and in repentance seek me with the understanding that I as the ultimate judge of all is able to forgive all sins I shall make whole.

They shall in their repentance and demonstration of continuous willingness to change be granted free access to my eternal kingdom but the foolish shall deny themselves access through continuous sin.

I love all human and to love them is supernaturally natural thing for me for it is in my image that I created man as you will find in Genesis chapter 1 verse 26.

However, man must remain with me to be part of me. They must walk in my ways not according to their fleshy desires.

To walk with me and to remain in me perfect man must reject the desires of the flesh and walk in the spirit.

THE MOTIONAL INTELLIGENCE OF THE SEVENTH SENSE

Life is about divine intelligence and to walk in the flesh is to stay compressed emotionally in the sixth sense. The sixth sense is fear of death in death and no man that is in the compression of the sixth sense shall walk in the motional intelligence sense and sensibility of the seventh sense, which is divine love.

To walk in the flesh is to do the things of the flesh and those who walk in the flesh shall never please me.[2] Why is it that those who walk in the flesh cannot please me? They cannot please me because the flesh reacts to what the physical eyes can see.

What the physical nose can smell. What the physical body can feel and what the physical hands can touch.

---

[2] Romans Chapter 8 verse 8

The flesh of man imprisons man in his sixth sense and the sixth sense is fear. The sense of sight captures information like a camera and it becomes registered in the mind. The sense of hearing provides man with the sense of sounds.

The sound as interpreted together with the other senses can be a sweet sound or an irritating sound.

What is a sweet sound or irritating sound all depend on the state of mind of the listener. Certain sound that is irritating to one is sweet melody to another.

The sense of smell as you know is the sense that enables you to tell the difference between a bad smell and a sweet smell.

The sense of taste also enables you to differentiate between a bitter or sweet taste.

The sense of touch is the sense that enables you to tell an object even when your eyes are closed. The sixth sense is a reactive sense and this reactive sense for a man in the flesh is fear. Fear is a human emotion that is common to man.

The sense of fear is an emotional flesh sense that leads a man to choose the wrong and reject the good.

The sense of fear is common to man because a man in the flesh is dead to spiritual senses. What you see, hear, smell, taste and feel in the natural does not provide the meaning of what it is in the supernatural.

The supernatural is opposite to the natural hence what looks good in the natural is the opposite in the supernatural.

The sense of fear therefore is a supernatural natural consequence that man suffers because of his entire mistaken sense in the natural of the supernatural and because of this mistaken senseless, he does not have any reality sense of supernaturalism.

However even though man is in the flesh unconscious his spirit is in search of awakenings from the darkness of fear, which is the sense that his spirit is locked on in his spiritual unconscious senseless supernatural existence.

It is the fact that his spirit is in the dark that his spiritual sense is in fear and in fear malfunctioning spiritually.

In malfunctioning of the spirit, man in the natural is in slavery of darkness emotions for the fact that what he needs to see as a spirit he cannot see.

No man is able to see in the supernatural in the natural what is of the supernatural unless I open your supernatural senses.

When your supernatural senses is open then you will see that what smell good is bad, what taste sweet is bitter, what taste bitter is actually sweet, and what sounds irritating is actually holy sweet sounds.

It is in the supernatural sense that a man is able to tell the difference between what is good and what is evil.

In the flesh, man sees sin as attractive and righteousness as offensive.

Man in the natural sense is blind to the reality of life for what man sees as dangerous is not and what they see as non-dangerous is what is dangerous to their souls.

For me to open your senses you must show willingness to walk in the seventh sense, this sense is the sense of divine love, and no man in the natural is capable of divine love unless I make them capable by the power and authority of my love.

To see the supernatural is to walk in the reality of life.

To have this reality advantage is by grace for all of man as sinners is lost in their sixth sense and in the sixth sense confused, man is only interested in trading in downward emotions. Downward emotions places man to be in deeper darkness out of deep fear and in deep fear man instead of going forward goes backward yet in spiritual blindness sees himself as going forward.

To have spiritual insight is a privilege for having such insight gives you an edge in the natural for what others are blind to and cannot see becomes open knowledge to you.

This privilege you have by grace of my love and my grace is what affords man the forgiveness that he needs to be able to operate in the seventh sense.

In the sixth sense, man is led and moved by his emotions and in sense of fear, man is of low intelligence yet sees himself as highly intelligent.

Intelligence in the reality sense is to be divinely intellectual and no one shall be divinely intellectual unless they walk in allegiance to the supremely universally divine which is I the I AM THAT I AM.

I know all things as the maker and creator of all things. Man from the beginning of their serving time has been engaged in answers seeking but the low intelligence of man makes man to seek in his own mind that which he cannot see for he is blindfolded by me until he demonstrates wisdom.

If you find yourself in an Island and you believe that this island just became on his own then you will always be in mind to reign supreme in the island.

In such mind you will never be in mind to seek the maker of the island for in selfish ambition all you desire is to convince yourself that there is no maker and that way you can pursue your plan of supreme reign.

To find the answer as to the how the island became or indeed how you ended up finding yourself on the island you must admit that only word self exist and as the self-existing the Most high God the creator uncreated.

If you believe no other self exist beside I Word the oracle of life then you will know that nothing besides me exist without a creator.

To prove that the earth self-exist my challenge to a man is to blow apart a house and see if the house will rebuild itself. It is the fact that I self-exist that I am the Most high God and as the Most high the

Almighty all power as the all glorious God the creator of heaven and earth.

If you believe there is a God who made all things then your first search must be for me to answer your question and to give you understanding of what is and what is not even though it appears as if it is.

If however you say there is no maker and you made yourself to be then you say you are the I AM for only I self-exist and this is why I am the Most High God as I said.

Man in blindness cannot appreciate who I AM because man in death is only after illusions not reality.

Man seek to be the king of his own fake castle in arrogance mind and in arrogance trusting in the foolish idea that he is the king of the universe with the power, mind and intelligence to give meaning to himself and to everything else that he can find with his ordinary eyes and mind of carnal reasoning.

As the Most high and Almighty God all power belongs to me and what spiritual life is all about is power and only the highest power shall stand in all eternity. Life is about victory, fulfillment, peace, rest, joy and satisfaction in all things.

Life is full of challenges and the victors in life are those that have the spiritual motional continuous movement intelligence, which is the necessary intelligence that a man needs to overcome whatsoever comes their way.

This motional spiritual intelligence, which is the seventh sense, is in my word power and this word power of mine is I Christ being my divine love revealed.

In the sixth sense, man in fear is void of peace, rest and joyful fulfillment.

The emotional sense of man in fear is of warfare orientated for man in darkness emotions is always in wroth for the fact that he is void and empty in his spirit.

Man in the sixth sense is by fear driven to walk in ludicrous ways of death darkness regiment forces.

In ludicrous ways of death man ridicules himself in his foolish actions by allowing himself to be driven by bitterness, envies, jealousy, selfish unfulfilling ambitions, lustful desires, hypocrisy and many more darkness emotions that is of darkness in the flesh of sin that man is locked into to be enslaved to suffer in fear until he repents from sin.

Sin is the root cause of death, death placed man in darkness of reality of life, and in such darkness, man became subject to time to serve time to repent and be free in eternity out of good behavior.

It is good behavior to repent and it is central to my divine character to forgive for if I do not forgive then no man shall be free from the imprisonment camp of sin.

Only in freedom from death shall man experience spiritual emotional freedom and such emotional freedom is only possible in love.

Man as flesh is in emotional imprisonment and this emotional imprisonment places man in worry mind of slavery and in worried mind in operative spiritual fear because the soul knows it shall perish if it does not find the way.

All of man on earth is on a mission and the mission is to find the way. In emotional darkness of the flesh, man is in confusion and in confusion; man sees good as evil and evil as good.

The flesh is the satanic element inherited by man in sin and this element contaminated the soul of man to place it in emotional darkness age in time era to remain condemned still in timeless era. For this reason man needed to be regenerated to be paced in true life motions to be in motion walk of goodness so that for eternity the soul is free from darkness in light of my glory.

This is what life is all about and this is why I made the few to commune with for the soul benefit of all man so that by the elected man hear the word and by making the wise choice he is saved.

Man in the flesh is his own enemy for whilst his spirit cries for freedom all he does as flesh is to keep his spirit locked up forever.

All man is spirit being and I the creator of all is the Father of all spirits. Nonetheless, I only see you as my son when you are my image and as God the Most High I am love hence if you are not of divine love I know you not nor can you see me or know me.

Love is the supreme order of the universe for it is by love that the moon shines and the sun shines.

Without love all there is, is darkness and this is the problem that man has as flesh that in hateful mind the soul of man keep on wondering in the dark endangered to perish forever. The flesh is emotionally evil and the driving force behind the emotionally flesh is the principalities evil regimental fallen angels.

The emotions of man brought on by the flesh are in the roots of his thoughts, and the thoughts determine the acts. In the spirit, you feel and hear the things of the spirit so the things that your physical senses feel become no longer a barrier to your spiritual growth. Reality is in the spirit and as God, I am the Spirit of Life and as spirit Father to all spirits that is of goodness hearted.

All of humankind is spirit and no man shall know me as I am unless a living spirit. As spirits, only by walking in the spirit shall any man fulfill their life's purpose.

I created man for fellowship and it is in fellowship that my relationship with man is established and only by walking in the spirit shall man walk with me.

Before man became flesh all creation was in the spirit hence man and woman had to be in the spirit first before I made them flesh.[3] Man I gave a physical body to feel and touch in the visible but even though man is flesh man is in all components a spirit being. Does it then mean that when man was in the spirit they could not feel or touch? The answer is no.

The spirit feels love and in love, the spirit touches the heart with loving deeds.

Man I made visible being to take my invisible loving kindness into another level and for this, I gave man a physical body but the body is only a shell the main being is the spirit in the body.

Man I created to live as a spirit as my flesh and blood forever and the initial flesh before the sin of man was the flesh of glory.

Mankind activated death by sin and in sin, mankind became separated from me and in separation; their flesh became the flesh of sin.[4] As I have said, life is about accountability and as the Almighty father obedience is the key to my heart.

Those who walk in obedience shall grow in my knowledge and wisdom.

---

[3] Genesis Chapter 1 verses 26-28. Mankind is made flesh from the dust of the ground as detailed in Genesis 2 verses 6-8
[4] Genesis Chapter 2 verses 15-17 and Genesis chapter 3 verses 19

As the all power, I am the king of kings and as a king I cannot be dethrone by any means. In my kingdom I have only Sons and together in joint glory my Sons reigns with me. In my kingdom Angels worship and glorify me and only saints that have been tried and truly tested are welcome in my kingdom.

NO MAN EXIST WITHOUT ME

As the Most high *Elohim* creator of heaven and earth, I know I exist as the only self-existing supreme ruler of the universe. Therefore, if a man says I do not exist he admits by his own saying that he does not exist for only in me shall a man exist as a living soul for as God I am life and as life the creator of heaven and earth.

You said why do I not just open the sky and speak to the whole world at the same time to end the debate of man about my existence which I know that I exist but for they do not know they speak in darkness of the truth.

My answer to that is that the dead will still not believe me because no man can know me in death for as God I am a God of the living and only a living soul can testify to my existence as the creator of all things the Alpha and Omega the beginning and the end. Even if I open the sky and speak audibly to the whole world at the same time the dead will say, it is the voice of alien enemies trying to invade the world. Any alien that is trying to invade the world is a heavenly outcast for the world is the world of sin and of sin of death; therefore, there is not point in invading the graveyard of the dead.

The earth and the fullness of it thereof is mine. My kingdom is eternal and just for the record let all man know that I need not invade what is mine. The earth as mine is under my arm of judgment and man for they are blinded by death will not see the light unless from a heart of repentance no matter how bright the light is shining around them. Even if I open the sky physically and speak to the whole world at the same time, they will still say if indeed you are God show your face. The fact is I have showed my face but even when I showed my face they said I am a devil because they are blinded by sinful death and as such said we still do not believe you are who you say you are.

Man is busy looking for aliens and I say aliens are living inside of the spiritual dead man and no canal telescopic objects can reveal them for what they are.

I know you have a question on aliens and I promise to give you a comprehensive answer as I continue in my revelations to you. For now know that aliens are heavenly outcasts and whosoever is cast out of heaven is a dead spirit and as a dead spirit will only be interested to invade the mind to lead it in sinful death so that the spirit suffers spiritual economic loss with no chance of recovery.

A dead spirit is a devil and a devilish spirit is a tempting spirit that will always tempt you to try to make you fall by asking you to do certain things to prove to him that you have extraordinary powers before he would believe you. Let all that aims to proper eternally open their ears to hear for divine faith comes by hearing not from natural sight of things.

As the Almighty God, I know I am the Almighty and so does the devil. The fact therefore is not for me to prove to man that I am God by showing any signs that is beyond my already visible goodness loving creations.

The evidence of my powerful self-existence as life in eternal life is already in my loving creations

If you believe I created all things out of my power and will as Almighty power of life then you must accept that I am indeed Almighty God that I say I AM THAT I AM.

The evidence that I am good on deeds is in my loving creations so the issue for man is to see my love for them through my loving creations.

In seeing my loving heart only shall a man realize that the entire trick of the devil in deceiving him to believe that there is no God is to rob him of his true inheritance.

You cannot see my love for you if you are in the devil's camp for all those that are in the devil's camp are in my consuming fire.

The devil as a tempting spirit always deceive man to have the illusion mind that to be evil is to have ultimate power and control and that only by being evil and wicked do you have total advantageous rewards.

The devil is a crook magician and magic is all an illusion and when your eyes is covered by the illusion of a deceitful magician you will not see that the house that he claims he has made to disappear is still standing right in front of you.

For you cannot see it you will be amazed not knowing that you have been fooled to believe in a total lie that you are witnessing some major mighty display of power that is compared to none.

It is the way of love to empower you with real power of life not with magic tricks and I anoint a saint for them to have real power of life through enabling them to have the mind of love.

The way of the devil is opposite to life and it is always to trick a man to believe truth is lie and lie is the truth to deny them from having the real power of life.

As the creator, I order the devil to remain silent always because the devil is an empty barrel making too much loud noise.

It is devilish principalities idea to say there is no God. A smart being in understanding of life purpose will not engage themselves in devilish principalities ideas.

For no good comes out of it and I say it is a devilish idea to say there is no God because God has not proved to you in the way that you would like for him to convince you that he exists.

You cannot see the air but you know it exist and if you came to the world naked with nothing how can you say there is no other higher power or authority behind all that you see on earth given that when you came you came with nothing whatsoever.

As God, I am a Spirit and the conviction a man needs to have is a spiritual one.

It is to deny man from having this spiritual conviction that the devil deceives man to be in mind of ordinary mind search not of the extraordinary spiritual search.

The truth of life is in the spirit realm and no man cut off from the spiritual realm of light can find the truth.

I am the most high God for goodness sake of life, so you cannot see me for who I am with ordinary eyes of wicked mind for if the evidence that you seek that I exist is ordinary still then you say you do not believe that I AM THAT I AM the creator of all things.

If you do not believe I am the creator then you cannot believe I exist as the spiritual God and Father let alone seek to find me to be in relationship with me for goodness sake of life.

It is spiritual wisdom to believe from the ordinary things that you see that I exist. From having that little mind of faith believe only will you embark on a soul search to have greater spiritual convictions of my divine power and existence as the Almighty God of the universe.

If a man say God does not exist then he will not attempt to seek for his lost soul and a dead soul at the end of time is a soul guilty of sin and in sinful guilt in condemnations walk of death everlastingly.

To say I do not exist is to say love, light and life does not exist for as God I am everlasting life and as everlasting life the source of life

A person that says I do not exist is a person that is void in life. Power of goodness is of life and to say there is no God is to say the only power that is in existence is evil. The devil deceives the dead spirit man to believe there is no God so that the dead mind of believe he has confidence to do extreme evil out of believe that the only power that is in existence is evil.

A man that has confidence in evil is a man in heavy-laden condemnation walk in death. For his confidence is in the evil that compresses him soul he will not see the need to be in mind of goodness spiritual accountability in his journey in time and at the end of his journey in time he will perish in eternal death by judgment from goodness.

Goodness is the universal ruling power for goodness is light and darkness can never stand against light for when light comes it simply eradicates darkness.

To say I that is the universal light does not exist is to say the entire universe is in darkness and this is an abomination saying for no one can see in darkness and as God I am all eyes and I see everywhere.

The power of life is love and I JEHOVAH God of the universe I am love and as love my power as evidenced by my entire loving creations is perfect works of life.

As love all power is subject to me and for all power is subject to me, I make everything work together for goodness sake of my name.

In love, you are meek, soft and gentle even though you are a mighty rock and as a rock lion king in the spiritual jungle of life.

For the fact that you are meek and gentle you appear as if you are weak even though you are mighty and fully strong.

Love is faithful and although love is faithful, you cannot see the faithfulness of love towards you in selfish mind of hatred.

A dead spirit cannot believe in me for as God only the living can know and see me and to become a living soul by my power you must believe that I AM from believing that I made the ordinary things to be from my extraordinary powers.

Faith of life comes from hearing not from seeing for as God I am a spirit and as a spirit the Immortal Invisible highest God of the universe.

If you say until you see me do something that, you consider extraordinary before you believe I AM then you say I am a liar for saying in the scriptures that I am the creator of all things. If you say I am a liar then you say you are all that you are because of who you are and as such are in no account to any higher authority and power that is beyond what the ordinary eyes can see.

If however you believe I made all things then you say from your believe that you have all the extraordinary evidence that you need to lead you to embark on a spiritual soul search to find me for you to obtain higher spiritual convictions of my existence.

Through the goodness of my heart, I have made way for man to become a living soul and if a man out of the wickedness of his heart chooses to remain in blindness of sin out of his desperate mind to sin then he carries the wages of his sin on his head.

The wages of sin is death and if a man carries on his head the mark of death then he cannot see the goodness of life in the darkness of his oppressed soul.

For goodness sake, of life, I afford man the gift of life by the giving of my own flesh and all that repents shall have the benefit of my total gift of life as king of kings in eternal life. If my own flesh does not satisfy a man then that man says he is a confirmed devil and a confirmed devil is always in mind to affirm the ways of his wicked devilish master as the right way.

This is a spiritual abomination for evil is darkness and as the Almighty ruling order of the universe I say I am light and the dominion power in the universe is light not darkness.

The entire sign of my existence that I have given to man is my flesh and heart of love revealed and this sign is I the son Christ Jesus

There is no greater sign of my existence to man than the perfect sacrifice that I made in my heart of love to save man from eternal death.

If a man fails to see my entire sign revealed then he will be going round the circle of death in his journey in time and believe he is progressing ahead in life. By the time he finds out that he has not managed to make any movement to step out of death circle, it would be too late.

This is the game plan of the devil to deceive the foolish minded to remain in circle of death to the end of day in time. The purpose behind this game plan is to entrap the foolish minded to remain in guilt of sin and in guilt of sin carry the wages of sin, which is death on their head forever.

A devil as a tempting spirit and in mind of temptations will keep asking for signs still when all signs is already made obvious for goodness sake of life.

For goodness sake of life, I have enabled you to write these things.

The truth is no matter how convinced you are that God enabled you to write these things do not be surprised to find that many will be in greater dark mind of conviction that it is madness for you to have such believe.

Do not be surprised to find that the more convinced you are that I AM THAT I AM the greater the attempt by the devils to confuse and discredit you as a total liar.

This is the way of the wicked and this is why only the wise will make it through the gates of heaven for heaven is the land of the wise and only the fool and the mad would say I do not exist.

I am love and as love, I am eternal life forever and my soft and gentle way as love is to make you a gentle soft and loving spiritual being for only by that are you a spiritual lion in eternal life forever.

Therefore by my entire spoken revelation word of power through my elected from beginning of time and from my perfect woks of remissions I have by so doing opened the skies to bring heaven down to earth.

From the look of things you can see that despite all said and done man still says I am not and to say I am not is to say there is no life and whosoever say life does not exist admits by his saying that he is void of life and as such a dead spirit that does not exist. When a person die on earth you do not count them as still living so also when a spirit dies they are no longer counted amongst the living.

To be amongst the living and counted as a living soul you must submit your will to love and my love revealed is I Christ Jesus for to love is to live and to hate is to die.

As the universal creator, I am love, light, joy, peace, rest, Spirit, power, life and as the total goodness joy of life the truth and as the truth I am the same today, yesterday and everlastingly.

As life, I am oracle of life that is eternal in my self-existing life forever. For a mortal man to say I that I AM creator of heaven and earth does not exist is to deny himself my immortal goodness benefit everlasting.

By that smile, I say you are satisfied with my answers and I see you have no more questions for now so I say the master will continue with his revelation in the next chapter and from now till then and beyond I say remain in my peaceful blessings.

ME: Thank you.

GOD: You are welcome and will always be welcome.

ME: Thank you.

GOD: You are welcome again.

CHAPTER 3

TO FORGIVE AND FORGET IS TO FULFILL DIVINE LAW

Luke chapter 17: verse 32; "Remember Lot's wife". Verse 33 "Whosoever shall seek to save his life shall loose it; and whosoever shall loose his life shall preserve it".

GOD: I continue my revelation by referring you to this scripture and I ask what would you say this scripture have to do with forgiving and forgetting?

ME: According to the biblical account in Genesis 19, you destroyed Sodom and Gomorrah but gave grace of salvation to Lot and his family.

However, Lot's wife looked back as you rained down brimstones of fire upon Sodom and Gomorrah and she turned to a pillar of salt.

So it could only mean that if a person looks back then they will become a soured salt and if soured they cannot move in line of salvation to the finish line.

GOD: Matthew 5 from verses 13 says **"Ye are the salt of the earth: but if the salt have lost his savour; wherewith shall it be salted? It is thenceforth good for nothing, but to be cast out, and to be trodden under foot of men".** Verse 14 **"ye are the light of the world. A city that is set upon a hill cannot be hid".** Verse 15 **"Neither do men light a candle, and put it under a bushel, but on**

a candlestick; and it giveth light unto all that are in the house". Verse 16 "Let your light so shine before men, that they may see your good works, and glorify your Father which is in heaven" and finally verses 17 says "Think not that I am come to destroy the law or the prophets. I am not come to destroy, but to fulfill it".

You are right in your answer and my referring you to this scripture is to clarify further the point that you have made that to have complete benefit of eternal life salvation is to keep matching on to the finish line without looking back and the world of death.

A man with benefit of grace is a light and salt and to have the full benefit of the grace that you have you must progress to the finish line for even though a man has grace if they do not hold on to the pillar of grace to the end they will not have full benefit reward of grace.

Lot's wife turned to a pillar of salt because she looked back and to look back is to become destabilize from progressive forward movement.

To walk in line of salvation to the very end is to continue to face Zion. A person that looks back at Sodom and Gomorrah will loose his sweetness flavor and without sweetness flavor shall be without his or her savior. Without sweetness flavor will find himself or herself in mystery Babylonia burning in raging fire and will be like ordinary sand trodden upon by the foot of principalities demonic spirits.

A man in the world shines as light when he is in the light and will be a salt of good flavor when he does not look back at Mystery Babylon.

Mystery Babylon is a place of great offence and the defenses that a man has in Mystery Babylon is my holy fire and to have this defense a man must stay in me to the end as his Lord and savior. To see things for what they are in mystery Babylon you have to look from the highest mountain and this Mountain that stands forever is Zion.

Mystery Babylon is centre command of darkness principalities regiment and the darkness world order regimental aim and objective of Mystery Babylon is to erect and empower the image of the beast and make mankind submit to the erected beastly image by evil force.

This is abominations and a criminal act punishable by death by rain of fire.

The fire is already raging in Mystery Babylon for Mystery Babylon as the opposite of life is in consuming fire of death of the beastly order that it is promoting. To seek to promote self-righteousness as world right is to be in beastly order and beastly order is raging fire of hell without chance of relief from extreme pain and sorrow.

Divine law is righteousness and this is the law fulfilled in the entire universal realm as the key to eternal life. The fulfiller of all divine law and life prophecy is the Lamb, all those that are in the Lamb shall be salt and light, and no evil principalities shall be able to oppress them to fail.

All those that look back shall partake in the offensive run of Mystery Babylon and shall become like Lot's wife sand and as sand shall not be a strong life pillar that cannot be moved or destroyed. For to be a salt that has lost its flavor is to be nothing but sand and all that is sand shall not see the end of salvation and from the middle ground of nowhere shall be washed away into the lake of fire where there shall be no resurrection from death.

However, the good salt shall be pillars of life in the highest mountain of the Salt Lake City of the New Jerusalem and shall have as their rewards everlasting all the benefit of the salvation of the sprinkled blood of the Lamb.

This is revelation, revelation is wisdom and let all those that have wisdom count the number of the beast, and the number is 666 as written in Revelation 13 verse 18. However the divine answer is 666=18=1+8=9=Vengeance for 9 is the number of vengeance and vengeance is mine.

Let the evil and the wicked that carry the death mark of the beast on their head know that my vengeance pronunciation on the wicked is eternal death by fire and let all those that seek to give power to the best know that the beast is by me pronounced dead everlasting.

This is my vengeance judgment and pronunciations on the evil and the wicked for the wages of sin is death but my gift of eternal life is only through my only begotten Son Christ Jesus the fulfiller of all divine law yesterday, today and forevermore.

This is wisdom, let all that have ears listen and hear for a word is enough for the wise and the only word that the wise needs to listen and listen to is the Holy Lamb the author and finisher of faith. Those that listen and obey my word shall have my forgiveness but those that fail to listen shall not for forgiveness by me is through my divine act of good faith and to obey my word is to walk in total divine solutions and free from all chains and shackles of sin both past, present and future.

This is the truth and the whole truth so let those that have ears hear and let those that have eyes see that mystery Babylon is on fire but if a man be in the Lion of Judah he shall go thought the fire and it shall not burn him.

To forgive and forget is to be free from hateful compression but a person that holds on to past offences will stay buried in past offences. A person that buries himself in past offences allows principalities evil to rule his mind. Principalities evil spirits rules the mind of man to disable their spirit from making any life progressive movement and unless a man rises from darkness offensive regiment, he shall not have benefit of entire life defenses.

A man that has allowed evil to rule his hearts and mind is my enemy for as God I am love and a person that evil rules his heart is anti love in his heart of hatred.

To forgive is divine and no one in death is able to have a divine heart of forgiveness. A soul in death is always into mounting grudges and when a person is busy building a mountain of grudge their heart will be of total darkness and in darkness of heart, they cannot see any light in their heart from beneath their high mountain of evil darkness resentment.

To forgive is to see in the light for a person that does not forgive will remain in evil darkness and darkness will blind his eyes to lead his mind to hate.

Forgiveness is different from you talking to someone because as I said, just because you are in talking terms with someone it does not mean you are in friendly terms with them. The most dangerous humans are usually least suspected by anyone to be so dangerous. Just because a person is charming on the outside does not mean they are lovely on the inside and just because a person does not appear charming does not mean they are not a saint.

This is the reason why human judgment is always wrong because whether you are a saint or a devil it is not about your outlook but your inwardness and man in blindness always look on the outside whilst I the utmost judge of all see all things from the inside out.

Whether or not you have forgiven or have not forgiven someone is a matter for the heart and even if the one that you have forgiven does not know that, you have forgiven them I know that you have for I see your heart.

My own forgiveness of your trespasses is the most important for if I do not forgive a man of his trespasses then that man is forever condemned to perish eternal damnation of death.

To have my forgiveness is to have no record of wrongdoing before me for when I forgive you of your sins I no longer keep record of the sins that I have forgiven you. I see you have a question.

ME: Yes. My question is about forgetting what the person has done when they keep doing the same thing all over again. As you said when you forgive, you wipe our slate clean and even though we continue to sin, you keep forgiving us so that we do not perish in our sin. My question is how can we as a human forgive and forget when the situation keeps repeating itself.

GOD: To forget is the hardest for human being especially if the offender keeps on repeating his offensive ways towards you.

However, even though I say it is the hardest thing for a human being it is the easiest thing if you understand forgiveness from a spiritual perspective.

What does it mean to forgive a person from a spiritual perspective?

TO FORGIVE IS TO STOP THE OFFENSIVE DEATH COUNT

To forgive a person from a spiritual perspective is to stop counting the offence against the offender.

If you count the offence against an offender then you increase in anger towards them and the angrier, you are for their continuous offence the more resentful and hateful you will be towards them.

If you add to the record of offence every time a person offends you then your reaction will not be to current offence but to every offence against you to the point of current offence.

Other human in witness of your reactions will consider it as disproportionate because they cannot understand that your anger is not just on the current situation but also on every offensive situation as you see it pertaining to you as a person.

Unless a person knows every offensive history then it would be difficult for them to understand your reactions and the devil's way is to make you appear as an irate talkative being in your attempt to justify yourself by your trying to make others see your pain and innocence.

I created your spirit to be willingly and lovingly strong and the game of the devil is for you to appear as someone that overreacts due to temperamental problems so that in the eyes of man you appear weak not the strong that you are.

When you appear in the eyes of man as a temperamental being then you become even bitter and resentful by the evil judgment and unfair criticisms of others towards you by those that does not really know you for who I have made you to be.

If you build up resentments, you cannot concentrate in goodness works of love and this concisely is the entire game of the devil for the devil is anti-goodness.

Knowing that the devil is anti-goodness is to never give the devil the opportunity to distract you from your goodness objective purpose of life for in smart knowledge of life you know that the devil is always bitter envious as a looser and liar.

To understand the ways of the devil is to shame the devil always.

You shame the devil by forgetting the previous offence of the human offender and it is through forgetting that you easily forgive the present offence.

 It is only by this way that you will always show forth your goodness character not the irate talkative character that the devil seeks that man sees you to be.

 If every human only deal with the offence at hand, things will be a lot easier for humans to resolve in their relationships.

The problem of a human being in their inability to forget is in counting the offence and adding the previous offences to the current and when you add many offences together and it becomes huge mountain of offence, small talks apology will not do.

This is because when you have many mountains of offence in your sight you build a mountain of defense round yourself to shield yourself from harm from your offender and this mountain of defense will usually be made of bricks of resentments.

If you see someone as offending you a little then a little apology will satisfy you but if you count all their offences together, you will not be satisfied with any amount of apology in your heart of huge resentments.

Unless you minimize the offence to the current situation not round it all up to arrive at a big resentment figure in your mind you will be greatly offended in any current situation than the previous time.

Your anger will not just be for the current situation but for all previous situations even if you say you have forgiven the person for all their previous actions of offensiveness towards you.

To forget the past as a human being like you said is difficult if you see the past as keep repeating itself in the present.

The only way to break free from the past is to focus on the joy that you have in the present and the hope of greater joy in your tomorrow.

The devil is a pest and as a pest does not seek for anyone amongst human to enjoy graceful joy at any moment and as such, a devil will always seek to place a person in mind of the past that they are trying to forget.

Most devilish beings will always taunt others with their past and this is because they have nothing to pin against them in the present and to keep being offended by such pest is to waste your valuable time. If you are in me and remain in me then you are free from every condemnation both past, present and future.

A person that has found my forgiveness need not keep any record of anyone's wrongdoing towards them because this is exactly the wish of the devil to aggrieve the mind by playing a tape of past offence in their head to lead their mind to hate.

By grace, I forgive you of your sins and if you have found my grace know that anyone that hates you hates you because they are envious and jealous of the glorious light that is upon your head.

Also, know that a person that seeks always to offend is a person that deeply hates himself.

If you love yourself, you cannot be in mind to offend others always for a person that love himself will always have joy and for they have joy will always be in mind desire to give the joy they have to others.

To let go of the past is to walk in full progressive courage of life. A devil always seeks to steal the joy of another not because it is of any use to him because a devil is a sad sorrowful beast and can never know joy but because he has no joy and does not wish for another to have joy he is always an offensive pest.

To forget the wrong of someone that persistently offends you is easy if you understand why they are the way they are.

A person that has love in their hearts is always full of courage in their heart of love but a person full of hate is a terrible coward that always tries to bully others to make them believe he is strong and mighty to get them to fear him and to hide his own fears and failures as a coward.

A persistent offender as a coward is always in mind to offend the courageous to tarnish their good image.

You do not show your courage to such a person by counting their offence to the point of deep aggravation reaction for this is their entire game plan.

Instead, you show your courage by remaining faithful to your loving kindness ways. Only by this way do you frustrate the hatred in them and not by reacting in the same manner that they react.

To act in provocation is their desire and this is the reason behind the continuous offending but when you focus your mind on your good works to remain justified you make it obvious to them that you are the courageous and they are the coward.

A hateful being is like a troublesome sleepless child that will not let the mother sleep. The best way to deal with such a child is to stay awake in patience so that anger does not carry you away into blind spot for no one can see anything from a blind spot.

Only by patience and understanding shall the mother of a tantrum child remain full of love courage and focused to do what is necessary to rehabilitate the child.

You rehabilitate the child by putting the tantrum spirit in the child to sleep so that the child can be peaceful and restful in his spiritual mind.

The intention of a tantrum child is to gain the attention of his mother through tantrum behavior.

What a wise mother must do is stay patient and by patience put the tantrum in the child to sleep to keep the child in lifeline free from tantrum pain.

A tantrum child does not know that the very first he gives headache by his tantrums is himself.

For his entire focus is to gain the attention of the mother by crooked means he will be awaken by tantrums to keep his mother awake and restless forgetting that a child that says his mother will not rest will also not find rest.

What the mother has to do is stay focused on important business of rehabilitating the child with patience for acting towards the child in blind fury will only bring out more tantrum behavior from the child and this will only make the mother to look and appear very ugly in her negative character display.

You counter bad behavior with good behavior for if you are both behaving badly then the situation will escalate to a high level of calamity and calamity behavior from two sides cannot calm a situation.

The mother is older than the child hence must stay above level of the child's frustrations to achieve a calm result.

If a child's succeeds in frustrating his mother with his tantrums then the mother will end up behaving just like the child and the mother will no longer be in a position to influence the child to behave positively.

IN MY HOLY SPIRIT COMFORT YOU ARE ABLE TO FORGIVE AND EASILY FORGET

A persistent offender is a weak being and if you are of love, you are not in weakness but in strength and in strength of love, you are able to forgive your offender easily just as you know I will easily forgive you.

You are able to do all things because you know greater is he that is in you and if the one in you is greater then know that there is no need to keep record of your offender's offending ways because as the utmost judge I will always bring every man into account for his ways.

As a saint, you are the rehabilitated and the whole essence of rehabilitating you is for you to rehabilitate others through your goodness action, character and behaviors.

To influence another to be of good behavior you cannot be acting in the bad manners and behaviors of the one that you intend to rehabilitate.

To be in resurrection of life is to be a new creature and as a new creature you cannot deal with things the exact same way that you use to when you did not know better.

When you became in resurrection of life all that is old is gone and anyone that seeks to place you in remembrance of the old, know for sure that they are a devils' mouthpiece.

The devil speaks through man and the ways of the devil he manifest through man for man to see that he is a doer of evil works for no man that is led by the devil can be up to any good.

A devilish man is a time waster and if you know a devil as a time waster, you will never give him a second of your time for whatsoever reason.

Your time is valuable and it is for productive profitability in time and in eternal timelessness era. You are in time era to be accounted eternal profit in timelessness era as an everlasting achiever of life business objectives in time and to give even a second to a devilish human being is to be in mind of counter productivity.

A saint must always be in mind of life business objectives as the wise for you are not called to sainthood to be foolish but to be wise and in wisdom walk you are to be in operative divine mind knowledge of good to counter evil for goodness sake of life.

To give the devil time is to dwell in negativity and it is negativity to keep an account of the offence of another towards you.

For doing so will only anger you the more towards them and by anger hatred resentment will mount in your heart, which is against my will for you.

The best way to proceed from negative to positive is to count your blessings and be thankful. Instead of operating in foolish mind of the flesh of counting hatred actions of another and by so doing allow anger to cripple you from making progressive movements. You display spiritual wisdom and prudence by appreciating grace and in graceful appreciations; you remain always in good cheer.

If you are in negative mind of anger you cannot see that you are blessed and if you do not see that you are blessed you cannot be productive with your time because all you will do is spend your time in self-pity due to your anger and resentments.

The aim of a devil is to cause you to give up on your goodness actions. If you keep counting offence then you will not just see the human person as the offender but me because your anger ultimately you will direct more towards your God for allowing you to go through all that you see yourself going through.

This is the magic trick of a magician with the aim of deceiving the very elect that his God hates him as evidenced by all he undergoes.

If you are in me and I am in you as the Holy Spirit of life then know that what no man sees or knows I see and know all and if I have justified you then let no man trouble you by their evil judgment of you. For no man is without sin and if a man with sin judges a saint that is justified by grace even though the saint is still a sinner as flesh then any man that sits to judge that saint only judge himself.

You do not know what a saint goes through to sit in a position of judgment of their character and if I that know all that you go through says you are justified by grace of my love then what is the use of weighing yourself down with keeping baggage of offensive actions towards you.

As a saint you always have to travel light and to keep counting a person's evil actions against you is to slow yourself down and if you are smart you will not allow this to happen for any reason.

It is important you fully forgive and forget every time because forgiving is forgetting and if you forgive many times then you must forget many times. I see you have a saying.

ME: Yes. I am just thinking how easier said than done.

If you forgive and the person continues to do the same thing continuously then it becomes difficult to forget something that keeps happening.

Although I understand, what you are saying but as a human being, I say it is just too hard. People always say all you have to do is forgive and let go and if it is that easy to forgive and forget the world would obviously be a different place. This is my saying.

GOD: To do these things as a human being is hard because if a human being is dead in their spirit then the being that they are human in is a devil.

To be in me is to be able to do everything that is difficult to do easily.

To forgive someone that you believe has wronged you is only possible if you are in nature of divine love.

The devil does not forgive or forget a wrongdoing as a perpetual wrongdoer and as a perpetual wrongdoer; the devil is always in mind of warfare not peace.

If a devil has no one to fight with, he will fight with himself because a devil does not know peace or rest of any kind.

To forget is the same as to forgive because if you do not forget then you cannot say you have forgiven and you are able to do all things in me because with love nothing is impossible.

All things for man are difficult but with love, what looks so difficult becomes so easy.

You forgive and forget not because the person has not wronged you but because you know that not to forgive and forget is to wrong yourself even more greatly.

A devil has no conscience so it does matter to a devil how many times he offends and a devil for he has no conscience of goodness always thrives in mannerisms of strife and malice. However, you have a conscience as a living spirit and your conscience always work for you when you allow me to take control of every situation to show you that all things works always to your advantage.

When you forgive and forget the wrong of a person, it is not because of them that you do it for if you because of a man seek to forgive and forget you will never be able to forgive or forget.

This is because as I said to you before the person that you see to have wronged you will also be claiming that you have wronged them even more.

If you believe they have wronged you more and continue to wrong you still then you cannot ever reach a point of forgiving or forgetting what they have done previously let alone forgive them for what they are doing currently.

You do all that you do for goodness sake of my name. For each time you are directly wroth towards someone you are indirectly directing your wroth at me and if I am in you and you are in me then I have not placed you in me to be in battle with you but to be friends with you and as your friend affirm you as victorious in all situations.

You are in me to be in victory always and if you know that, you are a winner then why bother yourself with a looser sorrowful offender that is offended in himself and in his mind of offence seeks to lure you by his offence to quit your joy to partake in his sorrow.

OFFENSIVE BAGGAGE KEEPS A SPIRIT IN THE CONDEMNATION OF THE PAST

To let got of the past is to be free from heavy laden of death for a man that is in his past is a dead man walking in the heavy laden of death.

Whosoever that is in heavy laden of death will be full of sorrowful debilitations and as such shall not be able to move and enjoy the freedom of the present.

You are not in me to be sorrowful and my joy is your strength and to always let go of any offensive baggage is to always see yourself as blessed and for you see yourself as blessed joyful always.

If you are offended by the past then you will not rejoice in the present and my desire for you is to always rejoice and for you to always rejoice, you must always see your justifications by me not the past condemnation that the offender tries to deceive you to believe that you have still from me.

If you have truly forgiven then you have forgotten also and to say you forgive many times is to forget many times for what you need to forgive is what you also need to forget.

You need to always forgive and forget because you understand and appreciate my love for you.

My love for all human has no dept and if you appreciate my graceful love then you will always travel light to do my will for goodness sake of my name.

For if, you are to run the race of time to the finish line you must stay focused on the way to get to the finish line and not be distracted by counting offensive ways.

It is only by appreciating the total defense you have in my love for you by which your soul remains everlastingly justified now and forevermore that you will always be in joy of every moment.

To be in joy of every moment is to have divine spiritual enjoyment with fullness of gladness in your heart at all times.

This is my desire for you and this is why the devil is envious because what he cannot have you have by grace of my love for you and if you know that the devil is a time waster you will never allow him to waste your time for nothing.

For your time is precious as I have always said to you and to bury your mind in offensive counting and in offensive counting be in wroth is to dwell in self-justifications and in self-justifications self righteousness.

The book of James Chapter 1 verse 20 says, **"For the wrath of man worketh not the righteousness of God."** The wrath of man worketh not my righteousness but my wrath will always worketh my righteousness.

My wrath is judgment, to walk in my justifications is to have my power of judgment, and all you have to do to operate always in my righteousness judgment mind is to walk in my holy character.

When you walk in my holy character, you will condemn the condemned dead that are in the sinner and love the sinner to remove the sin in him and in sin removal enlighten the sinner by your goodness walk of faith to be a champion of life that is everlastingly a winner in my holy redemption league of champions.

When you walk in self-righteousness, you give room for the condemned dead to try and judge you and the judgment mind of the dead is always in corrupt mind of death which is to silence the truth.

The truth is life and the power of judge met you only have in life. When the evil dead are judgmental it is evidence of their insanity for it is established rule of life that only the living shall have the power of judgment.

The dead judge to aggrieve righteousness and to allow the dead to aggravate you is to allow yourself to be angry for nothing for all those that are dead are nothing for to be dead is to be void.

To be in wrath of man is to be in unholy character and any man that is in unholy character will walk in mind of self-justifications and self-righteousness to justify his sin as right. You cannot be wroth out of self-justifications and in self-justifications self-righteousness and be in mind to give love for love is righteousness of life.

My life lessons to you is to enlighten your mind to operate in holy divine reasoning and to see things from a divine perspective is to understand that I see all that you see and all that you do not see and as the one that sees all the best judge of all situations and circumstances.

I see all that you go through and I understand that you have found your faith run experience to be quite a tough ride. I am divine love and as divine love I am the God of tough divine loving standards and your tough run is all to make you a tough lover just like me.

As such, instead feeling aggrieved for the offenders ways, thank me for allowing you to see the secret of evil through those offences for whosoever knows the secret of evil, evil can no longer oppress them.

It is blessing to see in spiritual light and those that have my blessings evil shall only do them a great favor to strengthen them to walk in benefit of their blessings not weaken them in any way.

By grace, I appointed you and every disappointment for the appointed is a blessing. Those that hope in vanity shall be disappointed and in disappointment, they shall miss their calling appointment in life and regret forever in death.

ALL THINGS WORK TOGETHER FOR GOODNESS SAKE OF LIFE

All things work together for those that are called according to my will and purpose as written in Romans 8:28 and whatsoever appears as evil it is to perfect you in goodness of faith.

Look beyond the person and see the one that has called you and if you focus your eyes on me, you will always see that all is well and good for you as the anointed in me.

All good and evil work for the goodness of the elected and a devil will only help the elect to reach their predestined destination.

However, woe to the man that allows himself to be used by evil in evil mind of hatred for if you are motivated by hatred to hate you cannot expect to have the reward of love everlasting.

The devil is a terrible beast and always seeks to lead the mind to operate in past sentences so that man is not able to hear the present, past, past participle tense word of freedom. I am the same yesterday, today and forever and those in me will in the present be free from condemnation of the past and in condemnation will be enabled by me to participate in glory walk of life to enjoy the glory of life everlasting.

The devil as a perpetual criminal is forever buried in past condemnation and as the everlastingly condemned a perpetrator of hatred and as perpetrator of hatefulness forever guilty of the wages of sin.

The devil as a hateful criminal knows that no man in hatred heart will inherit my kingdom to be in eternal life of peace, rest and joy.

You are not as I said called to be the fool but the wise and to be the wise is to always count all things as a blessing for if by grace you are called then know that by grace all things shall always work together for your goodness.

This is why you must always be in mind of goodness celebration not evil deliberations for evil deliberations always placed the mind in hateful connotations.

To be in hateful connotations is to be motivated by hateful suggestions and if a person is motivated by hateful suggestions they cannot move at all for hate does not motivate to move in any manner of goodness but cripples the mind to stay suppressed by evil.

To allow love to lead your heart to act, is to be in victorious walk always and if you are always in victorious walk then your spirit shall always flow in holy celebrations.

For joy is only in victory not in defeat and if you are in me, you are always a winner not a looser of any kind.

A saint is a heavenly celebrity, a celebrity is one that is celebrated, and if heaven celebrates you then you have no reason for not being of a good cheer always.

For by grace I have afforded you eternal victory you should always be in mind of celebrations and in celebrations be of a good cheer.

You are in good cheer always when you know that victory is yours everlasting for if I have assured you of victory you should not be without celebrating your victory at all times.

FORGIVE, FORGET AND GIVE THANKS THAT YOU HAVE DONE SO

When you forgive, forget and give thanks you will automatically increase in blessing for operating in divine holy mind of obedience to my royal law of life. Thanksgiving is evidence of good cheer in your spirit for if you give thanks you acknowledge gracefulness and acknowledging gracefulness gives you a daily renewal of everlasting hope of eternal life.

To have good eternal life hope is to be motivated to move in good faith at all times for if a person feels hopeless then their hopelessness will cripple then from going ahead.

If you count your blessing always and in blessing count remain in good cheer, you will always count all things as working together for your goodness advantage and not to your disadvantage.

If a person is in me all things will always work out for their goodness and if you know that goodness is always yours no matter what, then it is pointless wasting your time on things that are not of the goodness profit that you desire to have always.

A resentful mind is a mind full of complaints but a thankful mind is a mind full of appreciations. Resentments cripples whereas thanksgiving elevates and a spirit in elevation will always be in motivation of love and in goodness mind of elevation will always be of joy in every moment.

To forgive and forget is to say you are in mind of appreciations of my grace for you and those that are appreciative I will never depreciate.

All you go through will always give you a goodness outcome and if you see things for what I say they are you will always let go of any offence against you because you know you have my total defense and if you have my defense then all offences against you is in vain.

To forgive is to have a heart that is full of thanks always and just by you giving thanks you shame your enemy repeatedly for the aim of the enemy is to deceive you to believe that you have nothing to be thankful to God for.

To always forgive and by forgiving, forget is to walk in my righteousness. The devil is an enemy of righteousness, and to be an enemy of righteousness is to be in wroth of my judgment.

Know that the devil's game is to place you in wroth of my judgment through his tempting you to sin but I know the devil and I have not called a saint to place them in wroth of the same judgment that I have delivered them from.

Instead, I have called a saint to be accounted eternal blessings not for the devil to try them to fail and for me to eternally condemn them.

A saint carries my pass marks and I give my pass marks ahead of their trials to keep them in my eternal justifications for answering my calling and for performing my will of life for the entire glory of my holy name.

It is out of love that I called you and it is for goodness sake of my name that I delivered you from hatred oppression.

I called you to place you in my Holy Spirit and in gracefulness of my love; it is always my will and desire for you that you always have the benefit of joy in my Holy Spirit in every moment.

All you have to do to have this joy is be in mind of appreciations of my grace towards you always, in that mind forgive and forget always for goodness sake just as I have forgiven you all your trespasses past present and future to place you in eternal benefit rewards of life everlasting.

There is nothing a devil can do to shock me neither is there anything you can do to shock me. For I am eternal and I see all that is of today from yesterday and as God that is the same today, yesterday and forever I love you in my eternal existence before you even had a mind of loving me in time.

Love conquers all and with love, what seems so impossible becomes easily possible.

If you see my love for you in all situations, then rather than getting yourself aggravated by the devilish pest in man you will always be thankful and smile for the Holy Spirit in you.

You will be full of thanks for the Holy Spirit in you who by grace took the veil cover of darkness from your eyes for you to see that the devil is a looser and a liar.

The devil as a liar and looser is full of pestilence ways to cover the eyes of man for them not to see their true inheritance that they have in light of my glory.

The devil is death and as death an enemy to the soul of man and for goodness of my name, I gave my grace to humanity to afford them the benefit of life to their souls.

It is by my grace that I opened your eyes to see the truth that by light of my glory you are forever a winner and the devil as an enemy of goodness faith is forever a looser as a liar.

No man can be in spiritual free dominion in lies and the devil as a liar only knows how to tell lies as a condemned liar to oppress the soul of man in darkness of his own slavery forever. Only the truth shall set a man free from the wicked lies of the devil and it is so that man attains eternal freedom from death that I gave mankind my grace.

For you have my grace, the evil ways of the devil will only work to your benefit advantage in all situations for those that have my grace all wicked ways of the devil will only work to affirm them in the total victory that they have everlastingly in me.

The devils as a looser and a liar is a joker and there is no point in wasting your times on a dry pestilent joker for you know by grace all the devil's wicked jokes is upon him not you. As such do not waste your times on sentiments of dry jokes but be merry always in appreciative mind of the divine love you have in me through which you have eternal victory.

To always remember and appreciate grace is to be able to forget and forgive those that trespass against you always.

If at all times you remember that I have given you, grace to manifest divine love being able to forgive and forget becomes the easiest thing for you to do.

A conscience established in love is always in locomotion of goodness walk.

To be in goodness locomotion conscience mind is to be in continuous move in goodness faith of life and in goodness faith, you will always be able to manifest into others the love in your heart.

The evidence of love is good heart and to have evidence of love in your heart is not to act in evil mind of hypocrisy but through genuine heart of loving kindness.

Forgiveness is central to continuous walk in goodness faith for it is by your faithful heart of forgiveness that you will always remain faithful to me and kind and loving to your fellow beings no matter what the case may be.

It is through such kindness that you show that you are as my kind faithful to me always. For if you are faithful and committed to my ways and loving commandments only are you just like me and to be just like me is to forgive those that trespasses against you for you know that by grace you have my own forgiveness always.

You give love because you are in love and love is in you and as sign and gesture that you appreciate the love you have from me you do what I say is right because you see it as right for you to do whatever I say is right for goodness sake of my holy name.

If you entertain hate, you say you do not appreciate my love for you and this is not the way of love for love is always in mind of appreciations not depreciations.

You forgive and forget not because you are weak but because you are strong for only by strength of love are you able to forgive those that trespass against you and pray for those that curses you time and time and again.

No man that is motivated by hate is strong for hate is weakness and to hate is to remain in weakness.

A weak being will not be able to see his weakness and not being able to see your weakness is to remain weak yet believe you are strong.

Understanding that as flesh you are weak is to remain strong as a spirit. You depreciate your flesh to elevate your spirit for if a man appreciates his flesh then when he thinks he is strong is when he is weak.

Love in the heart maintains your spirit in strength of life.

Only in strength of life will your spirit continue to be in upward life promotions.

In weakness of hate no man can walk to the goodness, benefit of his soul for in hate, the heart of a man is wicked and the motivator of the wicked minded is demonic forces.

Wicked forces rule the mind through giving a man evil suggestions and a man that is a slave to sin will not be able to resist those wicked suggestions.

A man that hates denies himself the benefit of love promotions for hate never promotes you to have anything that is good whether in time or in eternal timelessness.

To love and in love forgive is evidence of your appreciations of grace of love towards you and those that by their ways walk in full appreciations of love will always have as their reward the full benefit of my grace to their souls everlasting.

However, those that seek to try them for they are faithful to my ways will face great spiritual trials and they will not have my justifications but those that by my grace are justified will always be free from any condemnation in all of their trials.

To say you are in love and love is in you is to be in appreciations and those that are in appreciations of love will never depreciate.

If you forgive others, just as I always forgive you then you say that you appreciate the benefit afforded to you by grace of my love.

Only in such appreciations shall you remain committed to walk in divine mind of goodness faith and in faithful commitment dedicate your mind to always confer benefit of the loving grace you have unto others for goodness sake of life.

In glorious mind of appreciations, you will always easily forgive and forget and it is only when you forgive and forget that you demonstrate that you are the wise and not the fool that the enemy is trying to get you to be through his wicked ways to harden your mind not to forgive.

As the wise, you forgive because you know that it is goodness, productive and profitable to forgive.

When you forgive, you will always increase in blessings because to forgive is to act in accordance to my will and purpose and it is always my will that those that walk according to my will and purpose remain forever blessed and highly favored.

To give love is to receive greater love and when you forgive and forget know that you will always be accounted my righteousness for doing my will.

Whosoever does my will shall always appear before me holy and holiness is love for as love I am always Holy, Holy and Holy.

It is my holy commandment that you forgive those that trespass against you just as I forgive you your own trespasses and to enable man abide by this holy commandment is the reason why I made my Holy Spirit available to you all.

If you are in my Holy Spirit, nothing is impossible for with me all things are possible.

To be in my Holy Spirit is to walk in active blessings for all works of faith from beginning to the end is to place you in my Holy Spirit.

My Holy Spirit is the Spirit of truth and as the Spirit of truth; it is by you being in my Holy Spirit that you are in my presence always.

If you are in my presence know that you are already in comfort zone of life for as the Holy Spirit I am life and as life the creator of all things the kings of kings as eternal life forever. For your soul is already in my comfort zone as one that is in me you will always be enabled by me in all that you go through to remain strong.

In strength you will be courageous to walk the good walk of faith and as the author and finisher of faith I am always faithful in rewarding all those that are diligent in good service and faithful in their ways towards me for goodness sake of my name.

As a faithful God, I am faithful to fulfilling my own promises and will always enable the faithful to have the benefit of the reward that I promise them both in time and in eternity.

It is out of my faithfulness to fulfill my entire promises to man that I made my Spirit available so that in my Holy Spirit man walks in vision of love and in vision of love in time focus on eternal life inheritance.

No man in the dark is able to see and to be in the world of flesh is to be in the dark. If a man that is in the dark and blind thinks he sees clearly, the one that he deceives is himself and the devil will only deceive such man to lead him to eternal death in the bottomless pits of hell.

The world of flesh is a world of many dead souls and dead souls are only mindful of evil to carry out the woks of the flesh.

A dead soul is always in mind to offend and defend their offensive ways due to their terrible heart of evil and wickedness.

To be the living is to be strong and a person that I have afforded the benefit of life I afforded that benefit to grow and mature for if the spirit upon realizing the benefit of life fails to grow in heart and mind of hatred such spirit will still eventually die.

To grow is the essence of life and to grow you must always walk in the strength of love for the purpose of sweet promotions of your soul in time for eternal life rewards purposes.

Without the strength and courage of love, no man in the world of flesh shall be able to be in continuous mind of goodness faithful walk in time to have the total goodness inheritance that I desire for him to have in eternity.

For man as flesh is desperately wicked and evil.

Every man is in time to acquire the right to eternal life rewards and unless you follow the right way, a man in time will spend all his time in acquiring condemnation of eternal death out of the wickedness of his hearts.

NO MAN SHALL FINISH THE RACE OF TIME UNLESS THEY ABIDE BY MY ROYAL LAW FROM BEGINNING TO THE END

To acquire the right to eternal benefit of life is the essence of my calling to man to enter my Holy Spirit so that in my Holy Spirit I enable them to walk the good walk of life. Only in my Holy Spirit is a man in visible understanding of my love for without my Holy Spirit all that a man sees is my wroth. Unless you understand my love, you cannot see the point in loving another.

The race of life is not for rats for a rat is a betrayer. The race of time will be run and completed by the lion at heart and at the finish line, they shall receive the crown of glory everlastingly.

To finish the good race of time and have the benefit of eternal goodness inheritance blessings you must always see the point of love, which is that it is righteousness of life to love.

If a man is not a contender in the race of life in time, he has no legitimate reasons to contest his eternal loss for a man that is not in the race cannot expect to have any kind of life position at all.

If you start a race but fail to finish it is as if you never took part in the race for only those that finish the race will the trophy giver consider as good runners for finishing the race.

If you are in my Holy Spirit, you have already reached the finished graceful line in the race of life in time and as such, all you have to do is to keep your focus on the trophy rewards that awaits you in eternity for being a committed good on deeds in time all the way to the very end.

No man is able to finish the good race of time unless they are in my Holy Spirit for man as flesh is weak and only the strong in me shall make it to the end. It is to give man the strength and courage of life that I make my Holy Spirit available to man in time out of my own gracefulness and forgiving heart.

My entire calling to man in time is to enter into my Holy Spirit through the door for unless you go through the door you cannot see the light of my glory.

Many is it that are called but few are chosen for although I call all man only those that is faithful to the end shall be chosen and no man can be faithful to the end in any mind of hatred.

Those that answer my calling and are by me selected for their goodness hearts of faith shall be justified by me and by my grace; they shall always have benefit of eternal life in me.

Only in my Holy Spirit is man in sight of the truth for if a man is in darkness he shall not see that his number one enemy is himself.

The devil is the spirit of lie.

To be hardened in your mind and be unforgiving is to give room to lie and any kind of lie does not place a man in heart and mind of divine truthfulness.

As God, I am the way, the truth and the life and no man shall be in knowledge of the truth unless they are in me and I am in them for to be in death is to trade with death and those that trade with death will only purchase lies in time to the eternal detriment of their souls.

As the Spirit of truth, only I can place you in discernment of right and wrong and if in me, you do what is right for I say it is right then know that you are by me blessed for so doing. Therefore, every time you forgive someone and by forgiving, forget their trespasses in accordance to my will and purpose, be glad for doing so for know that for doing that which is right for I say it is right I will always account it to you in my own righteousness to increase you in blessings of life.

For blessed are those that are in mind of peace and to always have the mind to forgive and forget is to have my peace always. I see in your smile that by my answers you are satisfied.

ME: Yes and thank you very much.

All that you have said just brings to mind that scripture Philippians 4:13 which says, **"I can do all things through Christ which strengtheneth me"**.

For me this scripture is accurately true and to say the bible is a lie is indeed to be a devil for if we all follow the goodness instruction in the bible then the world really will be a different place.

In the past many years of knowing you as my God, I have suffered a great deal of hurt by the attitude of people.

Many as you are aware seem to have gone out of their way to provoke me but I thank you for always steering my mind to love and not hate and as my teacher I know without a doubt that you are love for all you have thought and showed me is greater love than I can ever imagine.

You have always taught me to forgive and have encouraged me to keep going no matter what the case may be and I just want to say that I could not have gotten this far without your own faithfulness.

In all these things without your grace I could not have survived to get this far and for this I thank you for teaching me how to love and for motivating me to always love no matter what the case may be for the goodness sake of your name.

GOD: That is very sweet of you and what shall I say, I say blessed you are and for saying thank you know that you are always welcome to be in my presence.

On that joyful note, I say it is good for you to rest those fingers that I have given you.

By that, I say we shall end today's lesson of revelations here but before we do I want you to know that good courage is honor and cowardliness is dishonor.

Always be of a good cheer and courage and always be encouraged by the fact that I am a faithful God and know that to be faithful to me as love through walking in goodness way of life as I have designed it to be is to be forever blessed in my name.

ME: Thank you

GOD: You are welcome again.

CHAPTER 4

TO HAVE THE DIVINE HEART OF LOVE IS TO BE A LIVING ADVOCATE IN LIFE

> St. John Chapter 13 verse 34 "A new commandment I give unto you, That ye love one another; as I have loved you, that ye also love one another". Verse 35 "By this shall all men know that ye are my disciples, if ye have love one to another."

GOD: Life is all about relationships and as God; all I am about is relationships. To be in me is to be my witness and all those that are my witness advocate shall have everlasting life of peace, rest and joy. You cannot love the one that you do not know and without love, a relationship cannot work.

To love is to fulfill the law for no man is able to fulfill the law in hatred. Matthew Chapter 22 from verses 37 reads **"Jesus said unto him, Thou shalt love the Lord thy God with all thy heart, and with all thy soul, and with all thy mind."** Verse 38 **"This is the first and great commandment."** Verse 39 **"And the second is like unto it, Thou shalt love thy neighbor as thyself."** Verse 40 **"On these two commandments hang all the law and the prophets."**

This I the Son said in response to the question that a lawyer asked me which is, which is the great commandment in the law? Why do you think this question came from a lawyer?

ME: A lawyer is someone that many will regard as someone that knows the workings of the law.

I think as the scripture said he asked this question in mind of entrapment.

If you had said one commandment is greater than the other it would have meant attaching greater importance to one commandment than the other and this would have raised more questions as to why we need to abide by the lesser commandment if they are not so important.

GOD: You are right in your analysis. The keyword is entrapment and this is always the intention of the devil to entrap.

Everything that I have said so far about forgiveness is only possible if you are in the heart of love.

With love, you are able to do all things and only in heart of love are you able to fulfill the divine law of life. No man is able to abide in goodness unless they fulfill the law and no man is able to fulfill the law independent of love because the law is love.

My commandment that you forgive those that trespass against you is not something you can abide by independent of me because if you are without me then you are without divine love and a person that is without divine love cannot abide by divine law, which is love.

The natural way of man is commonly sinful and to do that which is divine your body must be dead to sin and awake in life.

The question asked by the lawyer as you said he asked in mind of entrapment and a devil's advocate is always in mind to entrap for evil sake. Goodness is in love and evil is in hatred. To understand the ways of evil you have to look at it from a fisherman point of view.

A fisherman knows that if he just drop the hook to the river he would not catch any fish but by hiding the hook in the bait, the fish would be hooked by the hook hidden inside the bait. The fish ends up hooked in the hook hidden in the bait because he thought the bait was food and because he could not see the fisherman waiting to entrap him he ended up in the plate as food instead of eating what he sees as food to his satisfaction.

This is the way of evil to entrap because evil knows that if his evil intentions are openly clear then he will make no catch.

Love is life and hatred is death. The way of death is always to entrap the foolish man to imprison his soul in death everlasting.

A devil's advocate seeks to entrap to bury in death A deadly spirit is a devil's advocate and as a devil's advocate is not in mind to learn instead ask to entrap to make the person that he ask appear as a fool.

To be in love is to be smart and what a devil advocate will seek is to make the lovingly smart look stupid so that no one believes the truth that they say.

A devil's advocate as the real fool always strive to prove a foolish point and the foolish point that the devil's advocate always tries to prove is that the truth is a lie and lie is the truth. To be in heart of love is to know that you are not in competition with anyone to prove any point because just for the fact that you are in the heart of love is prove in itself that you are the smart one.

For it is smartness to love and in love abide by the ways of love for goodness sake of your soul.

The way to deal with a devil's advocate is to make him see his foolishness and you do this not by engaging in some foolish entrapment debate with the foolish devil's advocate but by simply declaring the law for what it is.

You can quote the written law but this does not mean you understand the principle of what you are quoting. The law is about principle application and those that does not abide by my divine law principles shall be ruled by death principalities to perish everlastingly in death. The only one that can declare the law and give the meaning of the law is the giver of the law and when a devil's advocate seeks to pronounce the law it is always to denounce the just and promote the unjust and this is against universal justice law.

The law is for the protection of the just not the unjust and only those that are in mind of love are just and righteous before me.

The answer I gave to the lawyer's question as you can see is that every law and prophecy is all about love, which means if a man is in heart of love then he will walk in fulfillment of all divine commandments. This is clear enough is it not.

ME: Yes.

GOD: My question to you therefore is if I say all you have to do to fulfill all standards of divine law is love. More also, if due to divine legal implications in the soul, man agrees that all they need is love, sings about it, look for it and desire to be loved why do you think man is unable to abide by a commandment that looks so simple and straightforward.

ME: The reason as far as I am concerned is that we do not understand what love is.
If we say we want love then we must first understand what love is.
If we do not understand love then even if we see love we would think is hate and if we call hate love and love hate then this confusion in itself cannot make a person abide by the rule of love and to avoid the condemnation of hatred.

GOD: That is true. So my next question to you is what is love?

ME: I am sure different people will have different answers to this question.

For me given all that I know now I would say love is faithfulness, compassion, affection, mercy, light, joy, rest and peace. Love is enablement, forgiving, giving, comforting, endurance, tolerance, honesty, honor the list goes on forever so to round it all up I would just say my understanding of love through my relationship with love which is you is that love is total power of life over death and as total power of life absolute goodness of life as life.

GOD: That is very good. Let me round it up a lot more for you by saying love is HOLINESS and love, as holiness is life.

Life is all about goodness and there can never be any goodness out of hatred.

Every man is born with knowledge of good and evil and no man is able to choose good and avoid evil unless they are in heart of love.

The law is to make sin clear to man for if there is no law then sin will not be made obvious to man and man shall not see that the wages of the sin that he had sinned already through being a descendant of the first Adam is death.

ONLY IN DIVINE HEART OF LOVE WILL A MAN BE ABLE TO CHOOSE GOOD AND RESIST EVIL

The law is all about choosing good and resisting evil and if you cannot choose good and resist evil then you are a transgressor of the law and a transgressor of the law is subject to death penalty for transgression against the law is sin and the wages of sin is death.

Whether a person is good or evil is a matter of the state of the heart.

No man is able to tell just from looking at a person on the outside that they are good or evil. The law is all about goodness living and as I said the fulfillment of all law is only possible in love.

James Chapter 2 from verse 8 reads, **"If ye fulfill the royal law according to the scripture, Thou shalt love thy neighbor as thyself, ye do well"**: Verse 9 **"But if ye have respect to persons, ye commit sin, and are convinced of the law as transgressors.** Verses 10 **"For whosoever shall keep the whole law, and yet offend in one point, he is guilty of all".** Verse 11 **"For he that said, Do not commit adultery, said also, Do not kill. Now if thou commit no adultery, yet if thou kill, thou art become a transgressor of the law. Now if thou commit no adultery, yet if thou kill, thou art become a transgressor of the law".**

To fulfill my royal law is to be my holy grail and to be my holy grail is to be my royal blood and as my royal blood a body of love and vessel of goodness.

You fulfill every law by love and if you love me as your God and love your neighbor according to yourself then you really have fulfilled the law because this is what every law is about.

If every man fulfils this law then all man would indeed have a heavenly life on earth as it is in heaven. For if, you love your neighbor you will not steal from them.

If you love your wife or husband you will not commit adultery with your neighbor's wife or husband for in heart of love you will be faithful to your own wife or husband and what you do not want done to you, you will not do to another.

To love your neighbor you must first fulfill the first and the last law, which is to love your God with all that he has made you to be.

Only by loving me with all that I have made you to be shall you abide by my ways in total faithfulness towards me out of the goodness heart of love that you have for me.

You cannot love another except you love me first and to love me is to love yourself.

Unless you first love yourself you cannot love any other hence although man preaches love they are incapable of loving because although they preach love with their mouth they reject my love with their hearts and you cannot reject my love and be able to give the love that you do not have to another.

To give love you must find true love.

True love is of my Holy Spirit not in the flesh. For when man seeks for love, as flesh it is only in mind of lust and lust will only enslave the mind in darkness of hatred.

Many in hurt and pain of their lustful findings says love does not exist and this is a lie from the pits of hell for as God I am love and as love I exist as life in my eternal life forever.

To say that love does not exist is to say there is no life or light for only in love is life and total goodness of life you will only have in the light of my glory.

A person that says I do not exist confesses they are dead for if a person says I do not exist then they say they do not exist for only in love do you exist as a living soul for all in hate is dead.

If a person says love does not exist then they say to their spirit that the only thing they are interested in is hatred and those that are in mind of hate can never be motivated to love by hate. Love is life and I JEHOVAH God I am love.

To fulfill the law you must be in me, I in you for the flesh is only in mind of transgressions, and all those that is of flesh shall only be in mind to walk in transgression against the law not in fulfillment of the law. To love you must experience love.

Only when you experience love do you appreciate the importance of love and the need to give the benefit of love to others for the goodness sake of life.

If you do not know the meaning of love then you cannot be an expert on matters of love. The ways of a devil's advocate is to appear as an expert on matters that he has no idea.

The motivator of a devil's advocate is a devil and a devil only motivates to hate.

Whosoever hates motivates to act will walk around in evil blindfold and such a person will be in thick darkness and in thick darkness shall not be able to see the true consequences of his actions.

To love you must know that you are treasured and loved for if all you know is hate for you are not in love you cannot give the love that you do not have.

My lawful commandment as affirmed by this scriptures that I have referred you to is all about love and if you preach the law in mind of hate then all you will be is a devil's advocate and a devil's advocate does not advocate for any man to walk in fulfillment benefit of the law but condemnation by the law.

To be a respecter of man is to transgress against divine law for if a man does anything in mind of getting his reward for it from his fellow man or avoid condemnation from his fellow human being such man will be a hypocrite.

A man is only good when he is good in the closet for if any man is good in the closet then he says that he is only in desire to please me for the good that he does in the closet no man can see let alone reward him for it.

Every man wants rewards for their goodness just like every man desire to avoid punishment for their transgressions.

A man in evil mind of the flesh will always seek to deceive his fellow men to be awarded good marks by them and by so doing hope to avoid condemnation from them for the evil that he does.

Such a man is a fool for whosoever is evil carries the mark of a beast, which is the mark of death and whosoever carries the mark of death, is enslaved in their soul to death no matter how justified they appear before man.

TO PREACH THE LAW IN MIND OF HATE IS TO BE A HYPOCRITE

To be in mind of hate is to be a hypocrite and a hypocrite is a person that preaches the law to judge others in hatred mind. A hypocrite is a person that has self-certified himself to be an advocate and a judge of the law. Such people in their unlawful testimonials will be full of wickedness and hateful intentions.

A self-certified advocate is a corrupt judge and as a corrupt judge will walk in opposite line of the law that he preaches.

Such person for they are a condemned convict will be highly hypocritical and as a hypocrite will merely preach the law to punish others.

A hypocrite is someone that pretends to be good in the open when in real sense he himself knows that he is evil in every sense.

Such man only deceives himself for if you know you are evil and you pretend to be good it means you are not proud of the work of your hands and for you are not proud of it, you pretend to be good to avoid the real rewards for your ways.

This is madness for the real judge is not man but me and as the real judge of the law being the giver of the law no man can deceive me to give to them a reward that they are not entitled to have.

As God, I see the hearts. Whether you hate or love is not by open display of what man sees as love but rather it is all about the motivational aims and intentions behind your act.

A person may put on a show of goodness to fool his fellow beings to believe that he is godly and good so that he can steal from those that fall for his deceitfulness.

However, those that a person with heart of love seeks to give relief unto would normally hate him deeply because they are blind and as such, could not visualize his goodness heart for them.

Everything a man does is openly visible to me for man cannot see heaven from earth but all that is on earth is openly visible to the host of heaven.

Love is from the hearts and as such, my focus is always on the hearts.

The hearts is what is subject to trial before me.

Whether a person is justified or in condemnation is all about where their heart is established. If love is in the heart established, then the heart is of goodness and for it is of goodness such heart is before me justified but if the heart is in hate then it is in all condemnation of evil. Hatred in the hearts is evidence of total evil in the mind and a heart that hatred has established itself in is in sinful condemnation.

Only by your loving heart, will I deem you to be walking in fulfillment of my laws and it is for this reason that I focus on the heart of a spirit man always.

A hateful person is never up to no good and every thing that is good in life is only from love. It is with a loving heart that you forgive.

It is with a loving heart that you do what is right for you see it as right for you to do so. No one trades in heart of love to loose but a person in heart of hatred is a looser in their heart of hate.

Hate motivates man to be a transgressor and love motivates to walk in fulfillment of divine law for goodness benefit of the soul in eternal life forever.

Hate disables, love enables, and to hate love is to be spiritually unable to move for it is only in love that you walk in life abilities.

To love is to have the protection of the law whereas to hate is to have condemnation from the law.

Every divine law a man can only fulfill in heart of divine love, and any transgression against the ways and commandment of love carries the same penalty, which is death hence no one law, is greater than the other is.

The law is not higher than the lawgiver and commitment to advocating the law in evil mind of judgment does not equate commitment to the lawgiver.

Hence, such commitment to wrongful advocacy and corrupt judgment ways will only affirm the person in condemnation instead of help to avoid it.

The most high in all things is love and if you are in heart of love then you shall always be before me justified.

Only in my divine justifications do you have protection of the law and in protection of the law the total benefit of life afforded to you by grace of my love being the lawgiver, advocate and absolute judge of the law.

What is lawful and criminal is by me as love determined for left to the dead and hateful, everything that is good hate will deem unlawful and everything that is evil will be lawful deemed.

This is abomination for evil cannot criminalize good for good is the judge of all and as such goodness is the one with the power and authority that is over and above all things.

Only in goodness is life preserved for as I have said evil is all about destruction.

Everyone that says they are religious on earth will preach charity as the central purpose of their religion and charity I say is love but to preach charity does not mean to be in charitable hearts.

Many put up a charitable front to steal and this is because although they speak of charity they do not have anything good to give for their heart is all full of hate and anyone in hateful mind shall always be in mind of stealing.

Although a hateful being, have nothing good to give, he will deceive others that everything is at his disposal to give as he pleases.

The whole idea behind this is to entrap those that truly have to give away what they have to the deceiver so that the have not will now appear as the have and the have will now be enslaved and compressed by the one that pretends to have what he does not have.

This is the devil's gimmick to take from the foolish minded to oppress them and for being foolish to fall for his devilish gimmicks in the first place the devil will not intend for the person to be wise and be free from his oppression.

A devil is a slave and as a slave always wants to be a master to his man master ruler and if a man gives the devil, a chance the devil will rule him mercilessly.

A devil is a slave because he is a transgressor of the law and as a transgressor extremely hateful.

A hateful being as a transgressor of the law is always a loud speaker of the law and a transgressor that is established in the advocacy school of thought of the devil will always advocate in the mind to stir up hatred against the speaker of the truth.

TO LOVE IS TO HAVE WISDOM OF LIFE

The intention of the devilish man is to silence the truth because the devil is a liar and, as a liar does not want any man to hear the truth or be truthful in their ways.

The truth is wisdom of life and the highest in all knowledge and wisdom is love.

Only in life will you have divine wisdom and knowledge secrets of life. Life is all about dominion authority and only those that are in me established in my eternal life presence will have my permission to operate in life dominion power and authority.

If a man does not have dominion authority and power then he is a meat to the devil for the devil is a flesh eater and for ample supply, the devil is never interested in peace making or peacekeeping. For if, there is peace then the devil cannot feed.

The devil is a cunning spirit and the cunning ways of the devil is to deny man the truth for he knows that only the truth shall set a man free.

The devil always con man to desire lies and from having desires for lies the devil always leads a man to seek to silence the truthful voice that another man speaks.

Those that attempt to silence the truth are fools for they will only do their soul the total harm of remaining forever silenced in condemnation of death.

For just as man cannot cover the sun so it is that no man can cover the truth and to try to cover the truth is to stay buried in darkness for the truth is light and no man can see in the world without my shinning light.

The devil in man deceives man to be in mind to judge others to the detriment of their souls. For if, you preach the law to judge others then know that you will face severe judgment under the same law and by the standard of judgment you propagate for others is by the same standard that I will judge you.

Any man can preach the law but not all that preaches the law do so from the heart of love. All man is enthusiastic to preach the law as the judge but always wish to avoid the penalties from the law for their own wrongful doings.

This is evidence of the foolishness of man for if you transgress against the law then know that you will be by the law held accountable and unless I afford you mercy, you cannot expect to avoid punishment. If you are merciless then it is stupidity to expect mercy from me for I am only merciful to the merciful.

If you judge another by a standard then know that you are automatically judging yourself by the same standard.

If you are merciless then you cannot expect me as the highest judge to show you mercy. If you do not forgive, you should not expect forgiveness from a higher judge.

The foolishness of a man in focusing on judging another instead of himself, is centered round the false conviction he has in his mind that no one will see him as unholy and ungodly if he advocates the law as a judge of the law.

A person in wrong convictions is a person deceived to perish in wickedness mind of his wrongful convictions.

Such man in darkness veil cover of evil shall be deceived by evil to see himself as the judge to judge others when all he is in actual sense is a condemned convict that is deceived by a spiritual convict to remain convicted in death everlasting.

Everyman is guilty of sin and as the accused and lawfully guilty; no man can say they are holy through their own independent fulfilment of the law.

Every man is a sinner and when the accuse sit to judge another it will always be in mind of his corrupt soul to the further detriment of his soul.

No man is free from condemnation of sin except through forgiveness of love and to go against the wishes of love is to deny your soul the justification afforded by love to the soul by my graceful forgiving heart for goodness purpose of life as love.

Only in love will you have ability to love and in loving ability will you enable others.

To hate is to seek to cripple those that you hate from making any kind of goodness progressive moves.

To love is to focus your mind on the goodness of others and you cannot say you focus on the goodness of anyone when all you are interested in is to entrap that person to be food for the devil.

A hateful person is the devil's hook and as the devil's hook the devil's robotic killing machine that is controlled by the devil to remain in his own eternal condemnation.

Love is everything you have said and more and it is true also to say that to know love is to be faithful to love.

Sometimes love appears as hate and hate appears as love and to be spiritually smart is to be able to tell the difference between love and hate.

If you think hate is love then you will pursue hatred to end of condemnation and if you see love as hate, you will seek to be far away from love even though your desire is to be with love to be by love loved.

To remain faithful to love you must understand the ways of love.

If a man sees the ways of love as hate then hate will deceive such a man to hate true love and a person that hates love will loose everything that is good.

If you do not understand love then you will think love is hateful and hatefulness is loving kindness.

I have a question for you and it is, do you see from your experience so far how easy it is for a man to misunderstand love for hate and hate for love.

ME: Yes. There is this saying that God's ways is not our ways.

One of the things I struggled to understand in my relationship with you as I said before is in having to go through things that I consider unnecessary and painful hurtfulness.

More also, as I said before, the fact that instead of you simply ending the hurtful run you seem to encourage me to persevere in my going through it.

As a human being, I sometimes struggle to understand how God as all power and with his obvious love for me will allow me to go through so much stress when he can simply put a stop to it.

It is as if I am being slapped by one hand and comforted by the other but although the comfort is nice it would be nicer if the slapping stop altogether so that I can enjoy the comfort that I have in you in another higher dimension.

For me this is the area that most human must have trouble in understanding because if we say our God has every power and he loves us so much why is it that he allows those that he loves to go through so much suffering.

When I speak of God's love for me to others, it is always in relation to the comfort that he gives me in my trials and tribulations.

If I am more tried when I found God then the question remains still what manner of love does God have for me to allow me to go through all of this trials after I have found him.

If like I said before I cried on to you out of desperation and you answered my call out of your loving hearts then I am not expecting anything but solutions for the things that I cried on to you for.

I understand all that you have said before but for most human beings like I said it is difficult to see your love in pain and suffering particularly if we say as God you have all power to do all things and those that you love most appears to suffer most.

I think most human will struggle as I struggle to understand this things or perhaps I am just on my own on this.

I quite understand the whole essence of tough love but is it necessary to be tough still on a child that you love if that child has succumbed to your ways.

The way things appear is as if you are merciless to the faithful and lenient towards the unfaithful. I know this is not the truth but that is how it looks and this is why I think it is difficult for most people to stay faithful.

As humans, we are very weak and it does not take much before a man reaches a point that they just cannot keep going most especially if instead of things looking brighter it is as if everything is working against a person.

If I say, I love my child I will not allow that child to go through unnecessary pain after he has surrendered to me and appeared to have learned his or her lesson. I know for sure that your love for me as your child is higher than anything that I can imagine.

No matter the amount of love, I have in my heart I know it is non-comparing to yours because everything I know about loving and kindness I learnt from you.

However, as a human being with so much daily interaction with you I still cannot help but feel frustrated sometimes.

If after all you have said and done I feel the way I feel I honestly can understand why people will easily give up on their faithful run because it is hard for a human being to keep going when it is as if everything is falling apart around you.

To stay calm in the middle of a storm especially when that storm is blowing you all over the place is not possible. I hear you say you have a question.

GOD: Talking about storm so what do you say to the story of the calming of the storm that the gospel of Matthew 8 from verse 24 for instance gives the account?

ME: For me that story simply says that Jesus is God and the rest of us are human beings because as far as I am concerned what the disciples did is exactly what I would have done if I were to be in their shoes.

To stay calm in the mist of a storm is not the way of a human well not from my own experience anyway.

I find that as human beings it is easy to advice than to follow your own advice and from my experiences all I can say is that it is easy to say to someone stay calm in your situations than to stay calm yourself if faced with what they are faced with.

The only one that is calm always has to be you because you see all things and know all things and because you do not share in our panic, it is always as if you are sleeping.

When you try to calm us down by comforting us, it is as if you do not care about what we are going through.

Except you calm, the storm instead of comforting us to calm down in the midst of the storm it is difficult to remain in the same high conviction in our going through the heaviness of the storm that you care for us still.

To have the power to calm a storm and allow the storm to rage on whilst you watch me go through panic is beyond the understanding of most humans.

If I believe, you can simply save me all the trouble by preventing the storm or still the storm sooner enough for me to avoid greater panic it would be difficult for me to understand the manner of your love for me for allowing me to go through what I consider as unnecessary suffering. I hear you have a say.

GOD: Yes. My say is another question.

Why panic in the first place. If you are truly convinced that I am all power and as all power I love you with all my heart and because I love you I do not wish that you suffer any kind of harm what is the essence of your panic.

If you believe I love you then you must know that I have my hands around you at all times to shield you from every danger.

Therefore if you were truly convinced that no matter what the case might be you remain standing in fullness of my glory and not fall for you have my grace fully what would you say the rationale is behind your panics.

ME: Yes, it is true that if this conviction is there one will not panic. I hear you have another say.

GOD: So do you say the panic is due to lack of total conviction of my love

ME: No. I do not know about the story of others so for me I say the panic is like a human reaction that I am unable to help even though I know that you love me.

Indeed, for me it is because I am convinced that you love me that makes it even more difficult for me to understand why you allow me to go through what I see as unnecessary pain for me to go through.

If I believe you hate me then I will expect no relief from you but if I say you love me then I expect a form of relief that is meaningful to my entire human being existence.

If I undergo any form of suffering and I am comforted by you to persevere in my suffering then does it not mean that by you encouraging me to persevere is in itself evidence that you acknowledge that I am suffering.

If you love me, as I know you do why allow me to suffer at all in the first place especially given that I have surrendered all to you. This for me is the question and although I take on board all that you have said it is in my human mind easier said than done to keep smiling when you are being punched none stop.

GOD: If you are in the boat with me, and you know I love you and as one that love you I have, power over everything my question to you still is what is the essence of your panic?

ME: The only answer I can think of is that I am a human being and I cannot help but panic especially given that all it seems you are doing is sleeping.

Perhaps if it does not appear to me that you are sleeping, I may panic less but if despite all my shouting and screaming it is as if you do not hear me then as a human being, I will panic the more.

GOD: If you see me as resting, is that not an indication to you that I have everything under control and as such, there is no need for you to panic?

ME: You are sleeping because you know everything and my panic is because I do not know all that you know.

GOD: If you focus on the master instead of the storm then will you not see all that the master sees in the eyes lenses of the master and if you see as the master sees will you not relax as the master and not panic.

The master sees all that you see and as the master in all dominion dimensional realms is he not in full control of every situation and as such restful even though he may appear to you as sleeping.

As a follower of the master do you not know that the master never sleeps nor slumber and if the master appears as sleeping is that not an indication to you from the master that he has every situation in control and as such peaceful in his rest.

If the master that you are following is at rest no matter how heavy the storm, is it not to make things clear to you that you have no business worrying but simply rest just like him.

Therefore, if you trust the master for your safety as you say you do and believe he loves you as you say you do and have gotten his message that you are to rest and not panic because he as the master have everything under his control.

Why can you simply not rest in my restful assurances and trust in me that if I say you are going to a place with me on the other side you will get there in one piece with me and not perish on the way no matter how heavy the storm gets on the ways there.

ME: My panic is not because I do not believe you can take me to the other side in one piece. Instead, my panic is because for me as a human being it is difficult for me to relax in the midst of a heavy storm when the boat that I am to relax in is rocking from one side to the other with water gushing in everywhere.

For me the least I could do is to try to take the water out of the boat because if I simply relax and watch the water gush in then it is as if I am doing nothing to help myself whatsoever.

If I do not see myself as being able to still the storm and I do nothing to lessen the water in the boat and I see the master that can still the storm sleeping then it would reach a point when I would just jump out of the boat.

I will jump of the boat to take my chances with swimming when I start to see the boat that I am in to be near sinking because it is so full of water and all my entire efforts instead of reducing the water seems to bring in more water.

GOD: I must say you sure have a very good sense of humor.

Jumping out of the boat into the water to swim away from the master, how smart do you think that is?

Not very smart I would say because you do not know what is in the water. The water can be full of sharks and bloodthirsty deadly predators.

At least with the master you have every chance.

However once you swim away from the master, do you not see that to be equivalent to swimming from known safety to unknown danger?

ME: Yes. Nevertheless, if the master had wanted me safe at all cost then he will fish me out even if I am inside the fish.

GOD: But why tempt the only one that can deliver you out of temptations

ME: Okay I give it all up to you. This is what you always do to me and as usual, I say I surrender. The master is right it is wrong to panic when the master is in the boat.

GOD: Very good of you to see things finally from the master's perspective I must say.

Now the whole point of this is to make you understand that if I am with you then just as I always say to you all good and evil work for your goodness.

If you are on your way to fulfill a good mission and on the way to that mission a storm breaks out know that no matter how heavy the storm is if I am with you it cannot prevent you from reaching your missionary destination.

TO REMAIN WITH THE MASTER IS TO FACE AND WIN ALL CHALLENGES

A champion will always face challenges and the challenges faced by a champion are not to demote him from the champion's league of life but to affirm him to be in higher promotions there.

To reach the top of a mountain you must maneuver your way to the top and if half way there you say it is difficult to maneuver your way to the top you cannot find yourself standing on top of that mountain as one that has overcome that mountain.

The passage of a human being in the world is full of many mountains of trials and tribulations and this trials and tribulations is like a storm to prevent man from reaching his destination of victory.

If you are with me then nothing can stand between you and me and if in me, you have victory already then no point in panicking because of a storm.

My comforting you is to focus your mind on victory that you have and it is in no way acknowledgement by me that you are suffering as a spirit being.

You are a spirit being and if you suffer as flesh it is to walk in total victory in all dominion dimensional realms for if your flesh is tried to the justifications of your spirit then it is evidence that you are predestined to be established in total goodness reward of life by grace of my love.

All that you go through the master sees and the masters affords you his comfort to encourage you to move with him to the other side of the river where you will see in total eye vision that you have absolute victory all along.

If the master wishes that you perish then he will not be in the same boat with you for if the master is in the boat and the master has all power then know that the master's boat cannot capsize let alone you drowning.

The master is aware of the storm just as he is aware that you are in the boat with him in the midst of the storm and all the master seeks is that you rely on his own efforts and power not panic because you see your efforts as yielding no results.

The master sees all things before making it visible to you and he only allowed you to see the storm so that you can see through the eyes of the storm that the only real storm that no one is able to still is the master himself.

For when the master appear, he appears to blow all things that stand in your way apart to give you a free passageway all the way to the finish line.

The master is able to still every storm as all power but no one can stand in the way of the master for the master is above all powers.

For the master is all power the master is the only storm that no other can still and as such, the will of the master is by his power already done ahead of him making his will known to you.

If a man soldier is prepared to entrust his life in the hands of a human general who cannot see his ways. Then the question is, are you prepared to entrust yourself in the hands of the General of life that gave you life and sustained you in life for you to remain in line for reward of life everlasting. This is the question.

Faith is to believe, and to believe you are safe with me is to be full of my rest no matter what the case may be.

Yes, I understand perfectly all you have said and I know all about the common reaction of man. I also know as the king of kings that all of man is afraid of death and fear of death does not place a man to act in courage of life.

There is no fear in love for love is above all power and principalities and the power of love conquers all.

Love is faithfulness and to be faithful to love you must see that you have already conquered death and because you know you have conquered death you will not have fear of death in heart of love for you know there is no fear in love.

To be in heart of love is to walk in liberty and when anyone seeks to take any liberty that is not given to them by love, they will always find themselves in hot water.

Like I said before everything for a human in the mind of the flesh is hard but with love everything is possible for those that are in love are no longer in condemnation of death to perish in death eternally.

You are right my ways are not the ways of man and for man does not know my ways they always see my highest show of goodness as evil.

To stay faithful to love you must be totally convinced that I love you more and because I love you more I am more faithful to you.

If you are to think at any point that I do not care then you cannot be motivated to remain faithful to me.

If in your convictions you believe I love you no matter what and you understand my love for what it is then instead of panicking you will see every experience as a lesson point and every lesson learnt is growth in spiritual development and wisdom and this is a blessing.

A foolish child will seek to destroy himself but a wise child will always walk in his Father's footstep to protect the goodness name of his father. It is true to say there is no need to allow a child to go through unnecessary trials.

Love is wisdom of life as life and only love can say what is necessary and unnecessary in total visionary sights of all things.

As your God that sees all I will only allow you to go through anything to confirm, your victory to your mind not simply allow you to go through anything that is unnecessary for going through it sake.

It is not the way of love to do things without a learning purpose or life objective achievement aims.

For love is a teacher and as a teacher the one that rewards the diligent student that serves his masters objective purpose well.

All that love allows you to go through is to open further your eyes of understanding not to make you go through what you see as suffering for nothing sake.

Love often appear as hate and hate as love and if you misconstrue hate to be love and love as hate then you will not learn the lesson that you are meant to learn to grow as you are meant to grow and in growth promoted to operate in the level that you are meant to be operating from.

The only way to stay faithful from the beginning to the end is to understand the way of love for what it is for without such an understanding then you will not see the point of love in saying to you that he loves you.

THE STORY OF THE WISE SON

As God, I am a storyteller and to drive home my divine holy point I have a story for you and at the end of this story, I have some question for you to answer. The story goes like this:

There lives a king with great power and wealth.

This king is just in his ways and only wants a son that is just like him to rule with him in his kingdom.

Therefore, for this purpose he called all his sons and said to them that for them to learn the lesson of life he has decided to send them all out on a journey.

He gave them everything that they needed for this journey and said that although they are leaving as his son only the one that ends up just like him from going on this journey will he allow back into his palace kingdom.

As for the rest, he will disown them for no son can stay in his palace if they are unjust. So after bidding their father farewell they all left and they all followed one route until they reached a junction and at the junction the roads ahead was split into many parts and all except one looked beautifully paved.

All but one of the king's sons decided to follow the beautiful path and they all bid themselves farewell.

Many in their chosen path did not travel far before they found others that looked like them and they made them kings.

As kings, they were brutal and wicked and showed no mercy to anyone.

Many found all kinds of favors and did not favor others.

Others engaged in all kinds of ways that is wicked and evil and saw their evil and wicked ways as fun.

The one son that followed the not so attractive part did not walk far before he found some that appear like him and they arrested him.

Upon his arrest, they falsely accused him of treason tried and jailed him to serve a life sentence with hard labor by order of the king.

Although he did not come before the dominion king directly, the trial judge emphasized to him that the king approved his trial and sentence.

Whilst in prison he worked so hard to serve his prison time.

He helped his fellow prisoner in all manner of good ways and prayed daily for the safety of his other brothers for them to end up just like his father so that their father allows them back in his kingdom to be an heir to the throne.

He was very selfless in his prayers, loving kind and helpful in his ways to everyone.

After many years of serving his time in prison, the warden one day sent him a message for him to report to his office.

He was on his way to the field when he got this message and he quickly dropped everything and made his way to the warden's office.

Upon reaching the office, the warden sat him down and told him that the king has decided to set him free because upon detailed investigations the king found that he was wrongly accused and as such, the king is setting him free with immediate effect. Instead of jumping up in joy this son became very angry.

He looked at the warden in disbelief and said, "That is all, I am free to go. After all this years of suffering for nothing all you can tell me is I am free to go. No apology no compensation no nothing just you are free to go. How about the years I have wasted from being in prison. Did you by any chance know that my father is a king and he sent all of us as his son on a journey to learn the lesson of life to be just like him? What manner of king sentences a person without first investigating that they are guilty as charged? I cannot believe I have wasted all this years for nothing when I could be learning some serious lesson to be just like my father. I bet all my brothers are back home hoping for my safe return and wait till I tell my father about this and see what he will do to your king and by the way who is your king?"

The warden looked at him and said, "Does it matter who he is. He is setting you free does that not mean anything to you".

The son got even angrier and said "Of course not. I have suffered punishment for something I did not do and now I am set free after wasting all of my time suffering for what I did not do and you think I should be grateful. Why should I? The least your king could do is apologize to me for his unfair treatment and my father will never do any such thing that your king has done and neither would I. I have heard a lot about your king and have never met your king and to order that I am punished this way when he does not even know me is terrible and even to the very end he wouldn't even show his face to me. The least your king could do is at least show his face so that I can see the one that has done me this great injustice".

The warden asked him to calm down and told him to sit and wait whilst he sends a message to the king to see if he would grant him and audience.

Not long after the warden went inside to send this message he returned to tell him that the king has agreed to meet him and that the king messenger is waiting in a carriage outside to take him to the king.

He made his way to the carriage and to his amazement the carriage does not appear to have moved at all before he was told by the driver that they have reached their destination and when he looked the palace looked just like his father's palace.

As he was still standing their wondering he found himself right before his father sitting were he was before embarking on his journey still in his beautiful long robes and it was as if he never left the palace in the first place.

He looked at the father, the father looked at him, and the father said you are a true son of mine and as a true son of mine even though it is as if you have gone for you made the right decision to follow the right path I never left your side for a second.

The son looked at the father and said but father I was in prison for many years and I suffered so much and things were hard and why is it that you allowed me to go through all of that for nothing sake.

Then the father said "did you learn anything".

The son said "yes, I leant to be just always in my ways because I would not wish for anyone to go through what I went through".

The father said "is that all you learnt". The son said "yes".

The father said your real lesson is in the fact that because you are wise you are sitting here to your total consciousness right by my side which means because you are just like me wise in your decision making I have allowed you back in to be my heir to inherit my kingdom everlasting.

The son said, "How is it that I am wise like you".

The father said from choosing me you have my mind, my body, my heart and soul so even when it seems we were apart we were never separated from one another.

The son said but how did I choose you?

The father said you choose me in your chosen path because from going on your journey you cannot see your way back to me without me.

However because you are wise you choose the dirty and dusty road to find your way back to me because you knew as the wise that all that glitter is not gold.

The father said as for your question why did I allow you to go through what you went through my answer to you is I allowed you to go through all that you went through because I love you.

For the fact that I love you my desire is for you to be just like me to be heir to my throne everlastingly.

To be my heir everlastingly you must be just like me and you cannot be just like me unless you know justice and injustice and still be in mind of good justice for goodness sake of life. You insisted on justice because you believe you were just and for you are indeed the just as I have justified you to be out of my love for you, you will be my right hand son everlasting. The father said, "Son, you insisted on getting what you see as your entitlement, which is an audience with the king even though you see this king to have unjustly treated you. Why is that"? What answer do you think the son gave the father?

ME: It has to be for compensation for the sake of justice.

This is because even though he believes the king has wronged him by false accusations and for time spent in prison he must have considered it as greater wrong if he gets no compensation from the king for all that he has been through.

GOD: The question you need to ask to answer this question is why is it that the son became angry when the warden told him he is released and free to go but all the while in prison, he was loving and kind.

ME: Could it be because the son had no hope of becoming free hence he hopes to make good use of the time he has to give love and reach out to others around him.

But when suddenly he became free it became obvious to him what the entire purpose of his journey was that it is to learn and be just like the father so that he can be allowed back to the kingdom and if he sees his time in prison as wasted time then that explains his anger.

GOD: The anger of the son is all to do with the fact that he sees his entire missionary objective as achieved only upon his return to the kingdom.

The son did not hope to perish in his journey hence his wise choice from the very beginning for if he had no hope of ever returning to his father he would give up in his mind and if he gives up, he cannot be motivated to act in any manner of loving kindness whilst he was in prison.

If the son ends up not able to return to the kingdom then he cannot say he has fulfilled his objective. The anger of this son is because he sees his time in jail as wasted time that does not count towards his lesson of life that will certify him as just like the father.

A wise son is always in mind of accountability and a son that is in mind of accountability will always walk in heart of responsibility.

The father did not specify how the lesson of life will be learned but he said unless they are like him they will not be allowed back.

What it means is that if the son is just like the father then the father cannot deny him access back in even if all others try to deny him but if the son is not just like the father then the son cannot have access to return no matter how he insist that they let him back in.

My other question to you is how is the father's way in this story a way of love bearing in mind all I have said so far about love.

ME: I would say the father as the wise and the wealthiest clearly wants his son to inherit the riches of his kingdom.

However, the father has such a high standard and by wanting, the children to be just like him he says he loves everyone like a son and as such does not want any of his sons to be unjust to anyone so that the goodness of his kingdom is obvious and by all enjoyed.

Love is wisdom and only in wisdom shall the son be able to do what the father wants him to do and avoid what the father wants him to avoid and by so doing always have the blessings of the father.

I would also say the father as the wisest is love and as love also the richest and as the owner of the wealthiest empire the father obviously does not want foolish children out of greedy mind to wreck all that he has labor to build.

The father as love knows what is right for it is right and it must be because he knows what is right for it is right that he always get the outcome that he wants given that he is the most powerful and richest for he is the wisest.

Since love is wisdom, to love is to be wise in our choices of decision-making and it is in such wisdom of love that the son that made it back to the father chose the right path. All the other sons choose in foolishness.

The one that choose in wisdom of love they must have thought is the foolish and they the wise ones.

If love is wisdom and we choose in wisdom of love then we must always know that if we follow the way of love we would always arrive at the doorstep of love to have all the rewards promised that out hearts desire to have.

GOD: Very good. You see how your mind reasons now; it is all because it is operating in the corporate establishment of love for only in mind of love can you see the point of love.

If you operate in the wisdom of love, you remain in the domain of love to profit everlasting whatsoever the case may be.

The father wanted the son to learn two main lessons.

The first is to choose in heart of wisdom always and to choose in heart of wisdom is to know that not all that glitters is gold and just because a road is dusty and dirty it does not mean that it would not lead you to a pot of gold.

The second lesson the father wanted the son to lean is to persevere in patience and in goodness heart of love for to persevere in patience is to maintain good hope of life rewards and in goodness hope only shall you be faithful in your stance towards the objectives of life.

If you run out of patience it is because you cannot see any hope either for yourself or for another for as long as you hope in goodness reward even if it is for another for goodness sake you will always have the mind to persevere in hopefulness heart of love for goodness sake of life.

The father recognized the son has leant the first lesson by his wise choice of choosing what appears unattractive in hope to have every attractive reward promised by his father. The father being the wisest knows when you have leant a lesson and cannot be deceived to believe that you have learned a lesson that you have not learnt because the fathers knows everything and sees everything.

The road to love is dusty and unattractive and once you choose the road of wisdom you become in established heart of love due for continuous life promotions in corporate land of love.

- 333 -

You attain and enjoy your promotions through remaining in total conscious mind and understanding of loving ways and it is only by so doing that the rewards of love remains in your hands everlasting.

The return of the son to the father was not at the point when he saw himself sitting beside the father but at the point of choosing the dirty unattractive road.

This means that the entire suffering that the son believed himself to have suffered after his wise choice was not to his main being.

From the moment he chose the dusty road he was immediately reconciled with his father enjoying the comfort and rest of his father in his father's presence. It is because the son was with the father that he had the mind of love to give love for given his experiences amongst the sons he has greater reasons to be resentful and bitter because out of all the sons he was the only one that suffered what you might regard as greater injustice.

However, for his heart is in love he was the most loving and kind just like the father.

This is because for choosing wisely all that is good became automatically his rewards and it was only a matter of time before he sees that this is the case.

The other sons that choose foolishly became disengaged from the father and if you are disengaged from the father, you cannot be in relationship with the father to understand the ways of the father let alone be like the father to return to him.

The father is the most powerful and wealthy because he is as you said the wisest and if you are to be just like the father, you have to choose as the father would have chosen to get the reward of the father.

To choose a dusty and unattractive road is to choose in mind of good faith not of vanity for the road of vanity appears as if it is paved with gold when in actual sense, it is the road that leads to the pit.

If you choose in mind of love, you will always walk in total confidence of love to have eternal goodness life rewards forever.

The road to eternal life rewards appears dusty and dirty but it is in fact paved with gold, will lead you to the City of gold for you to enjoy the goodness of City of lights build and paved with gold everlasting.

To choose in mind of love is for love to assist you to receive the promissory reward of love. A person that chooses in mind of love will succeed in all that they do but a foolish person will always trade to loose.

The father also noted that the son has learnt the second aspect of the lesson of life from his experiences for despite all that he went through he was to the end faithful to the just ways of love for goodness sake of life.

The son had the mind to be just still in his ways despite the fact that he believes in his entire experiences that he has been made to suffer great injustice.

In his just mind, he was determined to confront a king that he believes to be unjust to have justice and you cannot demand justice unless you believed you have suffered injustice.

The experiences of the son made him to be in mind of goodness justice and to seek to give justice always you must know the pain of injustice.

 If you live in the palace all your life you cannot see those that you see as a peasant as nothing more than a pest and if you see the poor as a pest then all you will be in mind of is to control them as a pest not enable them to be free from their poverty trap.

A wicked being has no conscience and a person with no conscience is always in mind to control those that he sees as disable to disable them further to prevent them from enablement so that they will not enjoy the goodness comfort of life.

To be a merciful and just king you must labor in righteousness even though you are a king in righteousness.

Only when you labor in righteousness will you always be in mind to deliver freely what is good for you see it as good to do so.

The son insisted to see the king because he is confident that the king must have a conscience to at least set him free albeit the fact that it is some years late.

The son as the wise also know that for the king has a conscience he will be able to get some compensation if he can have his audience before the king, this is why the son insists on seeing the king, and this is still wisdom.

The son did not insist to have an audience before the king for the king to apologize to him but for the king to compensate him for the time he spent in jail.

The son as you can see for he is wise got everything he wanted from the father because the father as the wisest sees the son as the wise just like him from the beginning to the end. I see you have a say.

ME: Yes. Are you saying God that the son knew that the king was his father hence he insisted to meet him.

GOD: The son knew his father has sent him to learn the lesson of life and from being his father's son, he knows that he must account for any time spent if he were to be allowed to see his father again.

If the king sets him free without any form of compensation then it would be as if he had wasted his time and the son by insisting the king gives him an audience was in mind of accountability towards his father.

The king ordered his prison sentence which means the king is accountable for the time he spent in jail and if the king admits he has made a mistake then it is only just for him to be compensated by the king on account of his mistaken judgment.

Note that the son said neither him nor his father would wrongly judge a person.

Therefore, if there is a mistake from anyone the son believes there must be a redress if not from the one that made the mistake from his father that never makes any mistakes and if there is to be redress there must be evidence of wrongdoing.

What this is saying to you is that what matters most is to know your father because unless you know your father you cannot seek to be like him.

The son believes his father will never make the mistake of wrongful judgment and that he will always do what he says he will do.

The king that the son insists on meeting is not one that he considers his father because although he has never met this king, in his eyes this king must hate him for allowing him to have gone through all that he went through.

However, when the son finally met the king and realized that the king all along is his father he knew that everything he went through for he knows his father well has to be for his own goodness and not out of any kind of hatred in the heart of his father.

Otherwise, he would not be sitting at the right hand of the father as the heir to the throne. To be in mission of love is to find yourself in a position that seems you are facing trials and daily judgment from a wicked king to fulfill the objective of a good king.

Know however that all power belong to me and because all power belongs to me, I will always make everything to work together for your goodness and recompense you for all your goodness efforts in your heart of love.

All man in flesh is on trial and if a man faces trials as a dead spirit then the condemnation of his failures is to his spirit to remain in death and in death in sorrow of death.

A person that is justified in their spirit and in spiritual justifications in heart of love have my guaranteed pass marks and for he is guaranteed to pass free from all condemnation.

As such even though such a person faces trials as flesh, it is to their own spiritual promotions.

This is because once you are awake you are in me and once you are in me you are no longer in the flesh of the flesh but my own flesh and blood and as my flesh and blood you are established in my rest to have the total benefit of life everlasting.

Your trials as I said for you are in awakenings of life are to your flesh and if the flesh is tried, know that it is for the glory of the spirit.

If the flesh does not suffer crucifixion, then the spirit cannot enjoy glorifications. To walk in the glory of life you must abandon every way that leads to the vainglory of the flesh.

When you find the truth evil by his ways will try to discourage you to abandon the truth that you have found and if you abandon the truth because you are discouraged to abandon it then you cannot insist on compensation for you have not persevered to the very end.

Yes, it is hard to see my love for you when it is seems you are in a prison camp of hard labor.

However, if you understand that you are all along sitting at my right side in beautiful glorious robe of life for you are of life then it would matter not that it looks as if you are in prison because you know you are not.

Nothing is hard for love for with love all things are possible and if you are in the heart of love know that you are not in any kind of pain and suffering.

The other sons believed they were enjoying even though they were suffering and because they believe they are in enjoyment of life they will not have any mind to ask for any kind of compensation.

You can only ask to be recompense when you think someone has wronged you and you ask for compensation to place you in the position you would have been if the wrong has not occurred.

If you believe, you have had your reward you cannot insist on rewards but if you believe a reward is due to you, you will seek to receive it.

Anyone that follows the way of goodness will always have total reward of life and to follow the way through to the end you must understand the way of love that what is of high love always appear in the world of flesh as hate.

Promotion appears as demotions and backwardness appears as forwardness.

If therefore a person does not understand what is of light as light such a person will pursue what is of darkness and see it as light.

No man can see in the darkness of the flesh and as such, the only choice that I required you to make is to choose me as the way to eternal life.

For by choosing me and holding on to my ways, you stay guaranteed to reach your reward destination no matter how high the barriers may be that is in the way.

Love conquers all, and with love, all things are, possible.

This is why it is wisdom of life to choose love and whosoever chooses love will wear the crown of glory everlasting.

Therefore, I say again, persevere in all that you go through for it is only a matter of time before you see that you are free in all dimensional dominion realms.

If you are free and freedom in total liberations as a spirit being, then anything that appears as imprisonment is only false imprisonment appearing as real.

Life is all about learning and the best way to learn is through practical experience.

The question to ask yourself always is do you see the point of love in all that you go through or do you think you are needlessly been tried.

What would you say to this question bearing in mind your experiences to date?

ME: I see your point and it has reached the stage that in all I go through I am always looking for that lesson key point to hold on to and move on.

I understand the saying that a son that the father loves is the one that he chastises, but even though you know that the father loves you, you still cannot help but cry when he is chastising you. This is because one way or the other the chastisement hurts.

It is not as if I do not understand what you have been saying and I know you know I do for you can read my mind.

My point, which I am sure you know, is just to highlight that looking at things from ordinary human perspectives this things are somehow difficult to understand. I see the point in all that you have said and I love listening to your stories because they are always full of hidden lessons to open further my eyes of understanding.

Therefore, once again, for all you have done that, I see and for all you have done that, I am yet to see in the ordinary but you have made me to see through your extraordinary eyes I say thank you.

GOD: You are welcome says the Almighty that has all power of good and evil that forgives all sins out of his loving heart. On that good note, once again we shall end our lesson here today to continue another day after those fingers have enjoyed a good rest.

ME: Thank you

GOD: You are welcome again.

CHAPTER 5

THE LIGHT IS SHINNING STILL AND IT IS GAME OVER FOR THE HATEFUL BEAST

Revelations 5 verses 11; "And I beheld, and I heard the voice of many angels round about the throne and the beast and elders: and number of them was ten thousand times ten thousand and thousands of thousands". Verse 12 "Saying with a loud voice, Worthy is the Lamb that was slain to receive power, and riches, and wisdom, and strength, and honor, and glory and blessing". Verse 13 "And every creature which is in heaven, and on the earth, and under the earth, and such as are in the sea, and all the that are in them heard I saying, Blessing and honor, and glory and power, be unto him that sitteth upon the throne, and unto the Lamb for ever and ever.".

GOD: This is our final chapter for this part and before I proceed with my revelations I see you have a question to ask.

Before you ask, I just want you to know fist that I have been waiting for you all along to reveal your purpose to you just as I am waiting now for all those that are willing to discover their life purpose. Let all those that desire life come and become whole in me everlasting.

It is my desire that you find me and my reason for having this desire is to impact my knowledge unto you and unto all of man for goodness sake.

So now you may ask any question and I promise I will give you the answer that is of whole truth and nothing but the truth so help me, me.

ME: (laugh). Since I am laughing may I ask first although this is not my question that I wanted to ask do you laugh?

GOD: I am joy and joy is all about laughter. So as joy I must have laughter and you laugh because you have joy is that not so?

ME: Yes. However, sometimes I cry even though I am joyful. So does that mean you cry also?

GOD: Open your bible to the book of gospel of St. John chapter 11: v35.

ME: It simply says, "Jesus wept"

GOD: That is your answer.

ME: Okay I think I get the general idea.
You are a lot more fun than I thought. I use to think that as God you are fearsome and always in the mind to punish people.

However, I have found that even though you are awesome you are so loving patient and kind.

GOD: That is very kind of you to say such good things about me. All I hear from mankind is blame, blame and more blame. You need to know me for who I am to praise and worship me for goodness sake for as I said who is able to say let there be and it is. I created all with my word you know and like a potter, I formed and designed the body out of the dust of the grounds as it is written in genesis chapter 2 and with my final touch of breath, man became a living soul. Is that not something?

ME: It is something indeed and thank you, I must say on behalf of the human race for all your beautiful creations.

GOD: You are welcome.

ME: (More laughter). I am so full of joy thanks again.

GOD: You are again welcome

ME: (More laughter as I try to speak) Why can't I stop laughing? You know if someone were to see me laughing hysterically like this they will think I am mad because they cannot see why I am laughing

GOD: I know. You see, it just goes to show that spiritual sanity to the carnal minded is insanity before his eyes for he knows not that what is there is there.

Here you are speaking to the God that many say does not exist.

If you hear what you hear and by hearing, what you hear you rejoice is it not evidence that you know what you know and see what you see.

Just because no one else sees what you see as you see it or hear what you hear as you hear it does that mean you will react in the way that the one that hear not what you hear or sees not what is there as it is there expects you to react. That is the question. The answer of course is no for you cannot hide joy just as a sad person cannot hide their sadness so your laughter is evidence of joy in your soul.

Not all those that laugh however is of joy for many although are laughing are crying on the inside and many although are crying are laughing.

Your soul is full of joy and I am that joy in your soul what is insane about that.

You are speaking to the king of kings you know. I say, that is sufficient good reason to be full of joy and in joy laughter don't you think.

ME: (More laughter) I cannot stop please I just need to say something

GOD: Okay I will let you speak and I listen

ME: (Giggle then laughter stops). Thank you. I must say that feels good.

As for my main question, just to continue from the statement you made in the last chapter, you said as the Almighty you have all the power of good and evil and it is out of love that you forgive us our sins. If all power of good and evil belongs to you how then do you condemn evil being the source of evil power.

GOD: That is a very good question. What does it mean to be a God? To be a God is to have balanced powers.

As the Most high God, you cannot just have the power of good or the power of evil. To be the Most High God as I am means you are the overall undisputed, non-disposable, non-defeated number 1 and always and forever will be the undisputed heavy weight champion of the universe. How are you with boxing?

ME: I think is barbaric for two people to enter into a ring with the desire to beat themselves or knock themselves out all for nothing

GOD: That is true. To be a heavy weight champion of the universe is not a world ring contest instead it is because there is no one that can stand to contest you.

As the creator of all things, I have all the data and secret of all that I created.

Many that believe there is a God also believes that there is an ongoing contest between God and the devil.

Judging from the state of the world some will argue that it looks as if the devil is winning. This is a devilish lie from the devil to the fool.

The good on deeds does not wrestle with evil instead good controls evil by authority and power.

Wrestling is for the flesh and a man in flesh and blood will wrestle with evil principalities to loose his soul in death eternally.

A man that wrestle with dead spirits for he has no power of life will become completely compress, depress, oppress, suppressed and totally pressed, and flat out to suffer in eternal death for only with power and authority of life is a man able to destroy the poisonous effect of the deadly evil snake.

There never was a contest between Lucifer and me.

The contest was between good and evil with Lucifer in the minority of evil and Michael the archangel representing the majority, which is goodness and I allowed this battle contest to affirm life precedence that good will always prevail over evil.

To be in the minority is to always end up in a minus and if you are in minus always from goodness, you can never have a win in any contest in any context.

Michael the archangel and the other good angels representing goodness of course won the battle because whosoever I am backing is the winner.

As the king of kings, I am the heavenly life promoter and you will find throughout the bible that just like Michael the archangel of goodness won against the evil angel Lucifer so also is it that throughout history of man whosoever I am behind even though looks like a featherweight automatically becomes a spiritual undisputed heavyweight.

To be a spiritual heavy weight is to be an ancient rock in me and as an ancient rock whosoever seek to lift you or scatter you will end up scattering themselves into pieces.

As a God that is everlastingly victorious, I am a promoter and what I promote is goodness so if you want my backing to be a winner you must seek to walk in goodness for goodness sake.

A person that seeks to promote himself in evil will only find himself in a barbaric world ring fight with the beast to fight from death to death never to have any kind of winning over death.

Instead of winning, the beast will knock him out completely by many heavy blows because the enemy contender knows exactly where to hit hardest.

For the enemy is a crook fighter he never seeks to play by the fair rules of goodness.

A human contender that seek to promote himself will end up throwing punches into thin air hitting nothing whilst his enemy will always be on target landing every punch on the head to cause total brain damage.

Once there is brain damage, the foolish human will be in a permanent spiritual vegetative state. In such state, the eyes will be darkened and will not see at all and in total blindness the enemy will throw the final knock out punch in the end and it would be all over at the blow of the final whistle.

As the promoter of life I can assure you, I am no ordinary Don.

I am the king of kings the Lion king and as a Lion king the supernatural total power of life that can enable any human featherweight to be a spiritual undisputed heavy weight champion.

When you are a spiritual heavyweight, you do not engage in barbaric lost battle instead you walk as a champion by my backing and support simply by submitting your will to my goodness will for goodness sake.

In me, you are more than a conqueror and as more than a conqueror, you do not throw any missing punches.

In me, your enemy becomes your punch bag and as your punch bag, the only purpose it shall serve in all the challenges you face is to help you build spiritual muscles.

Your spiritual muscles will help keep your spiritual body in shape.

As a spiritual heavyweight you always must be in shape for if you are out of shape then the enemy will challenge you to a duet when you are not in good form knowing that you are in no position to throw any heavy punches let alone win for you are weak.

You become out of shape when you cease to live a healthy spiritual lifestyle.

You lead a healthy spiritual lifestyle through constant engagement with things of life most especially through effective prayer and fasting.

You do not fast to loose weight instead; you fast to gain spiritual muscle weight as a spiritual heavy weight of life.

If a person does not engage in effective fasting and prayer, such person will become dry boned in their spirit and what power can a skeleton have against the hype and tensioned dead beast flesh.

This from me to you is my lesson on spiritual boxing of life. You always throw the winning punch when in me for no man in me is a looser.

All in the devil is a looser for the devil is a lair and as a looser forever for no one wins in any way for being evil on deeds.

Therefore, to think that the devil is winning in any contest is to be in wrong mind of reasoning.

VICTORY FOR MAN IS ONLY THROUGH THE LAMB

The Lamb is light and as light victorious everlastingly. With one power punch, the Lamb has knocked out the beast for man and the beast stays knocked out and down forever. All in the Lamb will ride on high in the winning glory of the Lamb in eternal life everlasting.

However; all that is in the beast will wrestle the beast to loose as the beast and as joint losers will remain flat out in the world ring fight with the beast till the end of days when the winners will pronounce the dead forever dead still.

A person that sees the devil as a winner is a looser for the devil can never win for the devil is an eternal looser never to have the benefit of victory. Victory is in life and all that is in life will win forever.

The state of the world is evidence that man as flesh is desperately evil and wicked.

To be desperately evil and wicked is to see evil as strength and goodness as weakness.

To be in such mind is to engage in a barbaric ring fight with the devil to fight to death in death with the devil with no means of escape from the ring and no chance of smelling victory in the barbaric ring of death.

As the Almighty, I am all power and I am not the Almighty just for the sake of it.

As the Almighty, you have to have all offensive, all defensive, all assault, all onslaughts, all enforcement and all protective power to be the Most Highest power in all dominion and dimensional realms.

Humans for they are subject to death are mortal beings and I as God I am never subject to death thus as the invisible and the immortal God I

AM THAT I AM the Father of all spirits.[5] As the one with all power, I use all of my powers to promote goodness for goodness sake of life as life itself.

All of my power of good and evil I use together for goodness sake because in all that I do my desired outcome from the onset and outset is always goodness even though it may sometimes appear as evil at the onset.

I know what evil is and I know that evil does not bring joy, rest or peace. My utmost desire is eternal joy, peace and rest for all of living souls.

Therefore, if my utmost desire is joy for all living souls all that I do must be in intention and in my motive desire of goodness outcome in totality for all living souls.

I know as I said all evil and all good.

Good brings light and joy to life and evil bring pain and sorrow.

Being the all power I place myself in checks and balances in use of my power because if I am not mindful always of goodness then all that I will be in mind of will be in evil use of my powers.

Evil mind of power use by man is always for self-gratification and if as God self-gratification is all I am after then I would in selfish evil always

---

[5] Exodus Chapter 3 verses 13-14

place man in condemnation of evil without any care or concern whatsoever.

Man does not have to praise or worship me for me to be in high elevation for as God I am as the highest always in the highest elevations. Man does not empower me from their praise and worship instead I empower them from being a worshiper of I the Most High God for serving their purpose of creation.

Mankind are worshipers and only as good worshipers will they be in good fellowship with me and in fellowship in me they become in heavenly fellowship with me in my Most High domain and it is only by being a fellow in my Most high dwelling place that mankind is in fulfillment of their total purpose in life. If no man worships me for I am all power I can raise stones to worship me after all I created man from the dust and gave them breath of life and if all I am after is, self-gratification then I need not do anything with the mind of goodness at all.

Evil is not just self-gratifying but also instills fear.

As God, I am real fear and the only one to fear is fear.

For to have fear of your maker is to be wise and those that are wise I will place in my presence and in my presence I will give them greater wisdom and knowledge of life for I am all wise and as all wise the teacher of righteousness.

The evil spiritual minded knows the impact of fear and an evil doer in wicked human nature use fear in evil deeds for oppression, suppression, compression, depression and ultimately to bring others into evil submission to dominate for evil sake.

The ultimate submission of hearts must always be to goodness for goodness sake and not unto evil for evil sake.

To submit to evil is to be in condemnation of evil and because what the spirit is really in true desire of is goodness, evil always has to force submission on the weak evil man by use of fear through oppression, suppression, compression and depressive means.

The desire of evil is to bring about submission by force and as Good on deeds; I am able to force anyone into submission unto goodness for goodness sake by use of my enforcement powers on the mind and through open visible demonstration of my powers.

However, as love I gave mankind free will to use in manner of consent to love not to be forced to love.

For goodness sake as I said I will enforce my will to force the unwilling to submit to the will of goodness for the sake of goodness purpose and outcome which is always my desired result in all things.

Free will of consent is central to love and those that humbles themselves before love are giants of life in eternal life

As love, I know that the sweetness of love is in consent in willingness to love for goodness sake.

If you by force make someone to love you then it takes the sweetness out of it for love is only sweet when out of free will you choose in the willingness of your heart to love.

A central aspect of love is willingness.

Even though a man is capable of hate as a certified good on deeds, such man for he is in the regimental heart of I the Greatest on deeds will always choose to love for goodness sake.

It is by your choosing to love when you can hate and have reasons to hate but love that makes you good on deeds.

You show that you are good on deeds through exercising your free will to love instead of hate even though you have reasons to hate and not love.

To be good on deeds is to be strong in humility for although you are champion in the Lion kink you must always be a sheep to the shepherd of life and it when you are a sheep that you are really a true spiritual lion in the Lion of Judah.

The voice of reason in the visible is soft and appears weak and only by wisdom shall a man know that not all that appear tall, fearsome and strong is not necessarily of real strength just as all that glitters is not gold.

A bat in the visible sees himself, as an eagle bird but the wise knows that a bat may appear like a bird but it is no bird let alone an eagle bird the king of birds.

To love is to be a spiritual giant and even though many may see you as weak and too soft for you are meek and gentle do not let that bother you for just because a person roars does not make them a lion in the Lion of Judah.

David killed Goliath as the story goes in 1 Samuel chapter 17 for although Goliath appears strong and mighty in the eyes of man David in me is the real spiritual giant.

To be a spiritual giant you must first take off the coat and amour of hateful rebellion and this is the coat of Saul.

To have the coat of Saul is to walk as the dead seeing yourself as a king even though you are the disinherited due to your heart and mind of rebellion.

To be in my inheritance will is to be like a David who although as a man was a sinner but as a spirit being after my heart in goodness for goodness sake is full of respect and admiration for me knowing that he is who he is because of who I AM the Almighty God.

The stonehearted man would say; what else do you expect from such a man?

You choose him to be king and as king, you made him the head not a tail even though he was the last and you forgive him his sins generously.

The fact is David knew that no man can be king except made to be king by the kingmaker and no man shall continue to be king unless he walks in total submission to the kingmaker in reality mind of repentance and total submission to the will of life always.

A man is either like a David or like a Saul. A David has my backing and a Saul does not for although a Saul may prophecy as written in 1 Samuel 10 verse 12 the question is, is Saul amongst the prophets.

For a Saul to be counted amongst the holy prophets he must change his name from Saul to Paul as you will find in the story of Paul previously known as Saul in the book Acts chapter 9.

The name change is not a literal carnal change that will only change your visible record of death to be still of the spiritual mark of death but rather a spiritual shift of gear that would change your record, mission and character from death to eternal life.

This can only happen when a man gives his will to life for love to rule his mind so that he benefit from the ruler of life for goodness sake in eternal life.

The scales of blindness shall never fall from the eyes of a man that is only willing to remain in death to carry out the works of flesh.

However, a man that repent shall find mercy from me and in mercy; I shall change him from being a broken and useless vessel to a useful and productive vessel guaranteed to have everlasting life achievements rewards and awards.

A man that is adamant to remain in sin shall remain spiritually blind and in blindness shall walk in condemnation of death.

To be accredited life achievements awards a man must walk in mission of life to be in eternal life awards and rewards and this requires a heart that is committed to divine holiness love for the goodness sake of life.

A man that is bent on sin is a crook and his crooked mind shall not be made straight in his wicked commitment to sin and all those that are committed to sin are in destination destiny end of death to remain dead forever.

A man shall only change his course of destiny from eternal death to eternal life through repentance but a man that is of sin in sin shall not find the gift of life and shall be in the destiny reward of sin, which is eternal death.

David as a man was a sinner but in heart and mind of repentance found my forgiveness. By grace of my love and forgiveness from my grace of loving kindness, I established him eternally in covenant relationship with me to have everlasting profits and gain from my inheritance will of life for the living, which is eternal life of peace, joy and rest in my presence.

The coat and amour of rebellion is shackles and strong heavy steel tied to the spiritual feet. This weighs and slows the spirit down from engaging in real life spiritual freedom walk and if you are to conquer, fear to walk in spiritual freedom you must face fear head on and must be swift and smart in doing so.

DEATH IS THE LAST ENEMY OF MAN AND TO CONQUER DEATH YOU MUST HAVE COURAGE OF LIFE

Only by power of I the Lamb is a man able to walk in total victory of death for no man can face death without the power of resurrection of life and resurrect to live. You cannot face death without courage of life for to conquer death you must have courage to walk in honor of life.

You cannot conquer death in fear of death for if you are afraid of death then death will continue to scare you to rule you.

However, you do not show courage of life by suicide killing or suicide related death for by killing yourself for any reason you show that, that which you are is a slave of the devil.

There is no honor in killing yourself for death out of hatred of mind for death is a deceitful flesh eater with no honor of any kind whatsoever.

Suicide death is evidence of hatred frustrations in the soul and no wise man will make the mistake of loosing his soul to death for a wise man will reject hatred frustrations in his heart so that he can see in manner of goodness glory.

No man that kills himself in frustration of hatred shall find his way to my domain of peace for as God, I am a God of peace and vengeance is mine.

If you choose to take matters into your own hands, you say you have no respect for my peaceful ways.

Death wish in the soul is hard and conclusive evidence that the soul is in total disgraceful walk of death. As such, whosoever carries the death wish mark of death let them know that they are in disgraceful walk of death and shall only walk in honor of life if they change their ways to walk in honorary holy mark of life.

Who amongst man seek to live in the same house with a decomposed dead body?

Do you not dispose of the dead body and if the vain honor that you seek is of death, do you not say you are the disposed and as the disposed the reject.

If a man seek to have honor in death he by so doing demonstrate that he is already dead and as the dead a demonic possessed spirit willed and twisted by devils to promote the ways of the flesh to lead many to continue in hateful ways to remain in condemnation walk.

Many in the world are the dead mourning for the dead not knowing that their own soul is in deep spiritual mourning for fear of eternal death.

The soul of man is in mourning but man by his desperate wicked mind of sin seek to compress his soul further into mourning by his willful and desperate desires to sin.

The living shall seek to walk in the honor of life and you only shall walk in honor of life in heart of divine loving kindness and in such loving heart of kindness, you forgive those that offend you and pray for those that curse you.

That way only, shall you be spiritually uplifted and honored in time and in eternal life.

A man of real honor and courage even though other men may have treated him as the disgraced in one generation era he shall be highly esteemed in the next for he has real honor.

A man however, that is the disgraced shall walk in disgrace in all era both of time and in timelessness.

Such man shall seek to cover his disgrace through attempting to deceive others to confuse their mind not to see his real ways so that his lying secret remains secret but if lies goes on for a thousand years it can never be the truth.

All days is for the Ancient of days and it is one day that the Ancient of days shall reveal that he is the all glory in all totality.

A man at any given time will subject and submit his heart in his present mind existence unto those that he sees as his past heroes, adopted gods or by those that he considers as his godly agents.

If a man seeks to be in mind of revenge for what is passed down to him from a past that he is unsure of and fails to seek the truth in his present tense to see clearly what was, is and ever shall be then such man shall be taken for a fool.

As a fool the devil will drive such a man to crash into pieces for wisdom of life is to consider all things carefully before you make choice.

To know who you are you must trace you spiritual footsteps for if you simply accept hand downs, you walk still in genesis of sin.

To find love you must hate the hateful being that you have become and if all you behold is your own natural image in the mirror, you shall not behold my own existing glory of eternal life. If a man does not behold my glory, all he shall be in mind of is his own vainglory and in such mind of vainglory shall always seek to take his own revenge.

A man that beholds my glory will not seek to take revenge for himself or seek to take matters into his own hand by desiring to make those that he sees as his enemies to pay for what they do to him.

The enemy is within and when you do not see that the enemy is on the inside all that you engage in on the outside is a loosing battle that is of no honor whatsoever for what honor is there in engaging in a lost battle.

Honor is from winning and you win a spiritual battle only by grace of my love for no man in the visible is able to fight an invisible battle with visible weaponry and win.

The invisible holds the key advantage simply from being invisible.

To take advantage of one that has advantage over you, you must have a higher-level advantage in the realm of power and which advantage you have all depends on your connections.

If a spirit is in connection to dead spirits, such spirit cannot have advantage over the dead spirits that is in their spirits.

The advantage key that death holds is in the fact that as an enemy, he is in man and man in spiritual blindness seeks for his enemy on the outside.

This advantage key man will only take from death by commanding force of life through heart of repentance for in repentance and submission to life a man demonstrate that he wishes to separate from death and engage with life.

No man is able to trade to profit in death. To be in mind of sin is to remain in death for when you are in mind of sin you say by your willful heart of sin that you wish to trade only with death and in your trading be an enemy of life.

Trading in death places man in spiritual economic loss and in spiritual economic loss man is in mind of world trade to gain the world only to the eternal loss of his soul.

A man bent on sinning shall not as written in Revelations 13 be able to trade in goodness heart of life for a man bent on sinning shall give power to the beast to rule over him and shall make as his head the beast to oppress him in death.

Such man shall not walk in resurrection mind instead shall be in mind of death to remain in death for he shall see death as power not weakness.

Only the wise shall conquer death through resurrection from death and to resurrect from death you must first bind death for death shall not let you go just like that.

No man is able to bind death in death.

For although death is spiritual weakness, death as enemy of man is a very strong enemy for man to battle with and defeat. Man in sin is in slavery camp of death and in death slavery subjected in his spirit to the oppressive and depressive rule of evil dead.

 No man is able to free himself from a wicked master without the help of an overall merciful master with power above all powers and principalities in all dominion, dimensional realms.

Death as a master to man in sin has no mercy and no man can ever resurrect from death without my grace of love.

When a man hates my gospel of resurrection he demonstrate by his hatred that all that he is in death is a fool for the gospel is good news and as good news goodness soul food that the soul of man is hungry for to rise from death.

For all that a man shall hear in death is sad news of death and in such news shall always be in fear of his own dead end.

Only by my grace of love is man freed from death and this grace is afforded to man by my remission works on Calvary to free the soul of man from death by my binding death for man so that man walk in my grace not the disgrace of death.

The dead shall seek to walk in continuous disgrace of death yet shall see such disgrace as honor to promote death to deceive other men that death is an honorable choice.

If you choose to die in vain to honor your flesh that is already condemned to death forever you show that you have no understanding whatsoever what honor is.

The flesh is of death and as such smelly and decomposed body of sin. How then can you honor that which can be of no honor?

Honor is love, love is courage, and only in courage and power of love do you lay your life down for your enemy, for you know that they are weak and as the weak, they know not what they do. You know that by laying your life down in the natural for love sake and in love walk in spiritual honor of love, you shall gain total reward of life.

However, those that seek to gain self-pride through revenge in foolish mind of wicked self-righteous to proclaim false honor shall never find life.

Foolishness is to seek to take revenge for yourself for when you seek to take your own revenge you seek to walk in the disgrace of the flesh.

Grace is afforded to the spirit when a spirit submit to the will of life but a spirit that submits to the will of death shall fight to death to remain everlasting in death.

The battle is of the spirit and victory you have in the spirit when you use the right weapon. Carnal weapon makes a man shoot to miss in the spirit even though it may appear that he is on target in the visible.

The real battle is in the spirit and if every shot you take at your real enemy you miss whilst the enemy is always on target then you can never overcome the enemy.

To win you must shoot on target and to shoot on target you must have the key weapon that David used to kill Goliath and this key weapon is I Word the Alpha and the Omega the head of all as the all in all.

The key of David that I AM is I the Son the door to the Father in me for only the son of the Father shall the Father defend and protect from harm.

If you are not a son unto me then you are a slave unto death and you cannot be a salve of sin and be a king in righteousness.

To be a king in righteousness you must be a slave unto righteousness and as such dead to sin to be alive in your spirit.

Who is a king is a spiritual matter for even though Pharaoh was in his time regarded as a king he had no power, control and dominion of a king.

Even though man saw pharaoh as god that is strong and powerful Moses I certified as the good on deeds to prevail over Pharaoh as written in Exodus chapter 7 verses 1. With my certification of Moses as good on deeds over Pharaoh's the will of Pharaoh became subject to work for the advantage of Moses for Pharaoh as the evil on deeds is the dead and the ways of the dead is always to the advantage of the living.

The dead in hardness of mind helps the living to fulfill his mission.

This does not make the dead a friend of the living only that the dead is cursed never to profit no matter what the case may be albeit the fact that goodness is the outcome of his wickedness desire and aim.

This is because the dead does not wish for a goodness outcome and as such, the goodness outcome is the desire of goodness even though the deed in itself is still evil.

It is against divine justice to profit from an outcome that you have not intended for if evil is the intended outcome then the reward shall be evil even if the outcome turned out to be good for goodness sake.

Thus although the evil helps the living to fulfill their mission through the hardness of their heart to be evil the dead evil shall never profit from life for the reward of the wicked is to remain in everlasting wickedness of darkness evil.

NO MAN CAN BE GOOD ON DEEDS EXCEPT BY MY CERTIFICATIONS

As the creator of all I made all of man to be good on deeds. However, as the king of kings and God of gods, only I can certify a spirit to be a king or good on deeds and those that are not good on deeds are slaves. A self-declaration or self-certification certificate of a man of himself as a king or good on deeds is a criminal fraudulent act punishable still by death.

To say you are who you are not is to try to usurp power and anyone that attempts to usurp power is a rebel and just like the first and last rebel shall be subject to eternal condemnation. No one in hate is a king for to be a king is to have dominion authority power of life. Only in love shall man have dominion.

For in hate man cannot have dominion for hate is evil and I as the Greatest on deeds did not create the universe for the evil minded to have any control in any dominion dimensional realm for all evil is after is destruction. Even though it appears evil has control in the world it is all working together for good for all good and evil must always work for goodness sake.

Man in hate is a slave unto death ruled by death and in death; man is pro death and anti life and by so doing enslaved himself deeper in the hands of death.

If hate appears to have domination in any form, it is always to reveal the secret and the face of evil so that the cover and the veil of death on the face of man is lifted for man to see in the open eyes of spirit the shameful eyes of the wicked.

The day a man sees evil for what it is, is the day he buries evil and the day you see your enemy buried before your own eyes is the day you no longer shall walk in fear of such enemy.

So that man does not see evil for what it is; is the reason why the enemy tactic is all about internal affairs.

Through interfering with the affairs of the mind, the enemy of man from the inside leads the foolish man to believe weakness is strength and strength is weakness.

Through such interference, the enemy covers the eyes of man to see illusion and call it reality and reality illusion.

By so doing, man is fighting a lost battle with himself with the real enemy in control of his mind and in the enemy control; man is a robot programmed by the enemy to self-destructs himself.

The orientation of evil is always against the order of life but the will of life in all things must prevail hence the ways of evil is always subject to the will of good and goodness must always prevail.

The enemy knows that all that evil does is always going to work out for goodness and for he knows that he never shall profit in life he deceives man to remain in wicked heart of evil so that man like him trade always to loose.

Woe to the wicked for even though his evil shall always work out for the good of the elect the wicked shall carry the blame for his evil and wicked actions.

The elect shall walk in everlasting benefit of life from my inheritance will of life in their submission to my ways and as such the looser in all in all shall ever be the wicked not the good on deeds.

To be good is to never loose and if man is in mind of profitable gains he shows no spiritual economical sense by seeking to be wicked for no man profits from wickedness.

A real king is of love for who in their right mind seek for hate to rule over them.

In sin man seek for hate to rule over him and this is against his spiritual desire for no one is of peace, joy and rest in hate and the soul object is always to be of peace, joy and rest in eternity.

A man in the world is in darkness of spiritual truth and in such darkness must seek spiritual guidance from my Holy Spirit so that I make him to see things as they are in reality sense.

ME: Thank you. Things make a lot more sense with your explanations. I just have one more question for now if I may ask.

GOD: You may indeed ask.

ME: I now know that Christianity is not just a religion but life.

I also know for sure that only if we are in actual relationship with Christ and in Christ the Holy Spirit can we have life in our souls but for many years I thought I was a Christian and as far as I was concerned that was it.

I only found out when I became in awakenings in you that to be a Christian is to have a living relationship with you the Trinity one God the Father, the Son and the Holy Spirit.

I must say before all this revelations I had no idea what Christianity is really all about and even though I had called myself a Christian for many years I found out in mind of this revelations that I really was not a Christian as I thought in my mind that I was.

I mean words like principalities and powers never meant anything to me and today, many say they are born again Christians and some say they are Christians but not born again and I must say from my experience many in the world including Christians seem to have no idea what their belief is.

Even though for years I called myself a Christian, I must say I did not understand until your revelation the essence of my Christian beliefs.

Someone for instance once said to me that I needed to be born again and I was quite angry by their saying that I must be born again because it was like saying to me that they are perfect Christians and I am not.

I remember the one thing I said to the person was how can I be born again and can a person enter their mother's womb to be born again.

Most especially given that in my own case my natural mother is dead how then in the circumstances can it be possible to be born again if being born again literarily mean to be reborn.

I must also say I was amazed when I later found in the bible in your teaching to me that the exact thing that I said that Nicodemus said the same thing in gospel of John Chapter 3 in response to your saying to him that except a man be born again he cannot see the kingdom of God. What I mean to ask is can there be such thing as a Christian that is not born again given your statement in John 3 verse 3.

GOD: To see the kingdom of God as I said in John Chapter 3 verse 3; I repeat again you must be born again.

For as I said in the same gospel of John verse 5 "except a man be born of water and of the Spirit, he cannot enter into the kingdom of God".

Note that in John 3:3 I said except you are born again you cannot see the kingdom and in John 3 verse 5, I said you cannot enter.

The fact of the matter is if you cannot see it, you cannot follow the way of entrance. If because you cannot see it you fail to follow the way of entrance then such person although locked out but for they cannot see that they are locked out will think they are already inside and if you already think you are in when you are out then you cannot get in at all.

Many in the world today believe in their mind that they worship the God of Abraham, Isaac and Jacob and if you do not see me for who I am then you will be deceived to believe that I am who I am not.

I am a God of relationships and to be in relationship with me you must be my own flesh and blood. All of man died in sin of the first Adam and as God I am a God of the living not the dead.

To resurrect the soul of man back to life there must be shedding of blood and only my own pure blood is sufficient and good enough to redeem the soul of man from death back to life. If a man is to see me, he must be born again and this birth is a spiritual holy birth to place his soul back in goodness realm of life.

To be born again is to be in perfect covenant of life with me and to be in perfect covenant with me is to be free from all curses of death.

Many that say they are born again today are vain minded devils busy spreading vain messages of death.

They claim to be born again to lead man away from seeing or entering the kingdom by their vain messages.

For by their vain messages they promote a born again wrong image and as a result many see been born again as a cunning tool used by many to take from the needy to give to the greedy.

The food of the spirit is word and when the focus is on vanity instead of the word man in his struggles will be in state of hopelessness and in hopelessness will be in greater desperate mind of evil.

The church is a house of blessing and for man to be blessed from the church I gave the church many talents and gifts and the church is not the building or denomination that you attend but the spiritual man himself. Many denominations encourage demonisms for purpose of evil domination of the heart and soul of man through the back door evil demonism sold as denominations to place the soul of the foolish in eternal damnations walk.

I am one God even though I am the Father, the Son and the Holy Ghost and the corporate body of the Lamb is one in the Father as such, all in me must operate in my one mind, Spirit body and soul.

I Christ I am the head of the church and as the head of the church I am not impressed by vain ritualistic religious walk but by genuine heart of love.

No man in the devil has love to give for to give love you must have love in you and the devil is hate and as hate a hateful destroyer of souls as the destroyed before the foundations of the earth.

Just because a person goes to a born, again church does not mean that they are born again.

A person is born again when they walk willingly in their heart in the ways of my divine standard of love.

If a man willingly submits to my love then he avoids me forcing him to suffer the consequences of his actions for although man willingly chooses to do evil they are always unwilling to suffer the consequences.

The ways of man is full of hypocrisy and the main reason for their hypocrisy is to do evil in disguise that they are good to avoid judgment consequences not so much in their heart from me, but from their fellow human beings.

This is evidence of spiritual blindness and foolishness.

For like I said what a man sows he reaps and to think you will do evil and get away with it by fooling your fellow being is to be a confirmed foolish idiot for is unacceptable by my divine standards of supernatural justice for any man to reap goodness when they have sowed evil.

The will and standard of my Holy Spirit for man is to be genuinely good not hypocritically appear as good for if you are hypocritically looking good then you say you are really evil and not the good that you try to make others believe that you are.

I made my word flesh to afford man my Holy Spiritual guidance so that man in me remain in good heart of choices and by so doing avoid total perishing of his soul.

Every man must make a choice between good and evil out of his free will. It is to enable man to make this necessary spiritual choice of goodness and automatically avoiding evil consequences that I made my word as flesh for them to know and see that unless they are born again they cannot see my kingdom let alone enter it.

No man that is not born again can enter for a man that is not born again is dead and my kingdom domain is for living souls not dead spirits.

The place for dead spirit is hell for death is punishment to the soul of the wicked at heart and unless a man is born again and from spiritual birth engaged in holy covenant with me such man is in hell walking in the curse of the first Adam in danger of perishing in his soul forever.

As a God of relationships, I am a God of covenants. My covenants I only make by my own blood so if a man is not in blood covenant with me; he is in evil polluted covenant with the devil.

A man that is in evil covenant with the devil is only a dead man walking in the curse of death to perish in eternal death.

There is nothing like a Christian that is not born again. For the whole essence of shedding of my blood is to place the spirit of man in holiness of a new birth and through my own death as man afford the benefit of resurrection of life to the soul of man from placing them in my own resurrection as the resurrection of life.

The flesh must die for the spirit to rise for without the crucifixion of the flesh there can be no manifestation of the glory that awaits man eternally in the realm of the spirit.

When man crucified I the Son, it is for the purpose of resurrection of life to the soul of man so man by crucifixion serves a life purpose for this is the will of I the Father to crucify the flesh to resurrect the spirit. Man in foolishness gave his spirit to the devil to be just flesh and I Christ came to revere this order of evil by giving the flesh back to the flesh of evil to redeem the soul of man from wages of death.

For man to walk in the glory of I the risen Son such man must be dead to sin and walk in righteousness of I the Holy Spirit.

The righteousness of I the Holy Spirit is for man to obey my word and I Christ I am the word of the Father revealed to man and as the word revealed the only bridge and gateway to heavenly eternal rest in the presence of I the Father.

A man will only have the benefit of resurrection when he accepts me as his Lord and master for it is only by so doing that he rejects his flesh to death to rise in glory of life in me as the total power of life with power over all matters of life and death.

No one is good except I the Trinity one God. To be good just like me a man must choose me as goodness of life for me to certify him as good. Unless a man chooses me to obey, my entire word such a man will not have my good on deeds seal of approval.

To accept I the Son as Lord and master is to choose I the Father for as word I am in the son and the son is in me.

To Choose I the Son is to accept and fully obey my entire word standards of righteousness given to man as necessary to inherit my kingdom as sons, which is divine sacrificial love. Only a Son can inherit my kingdom.

I AM THE WAY, THE TRUTH AND THE LIFE AND THE FATHER AND THE SON IS ONE

The only way to be a son to the Father is through the Son for if you reject the Son you automatically reject I the Father given that I and the Son is the same for the Son revealed is my word and my word as I said is the same as me.

As the last Adam, a man in me is a son to me and as a son to me a son to the Father by my own adoption of him to be a son in me to have the total benefit of eternal life.

No man can have benefit of life in polluted mind of religion, to be a Christian is to be a living soul, and you are not a living soul just because you are in practice mind of vain religion.

Today end time so-called Christians are in total mind of darkness for to be a Christian is to be in the light and in the light a shinning light in the world.

If the world is in such thick darkness today despite the many that proclaimed they are Christians it is evident that although many say they are Christians they see not the kingdom and are not in kingdom mind for they are only in mind of vain religious rituals.

To be a Christian is to unite with me so that goodness of life is your soulful desire purpose. No man in death sees me, as the goodness of life for man in death is wroth at the mentioning of my name and this is due to the rotten will of his evil flesh to continue to walk in sin and in sin enslaved still to death.

The flesh is wroth by the truth for the flesh hates the truth and I the Son I am the way, the truth and the life.

You were angry when you were told that you needed to be born again because you were in the flesh walking in the flesh and to be in the flesh and walking in the flesh is to be hardened to the truth.

A person in the flesh will find the truth offensive.

A person that finds the truth offensive will be motivated by devils to be a defender of self-righteousness.

The devil will deceive such a man to hate the truth deeply to keep them far away from the goodness spiritual defense that they will acquire if they were to accept the truth.

For the devils lurked in the flesh he knows that a man in the flesh of the flesh is a spiritual captive and it is only by the acceptance of the truth will such a man be set free.

It is spiritual fact that a man must be born again to see the kingdom for if a man is not born again he cannot see the kingdom let alone enter.

The flesh hates this spiritual truth for to be born again is to accept me as your Lord and savior and those that accept me as Lord and savior will be born of water and spirit.

Those that are born of water and spirit only shall enter my eternal kingdom of life to have eternal life of peace, rest and joy.

If you say to a person in the flesh that they must be born again, they will always be offended just by the mentioning of the name of Jesus Christ for I am the truth and the flesh is always offended by the truth.

The devil that lurks in the flesh leads man to wroth at the mentioning of the name of Christ for the devil know the name of Christ is above all power and name.

The devil knows that to accept me as your Lord and savior is to walk in total glory of power of life in me as the master in all dominion dimensional universal realms.

Hence, a devils aim is to lead the mind of man to hate the name of Christ so that the man is without the defense of life and by that, the devil can continue to abuse the spirit of the man.

A man shall only walk in benefit of salvation when he obeys the commandment of love and this commandment is to love God with all your heart, soul, mind and spirit and love your neighbor according to your self.

No man can truly love me in the flesh. No man that walks in the flesh can love his neighbor and unless a man fulfils this divine lawful commandment, he cannot see or enter the kingdom of life to be of eternal life rewards.

This commandment is my divine order of life and no man is able to walk in divine order in hateful mind of the flesh for the flesh hates my good name and my goodness ways. Although man crucified I Christ, it is for my love to be obvious to man, as the everlasting power of all glory that I always AM.

Without the crucifixion of the flesh, then man will not see my love and my will power for them as the all power glory of life with all power over and above all matters of life and death. A man that walks in the ways of the flesh is dead to the reality of life and such man as the spiritually blind will walk in offensive minds of evil to carry out the works of the flesh.

As God I am a Spirit being and if a man is to know me such man must come to me as a spirit being and the only way a man can connect to me as a spirit is by being born again through my own blood, water and Spirit.

By my making way for the crucifixion of the flesh, I afforded man the benefit of my fertile virgin soil to be in goodness spiritual goodness productions of life in eternal life forever.

To say that a man is a Christian but not born again is to say that I Christ I am only of the flesh and as such not at all the divine power of love and as love eternal oracle of life that I AM and this is an abomination saying.

I am no ordinary flesh but, divine love. As the divine love, I am the flesh of righteous glory revealed and as the flesh of glory revealed, the only one through which man can see and enter the kingdom domain of life and dwell in it as the flesh and blood of I the Father everlasting.

If a man is born only of the flesh only then he is dead as a spirit and unless such man resurrects in his soul through my redemptive power such man does not know the Christ that he proclaims he is in unity with for only the living know me for who I really am.

My Holy Spirit leads the living and no man is able to see who I am as I am except by revelation from my Holy Spirit.

A man that my Holy Spirit leads will walk in life convictions and dead evil spirit shall not be able to deceive such man.

It is to afford the benefit of Holy Spirit convictions that I Christ came as flesh to place man in justification of life to afford man my Holy Spirit convictions.

For if a man is in reality mind of my Holy Spirit ways then he can no longer be deceived by the devil to walk in deadly false convictions that affords no spiritual justifications of life.

A man that is in deadly false convictions will only waste his valuable time for he will spend all his entire time chasing after wrongful convictions and in wrongful conviction walk will be a lost soul that cannot see or enter the realm of life to be in eternal life rewards.

To resurrect from death and in resurrection see in the light of goodness visions you must embark on a spiritual soul search and any man that seeks to find me in their spirit in humble mind and heart of love will find me.

You came to know Christ when you gave your heart and mind to me in your spiritual mind for me to lead you for goodness in goodness sake of life.

Although many say, they are a Christian they are the antichrist for their heart is in evil and their mind is set on wickedness and as such always offended just by the mentioning of name of Christ. To be in evil mind is to be a slave to death and if a man desire to be free in his soul let him submit his will unto me and I will make him whole.

You submit your will to me by seeking me in your spiritual heart to come into your heart and to guide you to walk in divine faith of life. If any man seeks me today in their spiritual heart and in mind of repentance, I will reveal my deity to them as the divine God of love and as love eternal life forever.

My mission to earth was necessary to call all of man to enter into me as the ark of life so that in me they walk in my holiness standards of life. As it is written in Matthew 11 verses 28, I say let all those that are heavy laden come and I am in wait to afford total rewards of life unto any man that repents in his heart to walk in holiness of life for goodness sake of my holy name.

If a man seeks to know me then let him first confess that, he is a sinner and say the sinner's prayer to be free from the wages of sin.

The sinner's prayer is simple prayer that you say in genuine soulful search of spiritual answers for only in such mind will you truly accept you are a sinner and as a sinner confess your sins in heart of genuine willingness to repent for goodness sake of life.

If you do not know me, and you have read thus far, then know that this is my word to you from my heart for you to see my heart desire for you that it is salvation for your soul everlasting.

I see the mind and I know the hearts and whosoever seek me with humble heart of repentance I will enter and open their heart to connect to me.

If a person is in me, they will be in visions of light and in visions of life in light will see in my revelations to them the eternal goodness reward that awaits them in my eternal life kingdom of goodness.

Life is eternal and the Christ that man crucified as Son of man is the glorified only Son of the Father in heaven and on earth in eternal life everlasting.

I am the righteousness of the Father and only in me will the Father as righteousness court a man as righteous.

If any man seeks to enter into divine righteousness to be in total benefit of life let him seek to be born again through confessing his sins and seeking in his heart for me to come inside his heart to make him whole for goodness benefit of life to be afforded to his soul.

A soul that is not born again is in death, death is darkness, and as God the Son, I am light.

As light, the light of the world by which any man can find his ways round in the wilderness jungle of life to enter into eternal glory of life in eternal life.

I am the way, the truth and the life as written in John 14:6. and I say now and again I am still the way, the truth and the life to eternal life everlasting.

Except a man be born again as I stated and now repeat as the Holy Spirit of life such man shall not find the way to the kingdom of life.

To walk in truthful ways you must be in the truth and if a man does not walk in truthful ways such man is not of life but a dead soul in darkness corridor of death row as a dead man walking.

This is wisdom and this is the truth and let those that have ears hear. I see by your smiles that you are very satisfied with my answers.

ME: Yes. Thank you yet again and I must say this is really all a revelation.

I must also say, as I am sure you know that I have many more questions to ask you and I am looking forward to your answers in the second part but for now thank you once again.

GOD: As I promised, I am prepared to answer any question that you may have and by any question, I mean any kind of question.

For this are the last days of time.

To make my grace obvious for what it is across the nations I say this is the time for me to reveal the meaning of revelations.

In revelations revealed, you will see that the beast even though he appears as if he is, is not for the power of the Holy Lamb has defeated the beast in all realms and those that carries the blood of my Holy Lamb walks in eternal victory over death.

The blood of the Lamb is my manifestation of my graceful forgiveness towards the sinful man for it is by my grace that I afforded life unto the dead spiritual man for him to have in me as the victory of life in all realms and dominion eternal life victory over death.

LET THE WISE SEEK ENTRANCE TO THE KINGDOM BY THE STRAIGHT LINE OF COVENANT

To wash man in the blood of the Lamb so that man is white as snow before me and in holy spiritual blood no longer subject to the condemnation of death is the entire purpose of my grace revealed.

If grace is revealed to you, it is so that you see to enter through the door for if you cannot see you cannot as I said enter through the door and no one can enter expect through the door.

Matthew Chapter 6 verses 33 say "**But seek ye first the kingdom of God, and his righteousness; and all these things shall be added unto you**".

I am the righteousness of life and as the righteousness of life the king of kings in all dominion dimensional realms.

No man can enter the kingdom when you reject the king for I Christ as the king of kings I am the kingdom of heaven revealed as manner from heaven and if a man seeks to find the kingdom let them seek me for whosoever finds me have the key to enter the kingdom.

If a man is not in me they are locked out of the kingdom and if a man is locked out he cannot see in spiritual light for any spirit locked out of heaven is an outcast and as an outcast in realm of darkness subject to abuse from evil demonic hell prisoners.

No man is able to see the kingdom of heaven until heaven became revealed to man by my grace and the things that shall be added to those in me is the total benefit of life in time and in timeless era everlasting.

If a man is able to see it is by my grace that he sees for no man is able to see unless I open his eyes.

I will only open the eyes of a man if he humbles himself before me through seeking in his spirit like a child to find me.

A man that seek me as a child admits in his mind that he does not know for if a man believes that he already knows then he will not see the goodness of grace.

Only if a man understands the essence of grace shall he be in goodness sightings of eternal life rewards and only in mind of hope of the seen goodness rewards shall a man walk to remain in line of the benefit rewards of the grace revealed to him.

A man in open mind of grace will be in faithfulness commitment to the ways of love for he shall know that all that he has is by my greater manifestation of my own love for him for his soul to have total benefit of life in time era and in timeless era forever.

If a man have found the meaning of my grace let him rejoice for all that is good is by my grace made good for without my grace no soul of man shall be eligible for rewards of life in eternal life everlasting following the fall of the first man Adam into sinful death.

If a soul is walking in banner of grace then let that soul know that it is by my grace that this is possible.

For no man can see the banner of my grace let alone recognize it in their evil mind of the flesh for the ways of the flesh is for the soul of man to perish everlastingly in death so that man never again has the rewards of life in eternal life.

I created man in my heart of goodness to be in blessings of total life everlasting.

If a man seeks to find eternal life as a spirit being then he is in search of my grace that I have revealed as I Christ for no man except by my grace is able to make his way to enter into my presence in eternal life to have the benefit of my eternal life rewards everlasting.

By grace I resurrected man from death to place back in heart of eternal life rewards and it is by the same grace that I made my Holy Spirit available to man to enable man receive my entire promises of eternal life rewards which I made to man out of my heart of love.

I Christ is the grace of love revealed and if a man rejects me, he rejects the fulfillment and benefit of my entire promises that I made in my heart of graceful love. I made my promises of eternal life blessing due to my love for man as their creator.

For in my heart of graceful love it is always in my willful desire for man to have goodness inheritance of life in me out of the goodness of my own will for them as their creator.

I created man in heart of loving kindness for them to have benefit of eternal life blessings everlasting for the goodness sake of my holy name. I am the Almighty God of Abraham, Isaac and Jacob and as God Almighty the creator of heaven and earth the Most High everlasting God of eternal life.

It is by heart of grace that I gave man dominion power on earth as the creator of all things. It is by the same heart of grace as I revealed it to man that I sustain man in goodness perfections in time era to be in total benefit walk of my entire goodness creations in the timelessness era that has no end.

This is wisdom of life and let those that have ears hear. I see that you have one final question.

ME: (Smiles and giggles as I am speaking) Yes, thank you. My question is why have you chosen me to give all this revelations most especially with all the controversy with Mary Magdalene because she was a woman and all?

GOD: The dead creates controversy to control the mind of the foolish man to walk in adversities of the death and only a fool will the dead fool with his fables from his graveyard of death. A dead spirit is a liar and as a liar always forgets that, the truth is neither deaf nor dumb.

I am the Ancient of days and as the Ancient of days the Holy Redeemer of life the savior of souls.

Mary Magdalene just like yourself was a sinner that needed salvation and I saved her just as I saved you being a savior that is in salvation business. For she was saved just like you, she served her life purpose in time just as you are now serving yours.

Therefore if any man carries on about the saved instead of finding their own salvation they will perish everlasting in the eternal lake of fire. I see that you have further questions relating to your gender. I promise to give detailed answers to your question as I continue in my revelations to you both in regards to scripture references to your gender, Mary Magdalene and on the Da Vinci propagated death codes. I also promise that the answer that I will give is the truth nothing but the truth so help me, me.

For the moment, to answer your specific question about why you, I say why not you. I made them both male and female says the scriptures, and if it is my will to speak through a female, then how is that wrong for is it not written my will be done on earth as it is in heaven. For did I not make Deborah a judge over Israel even though she was a female and did I not use an ass as I showed you in the story of Balaam as written in numbers 22 to reveal my word to Balaam and from Balaam to Balak that whosoever is blessed by me cannot be cursed. You are a female just like Deborah and surely a better vessel than an ass are you not?

ME: Well if you say so.

GOD: I know so and say so and whatsoever I say is final and as the one that has the first and final say in all things as the Alpha and Omega I say it is up to me to choose whosoever I am pleased with to speak through.

After all man that is in captivity of death say it is a free world of free speech. So if man that is in slavery of death consider that he is free to say what he pleases I ask how much more I the I AM, creator of heaven and earth master in all dominion. Is it not right as a matter of my divine right and law that I who created the heaven and earth speak freely through any creature as I please and freely through whatever channel that I have chosen out of my entire creations?

If any man in darkness mind refuse to see my word as shinning light and by not seeing remain a spiritual slavery everlastingly then they carry their blame on their head forever. They will be forever slaves and as slaves will be of eternal hard labor for failing to see that freedom in life is only from walking in eternal life of light.

If in the world of captivity a person believes that they are in a free world in their blind eyes of self-righteousness then they will not hear the real freedom message that I give now through you as my vessel.

For in their hardened heart of self-righteousness many eyes is covered by the veil of darkness and in veil cover of darkness, they will not see beyond their own flesh of sinful wickedness.

If any man refuses to listen to you for any reason then know that, the main reason for their not listening is that they are of the flesh blind in their spirit.

If such man accuses you of fabrications or blasphemy, know that they are the devils and as devils devilish and wicked minded to scare you to deny my divine righteousness in order to confirm their self-righteousness as right.

Woe unto such man for the risen Christ you crucify for blasphemy shall judge you to condemn you everlasting for your blaspheming of my holy name.

It shall profit no man to harden his mind to the truth for only the truth shall set a man free and I Christ I am the truth and as the truth the way to enter into eternal life of joy, peace and rest everlasting.

If any man refuses to listen to you know that they have not refused to listen to your human person but to me for all that you write is by the auctions of my Holy Spirit.

For it is by the auctions of my Holy Spirit I say let those that have ears hear for this is the time of revelations revealed and only in revelations is power of life revealed and only in understanding of revelations shall the blind see and the cripple walk.

ME: Thank you.

GOD: Blessed are you.

ME: Thank you

GOD: Blessed again are you

ME: Okay I get the general idea. Therefore, to the supreme general of life I say thank you for all of your blessings upon my life and upon the earth as the God that is love and as God that is love, my Father in heavens the all holy and all merciful everlasting Father of all spirits of life.

GOD: To thank me is to be blessed by me for to be thankful is evidence of willingness in your heart to walk in ways of goodness for a man that believes he has nothing to be thankful for will be full of wroth and in wroth shall seek to walk in opposite of my righteousness.
I say blessed again are you for your entire willingness mind to be good.
For to be willing to be good for goodness sake of life is to always walk in benefit of blessings of the word that is in you.

I Christ Jesus as manner and the bread of life from heaven that is revealed as the Son of the Father on earth to afford total salvation benefit to the soul of man is the word in you and if Christ be in a person then that person is a Holy temple of life.
I the Father made Christ my own flesh and blood available to man out of my heart of eternal loving gracefulness towards man and Christ as my heart revealed is the same as I the Father. As the Father I say if a man seeks to see and enter my kingdom let him seek my only begotten Son Christ Jesus the sinless slain for only if a man is in Christ is he holy and accepted by me as a perfect creature.

I made man to be a perfect sacrifice and the only sacrifice that is perfect and acceptable to me from the beginning to the end is my own flesh and blood Christ Jesus.
As the only perfect sacrifice, it is only by him that any man can be before me perfect and holy and only those that I certify as good on

deeds are my very own son for as God I only bear my kind and hence I am in all dominion dimensional realms the everlasting God of gods.

All those that are in I the Son will acquire through their being in me the benefit of Sonship to walk in total benefit of goodness rewards of life as son in me and in me son of the Father everlasting.

As such, even though they shall die, as flesh by my gracefulness loving power I the Father shall raise them up as I raised my one and only begotten Son Christ Jesus up from death to establish his name forever in all dominion dimensional realms as the only name through which man can have the resurrection of life.

I the Father say Christ is my righteousness and as my righteousness, death could not keep him underground.

That which death intended for evil I used for goodness and it is to say to man that all power of good and evil work together for goodness sake of life that I raised up the name of Christ to be the only name through which man will be afforded total power and benefit of life.

For Christ is my righteousness revealed only by the calling of his name shall a man walk in my righteousness to enter into my Holy Spirit domain of life to have eternal rewards of life everlastingly.

All power I have given to the name of Christ as the Father and if a man rejects Christ, he rejects me for between Christ and me, there is no difference.

Only by that name shall a man have the benefit of my entire eternal life promises and total rewards of life from me everlastingly. Christ is my word revealed and as my word revealed food of the spirit, that man needs to have to have spiritual fulfillment of life.

Christ as food of the Sprit is good news to the soul therefore, let all that have ears hear and as they hear rejoice in their souls for those that hear and receive in gladness of hearts shall have everlasting joy of peace, rest and joy.

On that big smile, I say gladness is in your soul for the goodness glory of my name sake.

As I have promised you I will not disappoint you in your reliance on me and I will answer all your questions in spiritual context as the spiritual master in all dominion for goodness sake of my holy name as eternal life forever.

In the meantime, rejoice and be rest assured that my grace is sufficient for you in all things. For in my graceful willingness towards you I promise I will open even wider your eyes of understanding by answering any question you may have as we continue in part two of my revelations to you as the Master that has all total power of revelations as the Alpha and Omega in all dominion dimensional realms forever.

As the Father I say peace of heaven be unto you everlasting and to all that persevere for goodness sake of heaven.

For all those that hear the word from heart of willingness to obey my total entire word as revealed by me as Christ I say also peace be unto you.

For all that hear my word and receive in gladness I will open their spiritual mind further to see by placing them in my Holy Spirit to walk in power of my total word which is revealed by me in time for man to see as divine holy perfect sacrifice.

I am a God of covenant as revealed in the scriptures and no man can enter into covenant with me except through my own door and acceptable open channel.

Only those that are in covenant with me through my perfect blood of sacrifice are my sons and as sons shall inherit my kingdom everlasting. I am the God of Abraham, Isaac and Jacob and as the creator of the universe the Alpha and the Omega.

This is the final hours of the end time and as such, my last and final call to all nations to see my kingdom and to enter through the gates from the door for just like in the days of Noah once I shut the door of the ark, no one shall be allowed to enter again. I am life and as life the only one that can give eternal life everlasting.

I am the Almighty God with power and might over all matters in time and timeless era and only those that walk in accordance to my righteousness standards of life shall have the benefit of total rewards of life in eternal life everlasting.

Let those that have ears hear and let those that have eyes see through the eyes of the master as I the master in all dominion continue to reveal the truthfulness of life as the way, the truth and as the oracle of life the king of kings and Lord of lords in eternal life everlasting.

Author Contact

If you have questions or comments about my book you may contact me at my email address listed below.

Pastor Olabisi Kufeji

Freedomhouse7@aol.com or kufeji@fredom-house.org.uk

Also please check out our Ministry Website:

http://www.freedom-house.org.uk